PENNSYLVANIA

OFF THE BEATEN PATH®

Help Us Keep This Guide Up to Date

We would love to hear from you concerning your experiences with this guide and how you feel it could be improved and kept up to date. Please send your comments and suggestions to:

editorial@GlobePequot.com

Thanks for your input, and happy travels!

OFF THE BEATEN PATH® SERIES

THIRTEENTH EDITION

PENNSYLVANIA

OFF THE BEATEN PATH®

DISCOVER YOUR FUN

CHRISTINE O'TOOLE

Globe
Pequot

Essex, Connecticut

To Jim, James, and Bill: great Pennsylvanians.
And to the memory of Bruno Lavoissier, 1988–2009.

All the information in this guidebook is subject to change. We recommend that you call ahead to obtain current information before traveling.

Globe
Pequot

An imprint of Globe Pequot, the trade division of
The Rowman & Littlefield Publishing Group, Inc.
4501 Forbes Blvd., Ste. 200
Lanham, MD 20706
www.rowman.com

Distributed by NATIONAL BOOK NETWORK

Off the Beaten Path is a registered trademark of The Rowman & Littlefield Publishing Group, Inc.

British Library Cataloguing in Publication Information Available

Library of Congress Cataloging-in-Publication Data

ISSN 1536-6197
ISBN 978-1-4930-6575-2 (paper : alk. paper)
ISBN 978-1-4930-6576-9 (electronic)

∞™ The paper used in this publication meets the minimum requirements of American National Standard for Information Sciences—Permanence of Paper for Printed Library Materials, ANSI/NISO Z39.48-1992.

Contents

Acknowledgments

This book has helped me relive some favorite moments in Pennsylvania history—my own.

As a native who started east, moved west, and eventually became a travel writer, my personal and professional footprints run all through the state. For their help in mapping every opportunity along the way, I thank fellow writers: my twin, Carol Denny, and Jim O'Toole, my husband, intrepid companion, and best editor.

To my father, Ned Hoffner, who bundled up seven kids and took them skiing in the Poconos, camping at French Creek, skating on frozen Delaware County ponds, and leaf-hiking at Ridley Creek, I owe a debt of gratitude for his boundless energy, example, and encouragement. He started me on this path.

About the Author

Christine O'Toole has written for *National Geographic Traveler*, the *New York Times, AFAR, Lonely Planet, Delta Sky, Hemispheres, Washington Post, Pittsburgh Magazine, Pittsburgh Post-Gazette*, and other publications. A native of Newtown Square, Delaware County, she has lived and worked in Philadelphia, Harrisburg, Washington, DC, and Pittsburgh.

Introduction

When I think of Pennsylvania, I think green.

Driving home to Philadelphia after a weekend at the beach, I used to roll down the window as I crossed the Delaware River and sniff the humid fragrance of an August night, so different from south Jersey's parched sand. On a spring drive down Route 6, I'll see a golden mountainside and know it's a week away from leafing out (unless it snows, of course—a distinct possibility in the Pennsylvania mountains). Whether observed from a bike seat in York County or a trail along the Chestnut Ridge, this state has simply terrific photosynthesis.

The natural end of all that transpiration is, of course, fall, and it's fabulous here. In October you bask in what I think is its most memorable weather: warm days, deep blue skies, and a palette of colors that Crayola (a Pennsylvania company) would kill for. Throw a few elk, bear, bikers, or golfers into that picture, and you've got the state at its finest.

Pennsylvania is an old state. Its central ridges and valleys are mind-bendingly ancient—about 250 million years old, geologically speaking. Evidence of human life in rock shelters in Washington County goes back at least 16,000 years. Ten thousand years ago Indians hunted mammoths and mastodons. Europeans first settled here in 1643. All those layers of history mean that however you slice it, there's always something new to enjoy and digest.

Spend lots of time in Philadelphia—it's as youthful as it is historic and has a collection of fabulous museums that would take weeks to visit. Walk around Old City, an authentic 18th-century neighborhood where young locals push strollers and scooters. In-line skate down Kelly Drive (but remove the skates when you get to the *Rocky* steps at the Museum of Art). Boo the sports teams—it's a tradition here—and ride the Market Street El, the Broad Street subway, or the trains to Suburban Station, because the Schuylkill Expressway can be a nightmare.

But Pennsylvania is a broad state. So, in planning your jaunt here, be broad-minded.

If you think state capitols are a snore, you'll be pleasantly surprised by Pennsylvania's neoclassical masterpiece on the banks of the Susquehanna. If you've ever seen the Grand Canyon, you owe it to yourself to compare it to Pennsylvania's version, a gorgeous gorge in Tioga County. And if you think Pennsylvania military history is all Gettysburg and Valley Forge, find out why native tribes joined forces with the French to battle the British for this land before the nation even existed—and why the redcoats hacked their way through hundreds of miles of deep, mountainous forest (more greenery) to claim their fort at Pittsburgh.

Pennsylvania is green because it's well watered. Between the peaceful upper Delaware and Lake Erie, ribbons of white water and terrific trout streams cut through the woods. In the valleys of Susquehanna and Lancaster Counties, lush farms snuggle against every rolling hillside, enjoying magnificent thunderstorms. And streamside county seats like Franklin abide like Brigadoon, charmingly unchanged.

Although Pennsylvania's tourist attractions often focus on industry, agriculture is still its biggest business. So, since you're being broad-minded, try a U-pick orchard or produce from a roadside stand. Visit the annual Farm Show in Harrisburg, which celebrates everything that grows in the state, from apples to zucchini. (Sweet-faced kids leading sweet-faced cows, butter sculptures, and rodeos, too—all for free every January.) Give Pennsylvania credit for the steady improvements in the state's 116 parks. Over the past few decades, the Department of Conservation of Natural Resources (DCNR) has worked to groom them and to create interpretive signs and exhibits. Nice job, DCNR (and thank you, commonwealth taxpayers).

Old industries have new purposes here. Many abandoned short lines built to haul coal are now being converted to trails. A bonus: Most of them run alongside rivers. Hundreds of peaceful miles that used to be rusting steel are now long, restful water-level pathways. (The state's prettiest country roads have also been linked in biking networks.) And in Elk County former strip mines have been converted to verdant meadows, creating a resurgence of elk. The herd is now one of the largest in the eastern United States—a rustbelt story with a wild ending.

Quick: What's the state's website address? If you're tailing a car with a Pennsylvania license plate, the answer's right in front of you: state.pa.us. Use that ubiquitous URL to find all things Pennsylvanian. Select the tourism page, "Visit PA" (visitpa.com), and type a keyword—say, apple—and you'll find museums devoted to apples, farm markets galore, even restaurants with apple desserts to die for.

Twenty years ago the state had a slogan that promised "You've Got a Friend in Pennsylvania." (Today you'll see front license plates in the same blue-and-gold style that say "You've Got a Friend in Jesus," a play on that old catchphrase. When you see one now, you'll catch the reference. That's true native lore.) The old ad campaign caught on because it's common sense and the real thing. With 12.8 million residents, you really are bound to know someone here. And I can vouch for the part about friends, most recently while writing this book.

In Donegal a fellow in a pickup truck tugged my car out of a snowdrift and simply drove off with a friendly wave. Dennis Tice of the Bedford Visitors

Brief History of Early Pennsylvania

King Charles II of England gave William Penn, a Quaker, a large tract of land in the New World as repayment of a debt the king owed to William's father. The tract of land that became known as Pennsylvania, or "Penn's Woods," was settled in 1643. Penn encouraged the Quakers and other persecuted groups to settle in Pennsylvania, saying, "No person shall be molested or prejudiced for his or her conscientious persuasion or practice." In Pennsylvania, he promised, they could practice their religious beliefs in a democratic way. Over time, Pennsylvania's freedom appealed not only to Quakers but also to Amish, Moravians, Slovaks, Poles, Jews, Catholics, Hungarians, Italians, Irish, Latinos, and many other religious and ethnic groups.

Penn established a legislature, making his mark as one of America's great visionaries. "He was the greatest law-giver the world has produced," said Thomas Jefferson. Penn originally intended the capital of Pennsylvania to be located in Upland, now known as Chester. In 1682 the capital moved upriver to Philadelphia. But as settlers in Pennsylvania began pushing westward, legislators decided that the capital should be in a more central location, so they moved it to Lancaster in 1799 and finally to Harrisburg in 1810.

Bureau insisted that my family drive to Gravity Hill, the most memorable of all my off-the-beaten-path destinations. Two shy Smethport teenagers, the only employees, kept me, the only dinner guest, company at the Courtyard Restaurant while I ate. And Ken Fosco made the early US Navy come alive for me on the Flagship *Niagara* while he guided me around. Ken's an enthusiast who'll never set sail (he gets seasick).

More help came from other authors. *Diners of Pennsylvania*, by Brian Butko, Kevin Patrick, and Kyle Weaver, is a great side dish for *Off the Beaten Path*. So is *Weird Pennsylvania*, Matt Lake's compendium of ghost stories, local legends, and other oddities from across the commonwealth.

You might say that hospitality is a cornerstone of the state, but in Pennsylvania we prefer that you say "keystone."

During colonial times Pennsylvania was the middle colony of the original 13 colonies. It held the colonies together as the keystone supports the arch above a window or door, so it's the Keystone State and has been at least since 1800. Actually, technically, it's not a state at all. Officially Pennsylvania is a commonwealth, as are only three other states—Kentucky, Massachusetts, and Virginia. The word comes from Old English and means the "common weal," or well-being of the public. In Pennsylvania all legal processes are carried out in the name of the commonwealth, although the word does not appear on the state seal.

Navigating the State

Pennsylvania's hills come in three flavors. From west to east, the state's topography slides from the Allegheny Plateau (an Ice Age leftover) through the central Ridge and Valley region, and southeast through the Piedmont, until it flattens at the coastal plain along the Delaware River.

From above, the Ridge and Valley region looks like folds in a blanket. The long, wooded ridges run southwest to northeast, with beautiful farm valleys in between. Roads generally run along those ridgetops or through the valleys. That's why the six slices of the state—three northern segments and three southern—don't follow a grid. In most cases they are bounded by the major roads (more about them later), which, in turn, find a way around the state's rivers and valleys that can seem a bit slanted. If you want straight lines, go west; if you want surprises, stick around.

YOU TAKE THE HIGH ROAD, AND I'LL TAKE ROUTE 30

Pennsylvania has the nation's fourth-largest highway system—more than 44,000 miles of highways under state control. And the Keystone State has the eighth highest count of highway miles—nearly 119,000 miles. Bottom line: It's real easy to get around. From four-lane highways with limited access to country roads that pass more cows than people, Pennsylvania has its share of concrete, macadam, and tarmac.

Most of Pennsylvania's busiest highways started out as Indian paths, as Indians had a genius for picking the most direct and level paths everywhere they went. The paths they created were no more than a foot or two wide, but they were later followed by European foot soldiers, then settlers with wagons, then modern road builders. Next stop: the interstates. When you drive any of the roads described below, you'll notice they often follow a ridgeline, a river, a valley, or a mountain pass. You'll now know why.

Among all these roadways, five highways deserve special attention:

- **The National Road (Route 40)** was the first federally funded highway (1818 to 1835). It connected Washington, DC, with points west, traversing Maryland, cutting across the southwest corner of Pennsylvania, running through Ohio and Indiana, and ending in Illinois. The National Road opened up land west of the Alleghenies and allowed a budding nation to expand westward. In the state's southwestern corner, native tribes had long used what is now Route 40 before the European settlers paved it. In those early days the route was called Nemacolin's Path for the chief who controlled these parts. (He was, in turn, controlled by the mighty Iroquois nation to the north.) You can see tollhouses in Petersburg and Searights and nearly 50 more structures that served as taverns and inns during the road's early years. The Stone House in Farmington still welcomes travelers after 200 years. Find all the attractions at nationalroadpa.org.

- **The Lincoln Highway (Route 30)** was the first coast-to-coast highway. When it was established in 1913, it was merely a line on a map, stretching from New York City to San Francisco by connecting existing roads. In 1925 the government began numbering highways. In 1928 the Lincoln Highway Association fabricated and installed (with the help of Boy Scouts) more than 3,000 concrete markers—one at almost every mile—across the entire country. Bands of red, white, and blue (with a big L) were painted on telephone poles to designate the highway. Alas, road widenings, snow plows, and natural disasters have destroyed all but about 20 markers. The Lincoln Highway Heritage Corridor (LHHC), a nonprofit organization, aims to encourage you to follow this ribbon of highway, where you'll discover nifty attractions that your grandparents might have seen. Within Pennsylvania, Route 30 covers 320 miles and 13 counties. At its westernmost Pennsylvania point, it's 4 miles west of Hookstown; it runs east through the state and crosses the Benjamin Franklin Bridge, connecting Philadelphia to Camden, New Jersey. Begin your Lincoln Highway Experience at the interpretative center at 3435 State Route 30 East, Latrobe 15650. You can also call (724) 879-4241, or visit lhhc.org.

- **Route 6** starts out mountainous in the east, then flattens out to a two-lane highway that strings together all the county seats of what's called the "northern tier." This is one of those in-between Native American paths: Big mountains flank your car as you drive through the Brokenstraw Valley, near the Allegheny National Forest. It may be a national road, but the speed limit is still a leisurely 50 miles per hour most of the way.

- **Route 1** is a mostly stop-and-don't-go path through dreary suburban strip malls around Philadelphia—but be patient. Follow it south into Chester County and you'll find the heart of the Brandywine Valley—home to Wyeths, mushrooms, historically Black universities (Cheney and Lincoln), and farmland.

- **The Pennsylvania Turnpike.** Talk about the beaten path—this one's been beaten just about to death. Those who drive it may frequently admire the feats of engineering that took it through four mountains (and over a few more), two rivers, and the state's major cities. But they can't bring themselves to admire its congestion, seemingly constant summer construction, and frequently foggy conditions. (I won't even mention the tolls.) The Pennsylvania Turnpike developed the Sonic Nap Alert Pattern (SNAP), which is the placement of rumble strips along the edge of the right lane to alert drivers who are falling asleep. A better way to stay awake: Grab a map and plot a route that takes you off the turnpike as much as possible.

DELIGHTFUL DRIVING TOURS

If you shun turnpikes, the state has some suggestions specifically for you in its "PA Roadtrips" page on the state website. Among the ideas to whet your appetite are visits to artisanal cheesemakers in the Cumberland Valley or the best pizza joints in Old Forge. Explore the history of the Underground Railroad on a driving tour of Kennett Square, Chester County. For classic country roads, consider the routes dubbed "Scenic Byways." My favorite, among a baker's dozen of quiet two-lane excursions, is the 60-mile meander through the Laurel Highlands, home to Fallingwater and handsome mountaintop vistas. See the suggestions at visitpa.com.

funfoodfact

Chocolate factories in Pennsylvania include Blommer, in East Greenville; Godiva, in Reading; Goldenberg, in Philadelphia; Hershey, in Hershey; Mars, in Elizabethtown; R. M. Palmer, in West Reading; and Wilbur, in Lititz. How sweet it is.

THE MASON-DIXON LINE

The English astronomers Charles Mason and Jeremiah Dixon surveyed parts of the colonies in the 1760s and drew a straight line—the stripe that became the Mason-Dixon line. Pennsylvania touches the north side of the line; Delaware, Maryland, and West Virginia touch the south. During the Civil War the North, the Union, comprised the "free states," and the South, the Confederacy, comprised the "slave states."

When Autumn Leaves Start to Fall

In autumn 127 varieties of trees change from summer green into 127 spectacularly brilliant fall colors. Choose this time to hike or bike Pennsylvania's trails. If you know where to look, Pennsylvania offers hundreds of miles of scenic biking paths, and a network of 7 less-traveled road routes take you near major cities but keep you far from clogged highways. You share the road, but safely. Check out the map on the official PennDOT website. For off-road riding, get some trail tips at trails.dcnr.pa.gov. And check the regional chapters of this book for local ideas.

WELCOME CENTERS

The Pennsylvania Department of Transportation (PennDOT) and the Pennsylvania Turnpike Commission operate welcome centers at highway entrances to the Keystone State. Knowledgeable and friendly hosts at the centers can offer directional assistance; provide detailed information about Pennsylvania's culture, history, scenic attractions, and activities; give you the weather forecast; report on road conditions; and arrange overnight accommodations. The centers have vending machines, picnic tables, restrooms, and pet areas. The welcome centers operate from 7 a.m. to 7 p.m., 7 days a week, including most holidays. Following is a list of welcome center locations.

- **Allegheny Mountains:** Warfordsburg, I-70 westbound, 0.5 mile north of Maryland border

- **Brandywine Valley:** Linwood, I-95 northbound, 0.5 mile north of Delaware border

- **Delaware Water Gap:** I-80 westbound, 0.5 mile west of New Jersey border

- **Dutch Country:** State Line, I-81 northbound, 1.5 miles north of Maryland border

- **Endless Mountains:** Great Bend, I-81 southbound, 0.5 mile south of New York border

- **Gateway to Route 6:** Matamoras, I-84 at exit 53, 0.5 mile south of New York border

- **King of Prussia:** Pennsylvania Turnpike, I-276 westbound, 32 miles west of New Jersey border

- **Laurel Highlands:** Mount Morris, I-79 northbound, 5 miles north of West Virginia border

- **Lehigh Valley:** Easton, I-78 westbound, 0.5 mile west of New Jersey border

- **Pennsylvania Great Lakes:** North East, I-90, 0.5 mile west of New York border

- **Shenango Valley:** West Middlesex, I-80 eastbound, 0.5 mile east of Ohio border

- **Tioga:** Route 15 southbound, 7 miles south of New York border

- **Washington:** Claysville, I-70 eastbound, 5 miles east of West Virginia border

- **York:** North Shrewsbury, I-83 northbound, 2.5 miles north of Maryland border

Kids Welcome

Children and inner children will find plenty of play time in Pennsylvania. Zoos abound (Philadelphia's is the oldest in the country, with 1,600 creatures; others in Pittsburgh, Hershey, and Erie are large and thriving). Philadelphia's Please Touch Museum is world-class; Pittsburgh's Children's Museum includes a salute to a local hero, TV's Mister Rogers. Sesame Place, in Bucks County, has been voted one of *Parents* magazine's top picks for its rides and Muppets. Easton's Crayola Factory (and its satellite at Philadelphia's Franklin Institute) is a rainbow of markers, stickers, glitter, and color. And amusement parks? Pennsylvania boasts some that are twirled and true: Kennywood and Idlewild in the west, Hersheypark and Dorney Park in the east, and Knoebels in Columbia County. Daredevils love Camp Woodward's skateboarding ramps and classes for extreme sports near State College, while toddlers prefer to feed the ducks at Dutch Wonderland in Lancaster County. And while you're driving the kids

Ten Keystone Food Firsts

- 1861: Julius Sturgis Pretzel Company, Lititz, becomes America's first commercial baker.

- 1894: Cracker Jacks are first manufactured in Philadelphia.

- 1900: Frank Fleer coats chewing gum in sugar. *Voilà:* Chiclets.

- 1902: Fast food is born at the Horn & Hardart Automat, 818 Chestnut St., Philadelphia.

- 1904: The banana split makes its first appearance in Latrobe.

- 1918: Frank Fleer does it again: Dubble Bubble.

- 1920: Emil's, 1800 S. Broad St., Philadelphia, makes sandwiches for Hog Island workers and calls them hoagies.

- 1936: Frank Ludens of Reading concocts the Fifth Avenue candy bar.

- 1937: Good 'n' Plenty candy is manufactured in Philadelphia.

- 1968: Jim Delligatti, a McDonald's franchise owner, invents the Big Mac, selling it first in Uniontown.

from one to the other, tune in to "Kid's Corner," a Monday-through-Thursday radio show. More than 40,000 kids call in each month, making the Philadelphia-based show the most popular National Public Radio program for under-tens. Find it on WXPN-FM, 88.5, Philadelphia, 88.7, Lancaster, and 104.9, Allentown; WXPH-FM, 88.1, Harrisburg; and WKHS-FM, 90.5, Worton, Maryland. Or listen online at kidscorner.org.

Pennsylvania Fast Facts

PENNSYLVANIA'S OFFICIAL DESIGNATIONS

- **Amphibian:** Eastern Hellbender

- **Animal:** White-tailed deer

- **Arboretum:** Morris Arboretum, Philadelphia

- **Beverage:** Milk

- **Bird:** Ruffed grouse

- **Dog:** Great Dane

- **Fish:** Brook trout

- **Flower:** Mountain laurel

- **Fossil:** *Phacops rana,* a small water animal

- **Insect:** Firefly

- **Motto:** Virtue, Liberty, and Independence

- **Ship:** Flagship *Niagara*

- **Tree:** Hemlock

GEOGRAPHY

- **Area:** 45,888 square miles

- **Capital:** Harrisburg, in Dauphin County

- **Counties:** 67

- **County with no traffic lights:** Forest

- **Geographic center:** Centre County, 2.5 miles southwest of Bellefonte

- **Highest point:** Mt. Davis, 3,213 feet

- **Lakes:** 1 Great Lake (Lake Erie), 50 natural lakes (over 20 acres wide), and 2,500 artificial lakes

- **Largest county:** Lycoming, which is larger than Rhode Island

- **Lowest point:** Delaware River

- **Miles of Appalachian Trail:** 230 (The midpoint of the 2,144-mile Appalachian Trail, where it's traditional for hikers to eat a half-gallon of ice cream, is in Pine Grove Furnace State Park, Cumberland County.)

- **Rivers and streams:** 54,000 miles, more flowing water than any other continental state

- **Rivers with the hardest-to-pronounce names:** Schuylkill (say SCHOOL-kill) and Youghiogheny (rhymes with sock-a-SAY-knee) Rivers

- **Size:** 46,055 square miles

- **Species of fish:** 159

- **Species of trees:** 127

- **State forest districts:** 20; 2,200,000 acres

- **State game lands:** 294; 1,379,002 acres

- **State parks:** 116; 282,500 acres; 5,000 miles of trails

GOVERNMENT

- **US representatives:** 17

- **State representatives:** 203

- **State senators:** 50

- **Municipalities:** 2,562 (more than any other state)

- **Sales tax on clothing and shoes:** Zero

PENNSYLVANIA FIRSTS

- **First hospital**—Pennsylvania Hospital, Philadelphia, 1751

- **First newspaper**—*Pennsylvania Packet,* Philadelphia, 1784

- **First national capital**—Philadelphia, 1790

- **First American theater**—Walnut Street Theater, Philadelphia, 1809

- **First brewery**—Yuengling Brewery, Pottsville, 1829

- **First zoo**—Zoological Society of Philadelphia, 1874

- **First all motion-picture theater**—Nickelodeon, Pittsburgh, 1905

- **First Jeep**—Bantam Car Company, Butler, 1940

- **First computer**—University of Pennsylvania, Philadelphia, 1946

- **First educational public television station**—WQED, Pittsburgh, 1954

AGRICULTURE (THE STATE'S LARGEST INDUSTRY)

- **Farmland:** 9 million acres

- **Farms:** 55,000

- **Leading farm products:** dairy products, mushrooms, apples, tobacco, grapes, peaches, cut flowers, Christmas trees, and eggs

- **Rural population:** 3,700,000

MASCOTS OF MAJOR SPORTS TEAMS

- **Philadelphia Eagles**—Eagle

- **Philadelphia Flyers**—Gritty

- **Philadelphia Phillies**—Phanatic

- **Philadelphia 76ers**—Hot Shot

Are You Feeling Lucky?

Lucky 13? Pennsylvania now allows table gaming and slot machines at select locations around the state. Five of the casinos are located at race courses: Parx Casino and Parx East in Bensalem; Presque Isle Downs & Casino in Erie; Hollywood Casino at Penn National in Grantville, near Harrisburg; the Meadows in Washington; and Mohegan Sun at Pocono Downs. The Poconos resort area also boasts the Mount Airy Casino. Rivers Casino commands a waterfront location in Pittsburgh as the name suggests, and Bethlehem's Wind Creek Casino occupies the site of a former steel mill. In the Philadelphia area, there's Rivers Casino downtown, Live! Casino Hotel in the stadium district, and Harrah's in nearby Chester, along with Valley Forge Casino Resort at the Convention Center. Nemacolin Resort in Fayette County operates the Lady Luck Casino.

- **Pittsburgh Pirates**—Parrot

- **Pittsburgh Penguins**—Iceberg

- **Pittsburgh Steelers**—Steely McBeam

FAMOUS NATIVES & RESIDENTS

- Christina Aguilera, *recording artist*

- Louisa May Alcott, *novelist*

- Marian Anderson, *contralto*

- Kevin Bacon, *actor*

- Samuel Barber, *composer*

- John Barrymore, *actor*

- Donald Barthelme, *author*

- Stephen Vincent Benét, *poet and story writer*

- Daniel Boone, *frontiersman*

- Ed Bradley, *TV anchorman*

- James Buchanan, *US president*

- Alexander Calder, *sculptor*

- Rachel Carson, *biologist and author*

- Mary Cassatt, *painter*

- Henry Steele Commager, *historian*

- Jimmy and Tommy Dorsey, *bandleaders*

- W. C. Fields, *comedian*

- Stephen Foster, *composer*

- Robert Fulton, *inventor*

- Martha Graham, *choreographer*

- Alexander Haig, *former US secretary of state*

- Marilyn Horne, *mezzo-soprano*

ANNUAL TEMPERATURE AVERAGES (FAHRENHEIT): MAXIMUM/MINIMUM

	Allentown	Erie	Harrisburg	Philadelphia
January	35/19	34/20	35/22	41/26
April	60/37	56/38	60/41	65/45
July	83/62	76/60	83/63	86/69
October	62/42	63/48	62/46	65/50

	Poconos	Pittsburgh	Scranton/Williamsport	Wilkes-Barre
January	31/16	35/20	36/20	33/19
April	56/36	61/41	63/40	59/38
July	78/59	83/64	86/64	83/62
October	58/40	63/45	64/44	61/42

- Lee Iacocca, *auto executive*

- Reggie Jackson, *baseball player*

- Wiz Khalifa, *rapper*

- Gene Kelly, *dancer and actor*

- Grace Kelly, *Princess of Monaco*

- S. S. Kresge, *merchant*

- Mario Lanza, *actor and singer*

- David McCullough, *historian and author*

- Margaret Mead, *anthropologist*

- Andrew Mellon, *financier*

- Mac Miller, *rapper*

- Tom Mix, *actor*

- Arnold Palmer, *golfer*

- Robert E. Peary, *explorer*

- Man Ray, *painter*

- Betsy Ross, *flag maker*

- B. F. Skinner, *psychologist*

- John Sloan, *painter*

- Will Smith, *actor*

- Gertrude Stein, *author*

- James Stewart, *actor*

- John Updike, *novelist*

- Wallis Warfield, *Duchess of Windsor*

- Andy Warhol, *artist*

- Fred Waring, *bandleader*

- Ethel Waters, *singer and actress*

- Anthony Wayne, *military officer*

- August Wilson, *poet, writer, and playwright*

- Andrew Wyeth, *painter*

Southeastern Pennsylvania

Philadelphia

As a native of the Philadelphia region, I love coming back to visit this historic city. To me, it's not only a place with lots of Revolutionary history—it's a hip, youthful city with wonderful art and architecture. Did I mention the fabulous food scene?

Philadelphia has the fifth-largest metropolitan area in the country. In 2015, Philadelphia became the first American metropolis to be designated a world heritage city. The region comprises five counties in Pennsylvania (Bucks, Chester, Delaware, Montgomery, and Philadelphia) plus two in New Jersey (Camden and Gloucester). In the 1960s Walter Annenberg, who then owned the *Philadelphia Inquirer* and *Daily News,* coined the phrase "Delaware Valley," essentially for marketing purposes. The term stuck for decades but has recently fallen out of favor. Now it's safe, once again, to refer to the Philadelphia region or to the Philadelphia metropolitan area.

Philadelphia was not always a bustling metro area of 6 million people. When William Penn received a gift of a lot of forestland in the New World—hence, Penn's Woods, or Pennsylvania—he became a 17th-century urban planner. The

SOUTHEASTERN PENNSYLVANIA

orderly street plan he created for Philadelphia is replicated in several other flat Pennsylvania towns, notably Lancaster and Carlisle.

Penn envisioned Philadelphia as a modern "greene countrie towne." Within his 2-mile-wide-by-1-mile-north/south street grid, he designated five squares to remain forever verdant. In the central square, cleverly called Center Square, the city built its *City Hall* in 1871. The surrounding 4 squares—Logan to the northwest, Rittenhouse to the southwest, Washington to the southeast, and Franklin to the northeast—remain delightful spots to stroll, meet a friend, or picnic.

Atop City Hall, crowning a 548-foot tower, William Penn surveys his city. He faces northeast, toward the spot where he made a legendary treaty with the *Lenni-Lenape Indians* in 1682. For the next four generations, the Penn Family and the Quakers dominated the city. You can find out more at the *Arch Street Friends Meeting House* (320 Arch St.; 215-627-2667; historicasmh.org. Still in regular use, the meeting house profiles Pennsylvania's amazing founder in "Penn the Peacemaker," a small permanent exhibit. A few blocks south, at Second and Walnut Streets, a small plaza called Welcome Park offers a small-scale version of Penn's city plan and a timeline of his tumultuous life. He died in England in 1718.

Liberty Bell? Check. Independence Hall? Ditto. Most of Philadelphia's most popular attractions lie within Independence National Historical Park. Start your visit there with a stop at the *Independence Visitor Center,* a perfect orientation to the neighborhood. Check out the free movies, plot your itinerary on

> ## trivia
>
> What better postmark than the signature of the nation's first postmaster? Get Benjamin Franklin's John Hancock on letters mailed from the US Post Office at 316 Market St., next to his home.

AUTHOR'S TOP 10 FAVORITES IN SOUTHEASTERN PENNSYLVANIA

American Philosophical Society

Barn Art Driving Tour

Brandywine River Museum

Chanticleer

Cheesesteaks

Fairmount Waterworks Interpretive Center

Franklin Square

Mt. Gretna

Rosenbach Museum

USA Weightlifting Hall of Fame

a giant map, get your timed admission tickets to free attractions, and quiz the helpful staff for suggestions. It's open daily at 1 N. Independence Mall West.

For more information phone (800) 537-7676 or (215) 925-7676 or visit independencevisitorcenter.com. Hours are 8:30 a.m. to 7 p.m. from Memorial Day through Labor Day; 8:30 a.m. to 6 p.m. during the months of Apr, May, and Sept; and for the rest of the year, 8:30 a.m. to 5 p.m.

Just north of the Visitor Center, stop by the ***National Constitution Center*** (525 Arch St., Independence Mall). The 2003 building by I. M. Pei includes a hectic first floor with high-tech, interactive displays that interpret all 8 articles and 27 amendments. Civic-minded kids can take the presidential oath in front of the capitol on live TV or don Supreme Court judicial robes. In Signers' Hall, mingle with clustered, lifelike statues of the document's 43 signatories—authentic to their well-polished brass fingertips. Because it's

How to Order a Cheesesteak

Ordering a cheesesteak—that overstuffed hot sandwich of paper-thin sliced beef on a long, freshly baked Italian roll—can be intimidating, and not just because the counter man usually looks greasy and vaguely unhappy. This toothsome favorite, known elsewhere as a Philly steak, will hit your stomach like a hunk o' hunk o' burnin' love.

Most Philadelphians pledge allegiance to a preferred vendor—just ask the nearest local for the best shop within walking distance.

Cheesesteaks are messy. They're usually wrapped in paper for takeout (you should also grab lots of napkins and remove your tie). They are best eaten when you are absolutely famished, and washed down with a birch beer—a favorite local soda that tastes a bit like a Dr. Pepper.

Here's what you want to decide before that scary cook barks questions at you:

Half or whole? A half sandwich is a 6-inch slab; a whole is the equivalent of roughly two full meals.

Cheese? Complicated. First decide if you want the cheese; if not, order a steak. If you want the classic provolone topping, order cheese. If you like soft processed cheese from an aerosol can, order with Whiz.

Green stuff? A cheesesteak hoagie means topped with chopped lettuce and tomato. Specify your onions cooked or raw. Peppers can be either sweet or hot; mushrooms, always cooked.

Sauce? In Philly parlance, sauce means spicy tomato sauce (feel free to specify lots or a little). You could ask for ketchup instead. Go for the burn.

After all that, don't be surprised if your order turns out wrong. Somehow, it's all good.

often quite crowded, with many school groups on weekdays, book your timed admission tickets ahead, either here or at the Visitor Center. Open Wed through Sun 10 a.m. to 5 p.m. Admission is $14.50 for adults and $13 for seniors (extra for other special exhibits); student and veterans tickets are $11, while active military and children under 5 get in free. For more information call (215) 923-0004 or visit constitutioncenter.org. Joining the patriot muster in 2021, the *Museum of the American Revolution* introduces the players on the stage of war, from Native Americans to British aristocracy. George Washington's war tent, his primary home for the nine years of the conflict, is on permanent display. Book in advance at amrevmuseum.org. Open daily except major holidays at 101 S. Third Street.

Franklin Square, one of Penn's original city parks, is an instant kids' antidote to Too Much History. Located a block north of the Constitution Center at Sixth and Race Street, it offers a cool fountain, an antique carousel, a playground, and a minigolf course (look for the pint-sized replicas of Philly landmarks that mark some of the 18 holes).

Franklin Square is also one of the best places in town to hear a good story—the true stories of the struggle for independence. Every summer Saturday, children are invited to meet storytellers like the griot, an African oral historian who recreates Black culture. Costumed re-enactors invite passersby to join them daily on free storytelling benches around Old City, or join them for ticketed themed walking tours through *Once Upon a Nation.* My personal favorite: the Tipplers' Tour, an evening stroll through the 18th-century pubs near the waterfront. Activities are seasonal; get details and buy tickets at Historic Philadelphia, which also sells tickets to Lights of Liberty and the *Betsy Ross House.* Find them at 600 Chestnut St., (215) 629-4026. Hours vary, but the center is open daily and also sells tickets online at historicphiladelphia.org.

phlashforward

Park your car and ride the *Phlash,* a small van that makes 18 touristic stops in Center City. It operates every 15 minutes from 10 a.m. to 6 p.m. spring through fall, and costs $2 per trip or $10 for an all-day family pass. Call (215) 440-5500 or check visitphilly.com/phlash for more details.

Most Old City tourists grab their souvenirs and meals along Market Street. Since 1745, locals have done their shopping a few blocks south, at *Head House Square.* Originally dubbed "The Shambles," meaning a butcher's lane, the brick arcade at Second and Pine Street still hosts Sunday farmers' markets in warm weather. A block away, South Street offers one of the city's funkiest shopping and dining scenes, with everything from antiques to tattoo parlors. My favorite Christmas ornament—a papier-mâché Mexican wrestler—came from *Eyes Gallery* (402 South St.; 215-925-0193; eyesgallery.com). There are more than 400 one-of-a-kind boutiques here; get the details at southstreet.com.

"Music is the most magical form of communication among people," said Wolfgang Sawallisch, former music director of the *Philadelphia Orchestra.* For more than 100 years the orchestra has been creating musical magic in Philadelphia and beyond. With Leopold Stokowski, Eugene Ormandy, and Riccardo Muti among its noted conductors, the orchestra has commissioned dozens of works of art, recorded scores of others, and entertained audiences from Ottawa to Osaka. By 1988 it was calculated that the orchestra had traveled enough to circle the Earth a hundred times. Its current home, the Kimmel Center for the Performing Arts, opened in 2001 at Broad and Spruce Streets. It's a block away from the century-old Academy of Music, called the "Grand Old Lady of Broad Street." For more information and detailed schedules, visit the Fabulous Philadelphians at philorch.org.

Philadelphia hosts a drop-dead collection of French impressionist and post-Impressionist artworks at the *Philadelphia Museum of Art* and the *Barnes Foundation,* neighbors in the museum district along the Ben Franklin Parkway.

trivia

The majestic plateau now topped by the Philadelphia Museum of Art was formerly a giant reservoir. Powered by the river, pumps raised water into reservoirs high atop the hill, which gave its name to the city park: Faire Mount.

With major renovations designed by Frank Gehry, the Museum of Art is a grand dowager who's had a little work done. For an off-the-beaten-time opportunity try Friday evenings when, in addition to seeing the artwork, you can order a cocktail, catch a live performance, and mingle with other aficionados. While the normal museum entrance fee is $20 per adult (students over 12 pay $14, and it's $18 for seniors), on Fri nights and the first Sun of every month, admission fees are pay-what-you-wish (but blockbuster exhibits require a separate ticket). Call (215) 763-8100 or visit philamuseum.org to find out what's on tap.

The Barnes is named for a private collector, Dr. Alfred C. Barnes, who ruled in his will that his vast stash, including French impressionists and African masks—should never be altered. A long court battle delayed the opening of the downtown museum until 2012; see the ingenious contemporary compromise at 2021 Ben Franklin Parkway Thurs through Sun. Book online at barnesfoundation.org.

In addition to the grand Swann Memorial Foundation, flanking the museums on the Benjamin Franklin Parkway, Philadelphia has plenty of impressive public art. Claes Oldenburg is represented by four fanciful works. Visit the **Paint Torch** on Lenfest Plaza at the Pennsylvania Academy of Fine Art (118 N. Broad St.; follow the signs to North Broad and Cherry Streets). His **Clothespin** stands at the corner of Fifteenth and Market Streets. **Split Button** lies on the campus of the University of Pennsylvania, nearest the intersection of Thirty-fourth and Walnut Streets. **Giant Three-Way Plug, Scale A, 3/3,** perches next to the Museum of Art itself.

A few blocks west, at the pedestrian-only intersection of Locust Walk and Thirty-seventh Street, take a seat on the bronze bench next to the bronze statue of Benjamin Franklin, founder of the university. Ben's reading his *Pennsylvania Gazette,* leaning on his cane, and waiting for you to sit down and relax. He knows he's a photo op extraordinaire. Two other relaxing perches near the Penn campus are *Cira Green*, a grassy oasis that's actually the 12th floor of a parking garage at 80 S. 30th St. Savor the views during morning yoga, have a picnic, or catch a big screen movie (ciragreen.com). A shady spot to watch the action on the boulevard and grab lunch from great food trucks is *The Porch at 30th Street Station,* on the southern side of the grand railroad terminal, worth a peek (universitycity.org).

For lunch you can't beat the *Reading Terminal Market.* Founded in 1892 at the terminus of the Reading Railroad, this is a traditional stall market with 75 merchants selling usual and unique kinds of fish, meat, produce, pastries, flowers, and more. That's far fewer than the 800 stalls that lined the place on opening day, but it's big enough to find precisely the spice or the sourdough roll you want. The market is particularly known for its Pennsylvania Dutch vendors, who bring fresh-this-morning produce and treats from the surrounding countryside each day. It's open daily from 8 a.m. to 6 p.m. and on Sun from 9 a.m. to 5 p.m. Restaurant and individual merchant hours may vary (see readingterminalmarket.org). Many stands sell delicious lunches at reasonable prices. Get your Philadelphia soft pretzel here.

Another in-your-face Philadelphia shopping tradition is the loud, messy, and lively *Italian Market.* It sprawls on both sides of South Ninth Street between Fitzwater and Wharton Streets, with 4 cheese stores, 4 fish stores, 7 butcher shops, 40 different international food vendors, and a larger-than-life mural of beloved former mayor Frank Rizzo, here called the Big Bambino. For more than 100 years, this district has been the city's favorite place to rub elbows and pinch tomatoes. Open every day but Sun. Get the details at italian marketphilly.com.

Don't overlook the excitement of other ethnic neighborhoods. The city's Jews, Asians, Latinos, and African Americans welcome you, too.

The *National Museum of American Jewish History* is the only museum in the nation dedicated exclusively to exploring and interpreting the American Jewish experience. The NMAJH was originally founded by the members of historic Congregation Mikveh Israel, established in 1740. Its new home at 101 S. Independence Mall East opened in 2010. Visit anytime except Mon and Jewish holidays, but note that tickets ($12 seniors, $11 kids, and military, free) cannot be purchased within the museum on Sat. Book online at nmajh.org instead.

Enter Chinatown at *Friendship Gate,* at Tenth and Arch Streets, and grab a meal and your bearings at *Joseph Poon Chef Kitchen* at 1010 Cherry St. Poon, a larger-than-life celebrity chef, leads 3-hour "Wok 'n' Walk" tours of his neighborhood by appointment. They include a 4-course meal and local color: everything from a Tai Chi demonstration to a vegetable-carving lesson. The tour cost, which includes a meal, is $45 for adults, and $39 for students. For more details call (215) 928-9333 or visit josephpoon.com.

Juneteenth Every Day

The City of Brotherly Love has a four-century history of the journey from slavery to freedom, and celebrates African American heritage. You may plan a trip to join the annual Juneteenth festivities Philly-style, but you can explore deeply rooted Black culture year-round.

Begin at *The President's House: Freedom and Slavery in the Making of a New Nation*. The Independence Mall site, with archeological artifacts, commemorates life at the nation's first executive mansion, where George Washington—with nine slaves—and John Adams lived. Admission is free. But linger at the *African American Museum in Philadelphia*, with four galleries. Philadelphia was the first city to create a museum honoring Black culture, and the museum, steps from Independence Mall at 701 Arch Street, confronts contemporary injustice as well as Black artists. A permanent exhibit showcases Black people's role in US history. Open Thurs through Sat, 10 a.m. to 5 p.m., Sun noon to 5 p.m. Admission is $14 for adults, $10 for seniors and children. Call (215) 574-0380 or visit aampmuseum.org. *Mother Bethel African Methodist Episcopal (A.M.E.) Church*, founded by Bishop Richard Allen in 1794, sits at 419 South 6th St., on the oldest parcel of land continuously owned by African Americans, and is the nation's first Black denomination. Today, Mother Bethel is a church (where the congregation worships weekly). Its museum and archive date to the 1600s, and founder Allen is entombed in its crypt. Reservations are required for museum tours: (215) 925-0616; motherbethlel.org.

The Underground Railroad Museum at Belmont Mansion, in Fairmount Park, is the former home of an abolitionist Judge Richard Peters, who opposed the Fugitive Slave Act of 1793. Plan a visit to the site, at 2000 Belmont Mansion Drive, at belmontmansion.org.

Northwest of downtown, the neighborhood of **Germantown** was a bustling village well before 1776. Today, it's a community recovering from tougher times, but several sites and a museum commemorate its grand past, which includes the only Revolutionary War battle fought within the city limits, as well as its role in the Underground Railroad.

Stenton is the well-preserved Georgian home of James Logan, secretary to William Penn. Logan was a powerful figure and a mentor to Benjamin Franklin, who borrowed his books (the collection was the foundation for Philadelphia's Free Library). Nearby **Wyck**, a Quaker home from 1690, maintains a 175-year-old rose garden. Cliveden, the imposing plantation home of slaveowner Benjamin Chew, was ground zero in the 1777 Battle of Germantown, but its historical facts and modern perspectives weave stories of privilege, oppression, independence, and slavery over centuries. Live summer performances and group tours are available. Go to cliveden.org. the how-to's, visit freedomsbackyard.com.

In the Johnson House (6306 Germantown Ave.; 215-438-1768; johnson house.org) three generations of a Quaker family championed abolition and hid escaped slaves. Family lore says Harriet Tubman was one of them.

Schools and cemeteries, including Concord School House and Upper Burying Ground in Germantown, tell more stories of local 19th-century life; the site is open to the public the second Sat of each month from May to Oct. Call 215-844-1683 or go to concordschoolhouse.org.

The Philadelphia Latino community calls the Fifth Street and Lehigh Avenue corridor "El Centro de Oro," or its heart of gold. Here you'll find **Taller Puertorriqueño,** a Puerto Rican cultural education organization dedicated to encouraging and sharing Puerto Rican and Latino culture through art exhibits and classes. Hours for the gift shop and gallery are 9 a.m. to 5 p.m., Mon to Fri, and Sat. 10 a.m. to 6 p.m. Closed from noon to 1 p.m. during the week and all day Sun.

Philadelphia's Center City has been the focus of a dynamic commercial and cultural revival in recent decades. The urban residential scene has kept pace with this revival, from the elegant towers of Rittenhouse Square to the leafy restored blocks of Old City, adjacent to some of the city's—and the nation's—most historic locations. Old City also boasts a wide variety of independent galleries, restaurants, and boutiques.

In the street grid south of Market, you'll find similarly walkable neighborhoods such as **Society Hill** and **Queen Village.** The vital residential street scene has spread north to restored neighborhoods such as Northern Liberties and Fishtown, once known as one of the city's tougher neighborhoods.

In a stretch of once-abandoned factories and warehouses just northeast of Center City, Fishtown is among the neighborhoods adding new restaurants and art galleries. One sweet spot for the tattooed and trendy is *Johnny Brenda's* (1201 Frankford Ave.; 215-739-9684; johnnybrendas.com). It's a gastropub named after a famous local boxer, and indie rock bands play upstairs. Locals pick up produce at Greensgrow, an urban farm stand on 2501 E. Cumberland Street (and another at 5123 Baltimore Ave. in West Philly). New shops dot nearby blocks on Frankford Avenue. But the sentimental favorite among local eateries is still *Johnny's Hots* (1234 N. Delaware Ave.; 215-423-2280), with award-winning cheesesteaks and a local sandwich specialty: hot sausage with a fish-cake smashed on top. Don't ask.

West of the Schuylkill River, the intermingled urban campuses of the University of Pennsylvania and Drexel University draw students from all over the world.

The Benjamin Franklin Parkway holds some of the jewels of Philadelphia—the majestic Museum of Art, the Franklin Institute, the Rodin Museum, the Museum of Natural Sciences, and the Free Library (founded by Ben himself). However, the Parkway Museums District is home to more than a dozen other spectacular collections. Visit parkwaymuseumsdistrictphiladelphia.org for details, maps, and discount admission coupons.

The Franklin Institute, along with other prominent institutions, including the Philadelphia Zoo, participates in the CityPASS program, which offers admission discounts. Prices vary depending on how many attractions you decide to include on your CityPASS. Check out the details at citypass.com.

While in the city, don't overlook some smaller gems with world-class special collections.

One of the city's oddest museums is preserved, quite literally, off North Broad Street, 3 blocks from the Temple University campus. The *Wagner Free Institute of Science* (1700 W. Montgomery Ave.) is an institution housing the private collections of the altruistic William Wagner. Since its founding in 1855, it has offered free public education courses. Fossils, taxidermy mounts, skeletons, insects, minerals, geodes, and shells—Wagner meticulously amassed a collection now displayed in a grand 3-story Victorian library. It even claims the first American saber-toothed tiger. It's both spooky and spectacular, a perfect setting for a horror movie. Admission is still free, though the institute suggests a $10 donation. Guided tours are $15. Hours are Tues through Fri 9 a.m. to 4 p.m. Visit wagnerfreeinstitute.org.

Just a few blocks from the Wagner, visit the only museum in the country dedicated to the collection and preservation of Black dolls: the *Philadelphia Doll Museum,* which highlights the story of how African American people have been perceived throughout world history by exploring the subtle cultural messages conveyed by its 300 handmade and manufactured dolls from Africa, Europe, and America. It's open Thurs and Fri from 10 a.m. to 4 p.m. and Sun from noon to 4 p.m. at 2253 N. Broad St.; (215) 787-0220; philadollmuseum .com. Admission is $4 for adults, $3 for all others.

In the Rittenhouse Square area, a beautiful spot for strolling and shopping, stop by the *Rosenbach Museum* at 2008–10 Delancey Place. It's the palatial town home formerly owned by two brothers: Philip Rosenbach, who collected rare furnishings, and A. S. W. Rosenbach, who collected rare books and manuscripts. Today you can gape at rarities on display from the museum's vast holdings: the original manuscript of James Joyce's *Ulysses,* Shakespeare folios, rare Americana, and works by children's author/ illustrator Maurice Sendak (for whom the museum's addition was named). The museum opens at noon Tues through Sun, closed Mon and national holidays. Admission is $10, $8 for seniors, and $5 for students, and free for children under 12. Guided tours are required for most galleries. Call (215) 732-1600 or visit rosenbach.org.

> roamifyou
> wantto
>
> Roll along the Benjamin Franklin Parkway—or any street in town— with Indego, the city's popular bikeshare. Rentals through your downloaded app start at $12 for 24 hours. Choose an e-bike or old-school ride. (BYOH: Please bring your own helmet.) Find the details at indego.com.

Like the Rosenbach, the *Pennsylvania College of Physicians Mutter Museum* is housed in a Rittenhouse Square town house and has its own unique niche, but there all similarities end. In fact, "endings" might be a good theme for this bizarre collection of skulls, lesions, a giant distended colon, the secretly removed tumor of Grover Cleveland. But there are excellent changing exhibits on motherhood, pandemics and more. Both medical and morbid, for certain members of certain families, it would be engrossing, as well as gross. Note to parents of teenaged boys: There's a gift shop and weekly movie nights. The museum at 19 S. Twenty-second St. is open daily from 10 a.m. to 5 p.m. Adult admission is $20; $15 for teens. Call (215) 560-8564, or visit muttermuseum.org.

The *Philadelphia Art Alliance,* located on ultra-fashionable Rittenhouse Square, displays innovative visual art. Built as a private home in 1906,

A Case of Nerves

The anatomical model outside the bookstore at Drexel University College of Medicine's East Falls campus looks eerily true to form, with good reason: It's the remains of a real human body. What appears to be string art is actually the nervous system of a college cleaning woman who willed her body to science in 1888. The school's foremost anatomy professor at the time spent five months manually picking out every piece of bone and flesh from the cadaver before wrapping each strand of the nervous system in wet gauze and preserving it with paint and shellac. See it at 2900 Queen Ln.; (215) 991-8100: drexelmed.edu.

the building was given to the Art Alliance in 1925. People initially joined the organization so they could imbibe alcohol on Sundays—the building was a speakeasy during Prohibition. The facility at 251 S. Eighteenth St. is open Tues through Sun from noon to 7 p.m. Admission is $5 for adults and $3 for seniors and students. Fri is pay as you wish. Visit philartalliance.org.

For those intrigued by Lewis and Clark, a visit to Independence National Park is definitely in order—not to gawk at the Declaration, but to view artifacts of the famous 1803–04 expedition at the *American Philosophical Society* next door at 105 S. Fifth St. Among the society's founders were Benjamin Franklin and Thomas Jefferson. The society, which directed scientific preparations for the Corps of Discovery, owns Lewis's original journals and exhibits them each summer. For more information call (215) 440-3400 or visit amphilsoc.org. A block away, Rembrandt Peale's luminous portraits of the explorers are displayed with those of other early American heroes at the Portrait Gallery in the Second Bank of the United States (closed for renovations; see updates at nps.gov/inde).

Go to jail. Go directly to jail. Do not pass Go, and do not miss a tour of the *Eastern State Penitentiary* at Twenty-second Street and Fairmount Avenue. You can stay for a short time, unlike Willie Sutton (who robbed banks because, he said, that's where the money was) and Al Capone. This was the world's first *penitentiary,* a place where criminals could be *penitent.* Constructed in the 1820s to rehabilitate criminals through solitary confinement, the castlelike penitentiary that was once the most expensive building and most famous prison in the world is now a crumbling, empty block of sky-lit cells and guard towers. The Halloween events—well, they're a scream. Eastern State Penitentiary is open daily 10 a.m. to 5 p.m. and stays open until 8 p.m. on Fri in June, July, and Aug. Groups of 20 or more can book ahead. Admission is $14 for adults, $12 for seniors, and $10 for students. Call (215) 236-3300 or visit easternstate.org.

The Mural Tour

Philadelphia has the most urban murals of any city in the country. On exhibit 24 hours a day, with no admission fee and no waiting lines, 2,300 murals tell the story of the city's vitality, history, and dreams. The brainchild of Jane Golden, the **Mural Arts Program** (215-685-0750; muralarts.org) has created 1,900 of those murals, inspiring hundreds of disadvantaged youths to work with professional artists. To everyone's pleasure, as the murals go up, graffiti decreases. Reflecting their popularity, there are multiple guided and self-guided tours of this urban gallery.

At Forty-third Street and Baltimore Avenue, in the pocket-sized Clark Park, is a **statue of Charles Dickens,** the only known sculpture in the world of the English author of classics such as *David Copperfield* and *Great Expectations.*

For over a hundred years, men (and, of late, women and children) have strutted along Philadelphia's Broad Street on the first day of the year, commemorating winter with costumes, comedy, and uncommon music. It's the internationally recognized **Mummers Parade.** The annual parade is an hours-long extravaganza of otherwise-normal people dressed in glitter, feathers, and organza. They march, dance, strut, and vie for prizes (and bragging rights). Thousands of enthusiastic revelers line city sidewalks at dawn each Jan 1 as the clubs, or "brigades," of Mummers dance to the music of tinny string bands. Think of it as Carnival, with overdressed middle-aged men instead of under-dressed hotties. Visit mummersmuseum.com or the **Mummers Museum,** 1100 S. Second St. The phone number is (215) 336-3050.

Philadelphia boasts **Fairmount Park,** the biggest planned urban park system in the world, with more than 8,700 acres of parkland, including natural and historical features, cultural attractions, recreation areas, and waterways.

The park comes within a 5-minute walk from downtown along Kelly Drive. Renamed for a famous Philadelphia rower (and brother of the late Princess Grace of Monaco), the road closes to traffic on Sunday so bikers, runners, and bladers can enjoy the riverfront scene from its east bank. Alongside are crew teams practicing for the city's many regattas; they finish their races close to **Boathouse Row,** the oft-photographed stretch of Victorian riverfront buildings. Bathed in floodlights at night, they're best seen either from West River Drive (where you can't stop your car to enjoy them) or from the promenade outside the Fairmount Waterworks.

The **Fairmount Waterworks Interpretive Center,** located in the largest cream-colored building in the group below the Museum of Art, is a great free introduction to what was once a worldwide wonder. In 1821 the city created an ingenious system that used waterpower to pump water. Waterwheels, installed in the dam below the Engine House, used 30 gallons of water to lift 1 gallon out of the river. The dam was the largest in the world and created a lake in the Schuylkill that was 6 miles long—which is why it's been a favorite rowing venue ever since.

With an emphasis on conservation, the center does a lighthearted job of showing kids how water is treated and transported (even the restrooms are educational, with displays on "The Journey of Your Flush"). Don't miss the wonderful short film that explains how the city turned the waterworks into a profit-making venture that beautified the entire riverbank, with parks, fountains, and promenades. The center is at 640 Waterworks Dr. and is open Tues through Sat from 10 a.m. to 5 p.m., Sun from 1 to 5 p.m. (except for city holidays). Call (215) 685-0723 or visit fairmountwaterworks.org.

trivia

Near Wissahickon Creek in north-west Fairmount Park you'll see Hermit Street, Hermit Lane, and Hermit Terrace. The streets commemorate a brotherhood of 17th-century German mystics led by Johannes Kelpius, who lived in a cave nearby.

On the western side of the Schuylkill, one of Fairmount Park's grandest structures is young at heart. The **Please Touch Museum** is located in Memorial Hall, built for the 1876 Centennial Exposition, filling the vast, 38,000-square-foot space with exciting exhibits for the under-7 crowd. It's a spectacular transformation. There's a carousel and family-friendly cafe on site. Open Wed through Sun from 9 a.m. to 4:30 p.m. except Thanksgiving and Christmas; admission is $19, no matter what your age (4231 Ave. of the Republic; 215-581-3181; pleasetouchmuseum.org).

The perfect trip to Philadelphia includes a visit to **Valley Green**—if you can find it. A 5-mile-long, dirt-and-gravel path called **Forbidden Drive** passes through Valley Green overlooking Wissahickon Creek. It's so called because it forbids automobiles, admitting only walkers, runners, horses, bikers, and bladers. Take Germantown Avenue northwest to #7900, turn left on Springfield Avenue, and follow signs (and the downhill topography) to the valley. Or take Henry Avenue northwest to #7900, then turn right on Wise's Mill Road, following signs to the valley. If you're on foot, access Forbidden Drive anywhere and stop for brunch, lunch, or dinner at the **Valley Green Inn.** Call (215) 247-1730 or visit valleygreeninn.com for reservations.

Northwest of downtown, the neighborhood of **Germantown** was a bustling village well before 1776. Today, it's a community recovering from tougher times, but several sites and a museum commemorate its grand past, which includes the only Revolutionary War battle fought within the city limits, as well as its role in the Underground Railroad (see "Juneteenth" above).

Creepy Crawlies

Talk about thousand-leggers: The country's largest bug museum is the *Philadelphia Insectarium and Butterfly Pavilion,* where swarms of live and mounted insects crawl through the imagination of children and adults. See (and sometimes touch) newly discovered and extinct species, bug out while watching insect movies, and creep through a man-made spiderweb. Butterflies in the tropical garden prefer that kids wear their brightest clothes. The museum, open from 10 a.m. to 4 p.m. Mon through Sat, is at 8046 Frankford Ave. in northeast Philadelphia. Admission is $15 for kids 3–13, $20 for adults; (215) 335-9500; myinsectarium.com.

Follow Germantown Avenue farther north and you'll climb to **Chestnut Hill,** a well-heeled historic district. Cobblestoned, tree-lined Germantown Avenue is loaded with blocks of pleasant shops and cafes; nearby lie the leafy campuses of Germantown Academy and Chestnut Hill College. To browse the many cafes in the neighborhood, visit philadelphiarestaurants.com.

Chestnut Hill is also the home of the **Morris Arboretum** of the University of Pennsylvania, a romantic 92-acre garden that emphasizes sculpture, trees, and research. Kids love Out on a Limb, a treetop canopy walk that includes a suspension bridge and play areas. It's a quarter mile off Germantown Avenue at 100 E. Northwestern Ave. You can enjoy lunch alfresco, or under a tent, during warm weather at the cafe next to the Widener Visitor Center. The arboretum opens daily at 10 a.m. Purchase tickets in advance: $20 for adults; kids under 3 are admitted free. Call (215) 247-5777 or visit upenn.edu/arboretum.

In nearby **Elkins Park** (take Route 611 north from the city) is Frank Lloyd Wright's **Beth Sholom Congregation.** Dedicated in 1959, months after Wright's death, the building is a hexagonal pyramid of glass. The design is based, in part, on ideas put forth by the synagogue's distinguished and for-ward-looking first rabbi, Mortimer Cohen. The building was intended to be self-contained and to stand apart from its suburban surroundings. It succeeds. Wright designed the fittings, too: the lighting, the seating, and the placement of the religious symbols. When the Museum of the Diaspora in Tel Aviv cre-ated a permanent exhibit of synagogues to represent 18 centuries of Judaism, it chose Beth Sholom for the 20th century. Tours of the sanctuary, at Old York and Foxcroft Roads, are given Sun, Wed, and Thurs. To book a tour, check bethsholompreservation.org or call (215) 887-1342, ext. 157.

Nyuk nyuk nyuk! From the sublime to the ridiculous: A few minutes north of Elkins Park lies a monument to the holy trinity of witless comedy. The **Stoogeum** immortalizes the head-knocking, eye-poking genius of the Three Stooges, Larry, Moe, and Curly, with exhibits, film clips, and memorabilia tucked into a space in a suburban strip mall off Bethlehem Pike in Gwynedd Valley. Can you tour it? Soitenly, but call or email first: (267) 468-0810 or stooge umstaff@gmail.com.

Got a few hours' layover between planes? Go fishing. It's actually possible, from Philadelphia International Airport, to hop in a cab and be transported across the highway into a national wildlife refuge. This one, the *John Heinz National Wildlife Refuge at Tinicum,* was created to save the largest remaining freshwater tidal marsh in the country. As planes soar overhead, 300 species of birds fly below. The interpretive center at 8601 Lindbergh Blvd. is open daily. Additional information can be found at heinz.fws.gov.

Another patch of green—one of the city's most venerable—lies a few miles down Lindbergh Boulevard. From its surroundings—the Philadelphia Gas Works and other flat and charmless industrial sites—you'd never guess that the site is a landmark in the history of botany. *Bartram's Garden,* the 18th-century home of a family of naturalists, is an idyllic Schuylkill River plantation that preserves native wildflowers, trees, and wetlands.

Father and son John and William Bartram are credited with sharing the plants of the New World with European scientists; John was named King George III's royal botanist in 1765. Both he and his son identified new species on field trips up and down the East Coast, cultivated more than 200 of them, and saved at least one from extinction: the *Franklinia,* a tree named for their good friend and frequent visitor Benjamin Franklin. (Thomas Jefferson and George Washington stopped by, too.) Today visitors can stroll the plantation and river trail, admiring the skyscrapers of downtown Philadelphia from a peaceful meadow. A map brochure identifies the locations of rare specimens, such as the country's oldest living ginkgo tree (circa 1785).

ON THE BEATEN PATH ATTRACTIONS WORTH VISITING IN PHILADELPHIA

Academy of Music	National Constitution Center
African American Museum	Pennsylvania Academy of Fine Arts
Independence Hall	Philadelphia Zoo
Liberty Bell	Barnes Foundation

A Voice for Justice

Paul Robeson, the 20th-century baritone, renowned actor, activist, and concert singer, was a mighty international voice for justice. But he retired to a modest West Philadelphia row house before his death in 1976. The building, with a small collection of artifacts, has been preserved as the Paul Robeson House and Museum at 4914 Walnut Street. Visit paulrobesonhouse.org.

Bartram's Garden is open daily, except for city holidays, and admission to the grounds is free. Garden shop hours are 10 a.m. to 2 p.m. Mon through Thurs and 10 a.m. to 4 p.m. Fri through Sun. Guided garden and house tours leave the Garden Shop Fri through Sun at 10:30 a.m., noon, 1:30 p.m., and 3 p.m. (2 garden tours, 2 house tours). The garden is located at Fifty-fourth Street and Lindbergh Boulevard but is hard to find (unless you arrive by boat: see below); call first for directions at (215) 729-5281 or visit bartramsgarden.org.

Boat tours along the Schuylkill stop at Bartram's Garden in warm-weather months. Fishing piers, docks, kayak rentals, and cycling paths are part of the newly bucolic Schuylkill Banks riverfront. Check the details at schuylkill banks.org or call them at (215) 222-6030.

Philadelphia gave birth to the nation's first horticultural society in 1827 and its first flower show in 1829. Today the *Philadelphia Flower Show* is an international success: 10 acres of soil, picket fences, orchids, and more—spectacular, enviable gardens created by nurseries and florists enlivening the Pennsylvania Convention Center. Crowds of more than 300,000 people cross-pollinate at the early-March flower show, the world's biggest to be held indoors. For more information call (215) 988-8800 or visit phsonline.org/the-flower-show.

Inner Suburbs

Harriton House was the northernmost tobacco plantation operated on the slave economy. It's at 500 Harriton Rd., Bryn Mawr. The grounds are open daily from dawn to dusk. House tours are available by appointment Tues through Fri from 10 a.m. to 4 p.m. Admission is $6 for adults; free for students. Call ahead (610) 525-0201, or visit harritonhouse.org.

Right in the middle of the beaten path is *Valley Forge National Historical Park,* where George Washington and his 11,000 soldiers slept fitfully during the winter of 1777–78. If you are a history buff, an enthusiastic kid studying the Revolution, or just a healthy visitor out for a country walk—if you are, in fact, anything but a British loyalist—you'll enjoy the natural and historical beauty of the park. The visitor center offers an excellent short free film introduction and other services, and bike rentals are available in good weather: The park is part of the Schuylkill River Trail into downtown Philadelphia, 18 miles away. The park grounds are open daily year-round from 7 a.m. till dusk. The visitor center and Washington's Headquarters are open 9 a.m. to 5 p.m. daily except Thanksgiving, Christmas, and New Year's Day. Valley Forge National Historical Park, 1400 N. Outer Line Dr., King of Prussia; (610) 783-1077; nps.gov/vafo.

Not far away is the *Mill Grove Audubon Wildlife Sanctuary,* on a bluff overlooking Perkiomen Creek. The museum features an array of wildlife art by *John James Audubon,* in a rural setting with 3 miles of trails. The first American home of Audubon, the site charges $4 for adult admission, $3 for seniors, and $2 for children. It's open Tues through Sat 10 a.m. to 4 p.m. and Sun 1 to 4 p.m. The grounds are open daily except Mon, from dawn to dusk. Find it at the intersection of Audubon and Pawlings Roads, Audubon. Call (610) 666-5593 for details about naturalist programs, some of which are perfect for children.

Consider, too, a visit to the *Wharton Esherick Museum.* This Philadelphia-born artist spent much of his life in this curious, rustic 5-story structure, creating designs mostly in wood. Like Barcelona's famed Antonio Gaudí, Esherick eschewed straight lines and right angles. The 2-story spiral staircase, carved from a single piece of wood, defies description but begs to be touched, as do many of the displayed pieces the artist designed for the 1940 World's Fair in New York. The hour-long guided tour is not recommended for young children. Tours of this National Historic Landmark for Architecture are available by appointment only Mar through Dec, 10 a.m. to 5 p.m. Sat, and 1 to 5 p.m. on Sun; groups of 5 or more may tour weekdays from 10 a.m. to 5 p.m. Adult entry is $15 and includes a 1-hour guided tour; seniors $13, students $12, and children $8. The studio is on the Horseshoe Trail near Country Club Road in Paoli, a western suburb. Check whartonesherickmuseum.org or call (610) 644-5822 for reservations and driving directions.

While nearby Longwood Gardens gets the tour buses and big crowds, *Chanticleer,* in Wayne, attracts the folk who garden for fun. I think it's the most innovative and lovable garden in Pennsylvania, and at its brilliant best in tulip season. Open to the public since 1993, Chanticleer's 2 manor houses are surrounded with bold shapes, modern contrasts, and a lighthearted approach. The result looks like a hip children's picture book, with oceans of color and shapes, punctuated by witty garden sculpture. Stroll an easy mile-long path, linking 8 separate plantings, that winds down a gentle green slope. Beds close to the circa 1913 house (the former home of the Rosengarten family) are pleas-

A Day on the Main Line

Built to shuttle the wealthy in and out of Philadelphia in style, the *Main Line* train became synonymous with old money and grand estates. The stops along the way—like Haverford, Bryn Mawr, Rosemont, and Villanova—also correspond to gracious college campuses and chic shopping and are well worth a drive west along Route 30, known here as Lancaster Avenue.

Start in Bryn Mawr for fine or hand-painted Italian ceramics at *Via Bellissima,* at 853 W. Lancaster Ave.; it's open Mon through Sat 10 a.m. to 5:30 p.m.; call (610) 581-7414 or visit viabellissima.com.

One block down the street, grown-up girls love *Skirt,* a tiny boutique crammed with everything from this year's most sophisticated couture to designer flip-flops. Personal stylists are available by appointment daily. Call (610) 520-0222 or browse shop-skirt.com.

Mushmina's motto is "Made With Love in Morocco." This Wayne boutique offers imported caftans, and handmade bags and jewelry at 164 East Lancaster Avenue, Wayne; 610-293-8089, or online at mushmina.com.

Pun's Toys has gotten "best of" honors from local magazines and lots of lucky kids. Skip the cartoon action figures—Pun's has marvelous tin soldiers from centuries of wars, velvety plush creatures, juggling equipment, puzzles, puppets, and more. It opens at 11 a.m. Tues through Sat. Find it at 21 Rittenhouse Place in Ardmore. Visit punstoys.com or call (484) 413-2561.

ingly structured. Those at a distance, like the Woods and the Water Garden, flourish seemingly undisturbed, with swaths of single colors, like red clover or blue camas, punctuating the lawns.

The whimsical sensibility of the garden's first director, Chris Woods, takes a theatrical turn in the Ruin Garden, 3 open-air garden rooms that were built on the foundation of a prior residence on the property. A large fountain, inspired by ancient sarcophagi, dominates the Great Hall, mirroring the surrounding trees in its dark waters; huge, sculpted stone books spill over the floor of a library; and in the Pool Room, marble faces gaze tranquilly from the watery depths of another fountain.

Chanticleer is located at 786 Church Rd., Wayne; call (610) 687-4163, or visit chanticleergarden.org. It's open Apr through Oct, Wed through Sun, 10 a.m. to 5 p.m. (until 8 p.m. Fri, May through Labor Day). Admission is $10 for adults, free for those 12 and under. Parking is free, but limited: Make a parking reservation in advance online. (If you time your visit for late afternoon, you may be allowed to park if space permits and you ask nicely.)

Another grand estate—turned—public garden, this one with free admission, lies only 3 miles away. It's **Stoneleigh,** the result of nearly a century of attention from the famous landscape architects the Olmstead Brothers. Look for the giant carved rabbits standing guard at 1829 East County Line Road in Villanova; stoneleigh.org.

Art aficionados adore the **Brandywine River Museum** (1 Hoffman's Mill Road, Route 1, just south of Route 100, Chadds Ford), one of the largest and most comprehensive collections of paintings by three generations of Wyeths (N. C., Andrew, and Jamie) and Howard Pyle, and other American artists. Expanded with a massive 2014 bequest from the estate of the Pittsburgh billionaire Richard Scaife, the collection lives in a 19th-century gristmill overlooking the stream. Exhibits change often, so you might see your favorites (like Jamie's *Portrait of Pig*) next to works you've never seen. It's open every day except Tues and Christmas, 10 a.m. to 4 p.m., and admission is $18 for adults, seniors $15, and $6 for students with ID. Call (610) 388-2700 or visit brandywine.org.

trivia

Baldwin's Book Barn in West Chester is just that: a charming 1822 barn crammed with 300,000 titles, both new and antique. Call it the anti-Amazon. Open daily except Thanksgiving and Christmas; call (610) 696-0816 or visit bookbarn.com.

At nearby **Longwood Gardens** (Route 1, PO Box 501, Kennett Square 19348), the extravagant, elegant, exquisite horticultural displays are open every day of the year, from 9 a.m. to 5 p.m. Jan to Mar, and stay open until 6 p.m. Apr through Oct, with extended hours in summer and at Christmas. The conservatory opens at 9 a.m. Exotic flowers thrive in hothouses, and illuminated fountains highlight summer concerts. Longwood is a carnival of 20 indoor gardens, 400 performing-arts events each year, a gift shop, and a restaurant. Daily programs and classes ratchet up your green-thumb quotient. Admission is $18 for adults, $15 for seniors, and $8 for children ages 5 to 18. Call (610) 388-1000 or go to longwoodgardens.org for details.

Follow Route 1 south until you get to **Lincoln University,** just northeast of Oxford. Lincoln, founded in 1854, is the nation's oldest historically Black college. Originally called Ashmun Institute, it was renamed in 1866 to honor President Abraham Lincoln. Among its famous alumni are poet Langston Hughes, chief Justice Thurgood Marshall, and jazz and soul legend Gil Scott-Heron.

In addition to being the cradle of liberty, Philadelphia also nurtured the helicopter industry. That's why you'll find the **American Helicopter Museum and Education Center,** a sure-fire kids' favorite, 20 minutes from Route 1 in West Chester. You'll learn about the history of the chopper and see vintage machines and the only V-22 Osprey on public display in the US. You can even hop into a helicopter for a quick flight. Family rides are offered at the annual

Family Fest and several other weekends spring through fall; check details and dates online. *Philadelphia Magazine* voted the museum its "best scientific outing for kids" a few years back, for the number of things that they can get into—wind tunnels, instrument cockpits, and hands-on exhibits. The museum is off Route 202 at 1220 American Blvd., adjacent to the Brandywine Airport. It's open Thurs through Sat 10 a.m. to 5 p.m., Sun from noon to 5 p.m. Admission is $10 for adults; $8 for seniors, students, and children; and free for little fliers under 2. Call (610) 436-9600 or fly to helicoptermuseum.org.

West Chester's downtown, another neat 18th-century grid designed by the Penn family, is worth a stroll, with eateries, galleries, and the campus of West Chester University.

If you'd rather bike, walk, or skate than drive, try the **Schuylkill River Trail** to get from here to there. It extends 30 miles from Center City Philadelphia along the Schuylkill River to Parker Ford. (When completed, the trail will extend as far north as Pottsville.)

On the northern edge of the metropolis, Doylestown, the Bucks County seat, offers a concrete-and-tile monument to one man's life. It's **Fonthill,** the home of Henry Mercer. Mercer (1856–1930) was a polymath of astounding energy. After training as an attorney and following a career as a globe-trotting archaeologist, he turned artist, designing and producing thousands of tiles at the height of the American Arts and Crafts movement. (The floor of the magnificent state capitol is inlaid with some of the results.) Mercer stuffed the walls and ceilings of his castlelike abode with his own work and added extensive displays of pottery, lighting, and furniture. One writer called the result "Colonial Williamsburg on amphetamines." It's less crazy when you learn that Mercer always intended his home to be a museum. The town's "Mercer Mile" comprises the next-door Moravian Pottery and Tileworks and the **Mercer Museum** a few blocks away, open Mar through Dec. For more information visit mercermuseum.org.

Both Fonthill and the Mercer Museum are open Tues through Sun (the museum is open Tues evenings, too) but are closed on certain holidays. Call Fonthill at (215) 348-9461 and the Mercer Museum at (215) 345-0210, or visit mercermuseum.org. Admission is $15 for either castle; get your timed admission online.

Upscale flea market may be a contradiction in terms, but it aptly describes nearby **Rice's Market** (6326 Greenhill Rd., New Hope; 215-297-5993; rices market.com). There's been a weekly market on this 30-acre site since 1860; now there are two, on Tues and Sat. It's a Bucks County tradition, located midway between Doylestown and the Delaware River, with vendors hawking everything from antiques to zucchini. Open Mar through Dec. Get there early.

As you travel west, drop south again to Chester County and **Historic Yellow Springs** (1685 Art School Rd., Yellow Springs). This village "has a connection with every era of American life," says staffer Pat McGlone. During the Revolutionary War, Washington's troops traveled here from Valley Forge for the medicinal waters. During the Civil War, Union troops recuperated at its hospital. Sixty years later, lured by the bucolic surroundings, the Pennsylvania Academy of Fine Arts established its landscape school here. In 1958 Steve McQueen spent his honeymoon at the springs while filming *The Blob* locally. For directions and details call (610) 827-7414 or visit yellowsprings.org.

Pennsylvania Dutch Country

About 300 years ago, groups of religious refugees from the Rhine region of Germany migrated to southeastern Pennsylvania. Amish and Mennonite communities still thrive throughout rural Pennsylvania, from Berks, Lebanon, and Lancaster in the east to Mercer, Indiana, and Lawrence Counties in the west. These settlers, mostly peasant farmers, came to take advantage of the religious freedom offered by William Penn. They included Amish and Mennonites—people of "plain" dress—and Lutherans and other Reformed groups of more worldly attire, sometimes called "fancy." Over time these people became known as "Pennsylvania Dutch," with the *Dutch* really a misinterpretation of the original *Deutsch*.

Wilkum to scenic Pennsylvania Dutch Country, where, despite the increasing encroachment of development, life moves at a slower pace and centers around time-honored traditions and values. Here you find beautiful scenery punctuated with one-room schoolhouses and wooden covered bridges, modern farm machinery pulled by mules, homemade clothing and quilts hanging to dry. You hear the clip-clop of horses' hooves on quiet country roads. The plain folks are less materialistic and less hurried than their urban counterparts, yet the highways through **Lancaster County** have grown touristy, as various people attempt to capitalize on the otherworldliness of these self-effacing settlers. Virtually any T-shirt shop, quilt boutique, or restaurant in the area can hand you a driving tour brochure. For a glimpse of a real Pennsylvania Dutch family, enjoy the movie *Witness* and leave these people alone.

A better idea: Go north to Lebanon and Berks Counties. Begin exploring off Route 72 in Lebanon County. It's the less-traveled part of the region, with equal numbers of "English" and Amish residents. While Lancaster County, to the south, hawks its "real Pennsylvania Dutch" attractions with ferocity, Lebanon County treats its Amish neighbors with deference and respect. Farms seated on the richest soil in the country sport immaculate barns and flourishing gardens.

Stern biblical quotes flank mailboxes. In the quiet, a syncopated trot heralds horse-drawn buggies before they come into view.

The region's German dissenter roots still flourish. In Schaefferstown, bright signs adorned with distelfinks, the folk-art icons of the region, adorn adjacent museums. The modest **Gemberling-Rex House and Brendle Museum** display 250 years of village history. The house and museum are open for tours from Apr 1 through Oct 6 every Tues and the first Sat of each month. Classes and other events are held throughout the year (717-949-2244; hsimuseum.org). A historic tavern operates nearby: The Franklin House (Route 419 on the town square in Schaefferstown; 717-949-2122) offers weekend lunches and serves dinner daily except Thurs.

Three miles west of Reading, there's a place to test an old adage: Give a man a fish, and you feed him for today; teach a man to fish, and you feed him for a lifetime. **Limestone Springs Preserve** (930 Tulpehocken Rd., Richland; 717-866-2461; limestonespringspreserve.com) offers recreational trout fishing Apr through Oct. For $1 admission and $4 for each pound you catch, you get your chance to introduce the kids to fun that isn't generated on a video screen.

Pennsylvania has more than 100 private fishing lakes; for a full list, visit https://pfbc.pa.gov/lakesreg.htm.

Barn Art Tour

Northern Berks County is a center for an 18th-century mural project: barn art, with vibrant geometrics and strong primary colors. Thanks to renewed interest by contemporary artists, there are over 700 restored and new examples of barn art in the region. You can begin your driving tour on the campus of Kutztown University. The Pennsylvania German Cultural Heritage Center here has created a step-by-step 47-mile route linking highly Instagrammable scenes. You'll see plenty of 12-point stars, or hex signs, the same designs used in the layouts of ancient European cathedrals. Borders and arches adorn some structures, huge animals some others. Look for "cattle murals," farm scenes that were added in the early 20th century. It's a magnificent meander. If you don't have time for the full itinerary, just drive north from Crystal Cave on Routes 737 or 143 and you'll spot some prime examples.

Slow your journey down, in local fashion, with stops at local eateries. **Deitrich's Meats** (660 Old Route 22, Krumsville; (610) 756-6433; deitrichsmeats.com) offers scrapple, kielbasa, pickled tripe, and whoopie pies. The Deitsch Eck Restaurant in Lenhartsville offers weekly specials in a dining room full of barn art; it's open Wed through Sat evenings (the-eck.com; 610-562-8520). Sun hours 9 a.m. to 4 p.m.

While the digital instructions for the tour are online at pa-mag.com/barnstar, they aren't easy to follow. Just grab a print copy at the Heritage Center, regional tourism offices, or merchants like Firefly Bookstore, 271 W. Main Street, Kutztown.

Head north toward Cornwall, a village with charm, history, and a pretty nice bike trail. You may have noticed how many eastern Pennsylvania towns end in "Forge" or "Furnace." There's plenty of iron ore below this land, mined since the 18th century. The **Cornwall Iron Furnace** is the only surviving furnace of its kind in the Western Hemisphere and was put to work during the American Revolution. Now a well-done state museum, it offers thoughtful displays about the region's development. The surrounding homes—grand for the owners, modest for the ironworkers—still stand. The redbrick museum is at Rexmont and Boyd Streets (717-272-9711; cornwallironfurnace.org). It is open Fri and Sat from 9 a.m. to 4 p.m. and Sun from noon until 4 p.m., with the last tour beginning at 4 p.m. each day. Admission is $8 for adults, $7 for seniors, and $4 for youths. Hours are subject to change.

Moving all that iron eventually required a short-line railroad that's now gone rails-to-trail. The Lebanon Valley Trail now covers 18 miles between the Lancaster county line and Lebanon. Get details at lvrailtrail.com. The 1830-era Cornwall Inn (717-306-6178 or 866-605-6563; cornwallinnpa.com), a bed-and-breakfast at the Cornwall trailhead, was once the residence of the furnace owner.

In the 1890s the Pennsylvania Chautauqua Society, attracted by the region's natural beauty, founded **Mt. Gretna.** The landscape is still just as inviting—gently wooded mountains, a stream, and a lake. Throughout the summer, the Chautauqua's genteel educational and cultural tradition lives on with music, theater, and arts events, and the Arts and Crafts–style cottages are treasured family heirlooms (a few can be rented, too). Follow Route 72 west from Cornwall to discover its charms.

The most well-known local attraction is the professional summer stock theater at the Gretna Theatre, where plays have been performed since 1927. Within strolling distance, on paths covered with pine needles, are the Greek Revivalist Hall of Philosophy (for lectures and chamber music), a gift boutique, and the Jigger Shop, jiggershop.com, an old-fashioned soda fountain that feels like the soul of the village. Among the highlights here are old-fashioned birch beer from a keg; fountain drinks you thought you'd forgotten, like lime rickeys; and chromebound counter stools that twirl until you're dizzy. Enjoy your lunch on the spacious deck.

Mt. Gretna's lake across the road is another throwback—a sand-bottomed freshwater lake with a beach, broad lawns, picnic pavilions, and a stationary diving platform with swing ropes in the middle. Daily admission is $24 for adults, $12 for kids and seniors; book online.

They say you can't revisit the past. Mt. Gretna proves them wrong. Get all the details at mtgretna.com.

Heading south, you'll see another monument to religious expression at **Ephrata Cloister.** At the zenith of this community in the 1740s and 1750s, about 300 German members worked and worshiped here. Today the National Historic Landmark is open for tours at 632 W. Main St. in Ephrata.

The charismatic founder of this community, Conrad Beisel, settled along the Cocalico Creek in 1732. He was followed by two groups of followers: celibate men and women, who lived in dormitories, and married couples with children. All expected that the Second Coming was imminent. The monastic Anabaptist community invented its own a cappella music, created Germanic calligraphy known as Frakturschriften, and operated a printing press. By 1813 its celibate members had died; children raised in the community were less enthusiastic about the celibate tradition, and the community dwindled. Its buildings remain. Visit Thurs to Sat from 10 a.m. to 4 p.m. and on Sun from noon to 4 p.m. Admission is $10 for adults, $9 for senior citizens, and $6 for youths 3 to 11. For more information call (717) 733-6600 or visit ephratacloister.org.

At the **Landis Valley Museum** north of Lancaster, you can see 18 historic buildings filled with artisans demonstrating the crafts, tools, and tales of German immigrants. Its shop stocks an interesting array of heirloom seeds for home gardeners. It's open Mon through Sat 9 a.m. to 5 p.m. and Sun noon to 5 p.m.; closed major holidays. Adult admission is $12. From downtown Lancaster, take Route 272 north to 2451 Kissel Hill Rd. For more details call (717) 569-0401 or visit landisvalleymuseum.org.

Landis Valley bills itself as a living history museum, usually a good indication that kids will find it a trifle dull. Little ones will prefer the next-door **Hands-On House,** a farm-themed attraction with an outdoor playground. It's at 721 Landis Valley Rd. Admission is $11 for kids, $10.50 for adults, with discounts some afternoons. It's open late on Thurs through Sat. Call (717) 569-5437 or visit handsonhouse.org.

The city of **Lancaster** served as the capital of the United States for almost an entire day: September 27, 1777. At the time, British invaders were threatening the capital in Philadelphia. The Continental Congress and the Executive Council of Pennsylvania fled to Lancaster, where they held one session of Congress. Believing that the British were in hot pursuit, Congress kept moving across the Susquehanna River to York.

The historic heart of Lancaster County, founded in the 1740s, is handsomely preserved and worth exploring. Stop at LancasterHistory (lancasterhistory.org) for an excellent introduction and special exhibits, such as the tradition of African American quilt-making. On Tues, Fri, and Sat, Lancaster's Central Market sells the best baked goods, flowers, and farm produce around—as it has since

1730, making it the country's oldest continuously operated farmers' market. The huge redbrick arcade at 23 N. Market St. opens at 6 a.m.; call (717) 291-4723.

A National Historic Monument, the **Fulton Opera House** in Lancaster was built in 1852. A gem of Victorian architecture, the theater's lush interior includes a sweeping staircase and crystal chandelier. Sarah Bernhardt, Al Jolson, W. C. Fields, Mark Twain, and others performed here. Each summer Friday, small group tours raise the curtain on the Fulton's history. Order tickets at thefulton .org. For more downtown cultural events, including a "first Friday" evening each month, visit lancasterarts.org.

trivia

Where did Pennsylvania's only US president live? Bachelor and youthful tycoon James Buchanan owned Wheatland, a stately Lancaster home now open to visitors.

In western and southern Lancaster County, the hills are more pronounced and the views more dramatic. Along the Susquehanna River you'll find many scenic overlooks that offer breathtaking views of the river far below.

Lancaster County features one of the largest concentrations of antiques in the country. In **Adamstown,** the "Antiques Capital of the United States," more than 5,000 antiques dealers gather to display and sell their merchandise. It's the essential antiquers' paradise. Dozens of shops line Route 272, with **Renninger's** (renningers.com) one of the best known and best loved. If you crave memories from any bygone era—even the 1990s—here's where to find what you're looking for. Take the Pennsylvania Turnpike to exit 286, then go north on Route 272.

Since 1875 **Groff's Meats** has been selling wholesale and retail meat in Elizabethtown. The fourth generation of Groffs—two brothers and two sisters— now run the business. Groff relatives and employees buy and slaughter cattle and pigs, then lovingly and painstakingly convert them into hams, bacon, sweet bologna, and, in the fall, mincemeat: a super—secret recipe of beef and suet, local apples, raisins, sherry, rum concentrate, and spices. No minces are killed to make this concoction. Groff's Meats makes 5.5 tons—*tons*—of mincemeat a week during mincemeat season, which coincides roughly with autumn leaves. (If storage space fills up, they might skip a week.) Visit Groff's Meats at 33 N. Market St., Elizabethtown, or place a 2-pound or 35-pound order by calling (717) 367-1246 or search for them online at groffsmeats.com.

You want corn chips? You want onion rings? **Herr Foods** is one of the largest snack food companies in the country, employing 1,000 people and distributing its munchies in 10 northeastern states. The factory tour includes a 25-minute video (great for kids). Then you walk through windowed corridors, watching people and machines washing, peeling, slicing, cooking, and seasoning the food—then bagging, boxing, and preparing it for shipment. Reach onto the conveyor belt and pick up a free handful of fresh, warm chips. Yum. Herr's is at the intersection of Herr Drive and Route 272 in Nottingham, just south of Lancaster. The visitor center gift shop is open weekdays year-round except for major holidays, 10 a.m. to 4 p.m. Mon through Fri. Visit herrs.com for information.

Visit the demonstration garden and see the sustainable agricultural experiments taking place at the **Rodale Institute.** Rodale, which publishes *Prevention* and other magazines, welcomes visitors just outside Kutztown. Take a self-guided tour Thurs through Sat 10 a.m. to 3 p.m. or take a leisurely stroll through the gardens on your own anytime, 24/7. Call (610) 683-1400 or visit rodaleinstitute.org.

People in the East know **Reading** for its outlets, its Pennsylvania Dutch heritage, and its antiques marts. But few people recognize that in some ways, Reading is the East—the East as in Orient, China, and pagodas. At the top of **Mt. Penn,** the 7-story **Pagoda** dominates the town's skyline. In the early 1900s William Abbott Witman bought this land to quarry its stone. But the quarrying operation defaced the mountain, which he hid by building, of all things, a pagoda, hoping it would become a luxury hotel. When Witman's license to serve alcohol was denied, the building fell into the hands of a bank. In 1910 an investor bought the full catastrophe, then sold it to the City of Reading for a dollar. You can visit, free, daily from 11 a.m. to 5 p.m. A gift shop is open Fri, Sat, and Sun on the first level. To get there, start in Reading and drive uphill. For precise driving directions call (610) 375-6399 during operating hours or check pagodaskyline.org.

Daniel Boone, the legendary pioneer, was born and raised in **Birdsboro.** You can visit his family's Quaker homestead and learn about 18th-century rural Pennsylvania. From Reading, take Route 422 east to 400 Daniel Boone Rd., Birdsboro. From mid-June to mid-Aug, the modest exhibit on his life is open in the visitor center Tues through Sat, 10 a.m. to 4 p.m. and Sun noon to 4 p.m. (reduced hours in the off-season). You may visit part of the grounds for free; take a self-guided tour for $3, or pay $6 for a guided interior tour. Call (610) 582-4900 or visit danielboonehomestead.org for more details.

The **Greater Reading Trails System (GRTS),** overseen by the Berks Area Mountain Biking Association, covers more than 125 miles of trails in 5 major preserves, and all are connected to the Schuylkill River Greenway Rail Trail. The International Mountain Biking Association gives the network a bronze star. The trails range in difficulty from beginner-friendly to some of the most technical, rock-strewn trails you'll experience anywhere. You'll note an abundance of in-town amenities for hobbyists, including bike shops, craft beer

Saving Grace

Lancaster County boasts that it has the most productive nonirrigated farmland in the United States. There are more than 4,500 farms here, mostly small and family owned. The pace of urban sprawl severely threatened these farms during the 1980s and 1990s—the *Philadelphia Inquirer* estimated the rate of loss at an acre an hour.

To the rescue came the Lancaster Farmland Trust. The trust helps farm owners obtain conservation easements to preserve their lands for agricultural use forever. And it's stemming the tide of development: Since 1994 there have been two county acres saved for every one lost to development. To date, it has permanently preserved more than 32,000 acres of farmland on 530 farms, making Lancaster County a national leader in the preservation of farmland, and plans to acquire another 50 farms over the next few years.

bars, hotels, music venues, restaurants, and sporting events. For more information on where to ride refer to berksmountainbiking.org.

A cozy and well-done little museum in Womelsdorf pays tribute to a very early American, Conrad Weiser. His amazing gifts as a linguist put him at the center of Pennsylvania history from 1730 to 1758. Fluent in a half-dozen tribal languages, English, and his native German, he negotiated with the Iroquois, served as a magistrate and militia leader, and fathered 10 children. Somehow, he also found time to join the Ephrata Cloister for two years. The **Conrad Weiser Homestead** is open seasonally at 2588 Weiser Ln.; call (610) 589-2934 or visit conradweiserhomestead.org.

A completely modern diversion, the **Spooky Nook Sports Complex** in Manheim is a 14-acre indoor sports complex that welcomes even the youngest athletes. It bills itself as the largest such complex in North America. Day passes ($15 for adults or $40 for a family of three or more) are available for tennis, volleyball, field hockey, batting cages—name your workout and have at it. It's a popular site for youth sports tournaments; hence the onsite Warehouse Hotel. Look for the complex at 2913 Spooky Nook Rd. The Complex is open Mon through Fri from 5 a.m. to 10 p.m., Sat from 7 a.m. to 10 p.m., and Sun from 8 a.m. to 9 p.m. Call (717) 945-7087 or check the online events calendar at spookynooksports.com.

Also near Manheim is a gorgeous outdoor laboratory: the Penn State **Trial Gardens.** Here's where hundreds of varieties of flowers are evaluated before coming to market. Casual gardeners, photographers, and families are welcome June 1 to Aug 31. Look for the Penn State sign at 1446 Auction Rd., Manheim; call ahead to (802) 309-3814 or visit trialgardenspsu.com.

In Columbia, make time for the **National Watch and Clock Museum,** a deft and thoughtful look at how humans tell time. It found a home here because Hamilton watches were made here. Don't waste a moment wondering if you should go. You must. Look for the clock tower at 514 Poplar St. Hours vary; admission is $12 for individuals, $30 for the whole family. Call (717) 684-8261 or visit nawcc.org.

Capital District

My husband used to joke that my intellect was like the Susquehanna River: broad but shallow. It's a good description, both of my brain and of the river at **Harrisburg.** Here little forested islands dot the stream, and the only boats that can maneuver are of the pontoon variety. But Harrisburg's small downtown makes good use of its waterfront, and its state capitol complex, lavishly restored and expanded over the past few decades, is no snore—it's a stunner.

In 1906 President Theodore Roosevelt dedicated the gleaming granite capitol, declaring it "the handsomest building I ever saw." Lots of folks would argue that it outshines even the US Capitol, which stylistically shares its distinctive flights of steps and domed rotunda.

Free tours start at the foot of the grand staircase, copied from the Paris Opera House. Look up—272 feet—to admire the grand dome. Look down, too: Interspersed with the terra-cotta floor tiles throughout the building are 377 mosaics by Henry Mercer's Moravian Tileworks. These mosaics depict a visual timeline of Pennsylvania, from its native animals, like the elk and robin, to the factory and automobile.

Images of women abound in the capitol, which adopts different styles for its major chambers. In the state senate chamber, you'll find the mural "Unity" by muralist Violet Oakley in which goddesses holding up light fixtures preside in pre-Raphaelite style. In the Italianate House chamber, women representing "The Hours" are featured in the dome painting by Edwin Austin Abbey, and still others are found glowing with light in the stained-glass windows designed by Philadelphian William Brantley Van Ingen. Free guided tours are offered every half hour Mon through Fri 8:30 a.m. to 4 p.m. Weekends and most holidays (except major ones), tours are offered at 9 a.m., 11 a.m., 10 p.m., and 3 p.m. Reserve your timed visit at pacapitol.com.

The guided tours are well worth an adult's time, but kids will prefer the attractions of the capitol's newer east wing: a skylit cafeteria and the welcome center's free, lighthearted interactive introduction to state government (the state dog is the Great Dane because William Penn owned one). There are lively state factoids embedded in the floor (stomp on your answers), a model of the capitol statue in Legos, and plenty of action and music. Don't miss the wonderful Rube Goldberg contraption called "Making a Bill."

The next-door **State Museum of Pennsylvania** (300 North St.) offers few surprises, but toddlers may enjoy the museum's Curiosity Connection, a cute hands-on space on the ground floor. Closed Mon and Tues; $7 admission for adults, $6 for seniors, and $5 for children. Get the details at (717) 787-4980 or statemuseumpa.org.

Elsewhere along the gentrified riverfront that radiates from the Capitol's west front, there's a livelier restaurant and retail scene that builds on and transcends the lobbyist-and-legislators culture of this company town.

Security precautions prevent visitors from parking in the garage under the capitol, and on-street parking is fiendishly difficult. Leave your car instead on **City Island,** a short walk across the Walnut Street pedestrian bridge from downtown. City Island is the site of Riverside Stadium, the summer home of the Harrisburg Senators, an Eastern League AA pro team (check the schedule at milb.com). But it's got plenty of other fun. The **Pride of the Susquehanna** paddleboat departs for river tours from its marina (call 717-234-6500). A miniature steam train, mini golf, food stands, athletic fields, and paved paths are open most of the year. If you're feeling unathletic, just take a horse-drawn carriage ride from the Harrisburg Carriage Company (717-234-1686).

Farther from downtown, Harrisburg's attractions dwindle, but firebugs may enjoy the **Pennsylvania National Fire Museum** in an old Victorian firehouse at 1820 N. Fourth St. ($6 adult admission; 717-232-8915; pnfm.org). Nearby is the capital's answer to Philadelphia's Reading Terminal: the 1860s-era **Broad Street Market** (broadstreetmarket.org; 717-236-7923), with farm-fresh food, candies, preserves, and snacks. Open Thurs through Sat. Eat here or carry a take-out picnic to the river along Front Street. Two miles east of the capitol you'll find the **Greystone Public House,** a sleek contemporary bistro that's actually been serving beers since 1805. Open daily (Sun for brunch only); greystonepa.com.

winetrail

The Susquehanna Valley is wine country, and the **Mason-Dixon Wine Trail** lets you meander through 14 vineyards. Find maps, seasonal events, and discounts for B&Bs and hotels at masondixonwinetrail.com.

While Gettysburg gets the most Civil War tourists, Civil War skirmishes reached right into **Camp Hill,** now part of the Harrisburg suburbs. Harrisburg's bid to lure some of those history buffs is the **National Civil War Museum,** which portrays personal experiences on both sides of the conflict. One thousand artifacts and lots of multimedia illuminate the lives of common soldiers, men and women on the home front, and African Americans in the conflict. It's open daily. The hilltop location, somewhat isolated from town, is One Lincoln Circle at Reservoir Park. Admission is $14 for adults, $9 for seniors, and $8 for students. Call (717) 260-1861, or visit nationalcivilwarmuseum.org.

The two giant cooling towers by the airport south of Harrisburg are the site of the country's worst-yet nuclear disaster, at *Three Mile Island.* The affected reactor was shut down immediately after its partial meltdown in March 1979; low levels of radiation were released. Take a photo (from a distance) and continue into Middletown. At *Alfred's Victorian,* the restaurant specialty is the Flaming Victorian Salad, which bears absolutely no relation to other kinds of leaking fuel. The address is 38 N. Union St. For more information call (717) 944-5373 or visit alfredsvictorian.com.

A short drive down I-83 from Harrisburg brings you to *York,* a biggish town (or a smallish city) whose history is everywhere. York, briefly the US capital in the 18th century, is now a genteel county seat just north of the Maryland state line. The Articles of Confederation were signed here in 1777. But the northern edge of town gets lots of traffic these days, and not simply because of nearby strip malls. Here stand the muscle-flexing power of two macho monuments: the *Harley-Davidson Vehicle Operations and Tour Center* and the USA Weightlifting Hall of Fame at the York Barbell Company.

The visitor center at Harley-Davidson (1425 Eden Rd.) celebrates the lure of the open road—and the choppers that frequently cost more than 4-wheeled cars. The well-designed exhibits and the factory tour are free. More than 60,000 visitors come by each year—double the number of those touring the town's colonial district. The factory tours are relatively quiet (you'll hear your guide through earphones) and are offered to guests over age Mon through Fri. (check post-pandemic hours). When open, a play space at the center entertains younger kids, and the gift shop offers everything from leather jackets and caps to Harley-Davidson Yahtzee games. Call (877) 883-1450, or roar over to harleydavidson.com.

Up the road, look for the larger-than-life weightlifter jerking his barbells high over I-83, 5 minutes from the Harley factory. A latter-day Atlas, he lunges forward, twirling continuously above the York Barbell Company. The *USA Weightlifting Hall of Fame* next door chronicles competitive strength from ancient Greece, through its late-19th-century heyday when celebrity strongmen toured the world, to the present.

Really strong guys, at least in cartoons, favor leopard-skin leotards and handlebar mustaches. That's all due to Eugen Sandow and Louis Cyr, the trend-setters whose stunts awed Victorian fairgoers. The exhibit traces them and their descendants to the well-oiled era of Schwarzenegger and Steenrod (as in Vicki, a contemporary Hall of Famer). Most of the memorabilia here was acquired by York Barbell's founder, Bob Hoffman, who advocated weight training, health foods, and isometrics. Practicing what he preached, he lived to the age of 87. Free admission Mon through Sat at 3300 Board Rd., exit 24 off I-83 (800-358-9675; yorkbarbell.com).

York County bills itself as "The Factory Tour Capital of the World." "Conveyor belts are great!" says its guidebook. You'll find Pfalzgraff, the pottery maker; Hope Acres Farm, where robots milk the cows; Snyder's, the pretzel people; and more. A good place to sort out all the man-made possibilities is right at the Harley-Davidson Tour Center, where the county maintains an information office (888-858-9675 or visit yorkpa.org). One-stop shopping.

Among the kitschy roadside attractions of the Lincoln Highway is the **Shoe House,** just off Route 30 at 197 Shoe House Rd. in Hellam, Adams County. It was built in 1948 by Mahlon Haines, who made shoes, then boots, then a house for honeymooners shaped like a shoe. A really big shoe: 48 feet long and 25 feet high. You can tour the shoe June through Oct (or other months by appointment) for $5; call (717) 840-8339 or check hainesshoehouse.com for hours and directions.

Hersheypark, the famous amusement park, may be too crowded for you, but consider **Chocolate World** at the entrance to Hersheypark in Hershey. A sweet 9-minute ride takes you through a simulated chocolate factory. Hours vary by season and week; closed Christmas. During some festivals, the hours may be extended. Call (717) 534-4903 or (800) 437-7439 or visit hersheypark.com. You can't beat the price (reserved passes are free), and of course there are treats.

The Moorish architecture of **Hotel Hershey** is worth a peek into the lobby, even if you can't afford its 4-star prices. And the fabulous rose garden outside the hotel blooms freely (and is free for public viewing) well into November. For 23 more acres of floral displays, visit **Hershey Gardens** next door (170 Hotel Rd.; 717-534-3492; hersheygardens.org).

Battlefield Territory

Don't miss **Gettysburg.** Union and Confederate soldiers fought the bloodiest battle of the Civil War here in 1863. The area is well-organized for tourism, with the absorbing history communicated in virtually every medium.

War, they say, is hell. That's never more true than on a summer weekend at Gettysburg. The crowds are daunting. If at all possible, plan on a weekday visit, preferably in the off-season.

The Museum and Visitor Center should always be your first stop: It orients you to the war, the battle, and the battlefield. You can stop in for just a snack, restrooms, and free maps, but it's worth paying the $12.25 admission for a fine 20-minute film, a museum with 1,600 artifacts, and—the pièce de résistance— the miraculous **Cyclorama.** The latter is the world's largest painting, created in 1884 by Paul Philippoteaux. The 377-foot picture in the round depicts Pickett's Charge in images so realistic the first visitors wept. You can also build your own itinerary, from "quick raid" (a half-day tour) to "full campaign." Purchase tickets online in advance at gettysburgfoundation.org, or upon arrival at the center at 1195 Baltimore Pike. It's open except for Thanksgiving, Christmas, and New Year's days, with extended summer hours.

Make the most of your visit to this well-preserved battlefield with the help of a licensed tour guide—each one must pass a detailed oral exam. Gettysburg offers bus and car tours where experts will accompany lay visitors on 2-hour trips. Car tours start at $75 for up to 6 people; bus tours, which depart from the visitor center, are $35 for adults, $21 for those aged 6 to 12.

Also at Gettysburg, the **Eisenhower National Historic Site** commemorates Dwight D. Eisenhower's military and presidential years. The only way to get there is on a tour that departs from the visitor center. Your site visit includes the Eisenhowers' 230-acre farm and farmhouse, the only home the First Couple ever owned. The tour costs $9 per adult, $5 for youths.

Gettysburg also offers bicycle, horseback, and Segway tours of the battlefield—an ideal way to cover ground and to bypass crowds on the battlefield roads—with guides who know their stuff.

Horseback tours are offered not by the National Park Service but by two local firms: the **National Riding Stable** (see nationalridingstables.com) at Artillery Ridge Camping Resort, 610 Taneytown Rd. (1.5 miles from the visitor center), (717) 334-5100; and **Hickory Hollow Farm** (hickoryhollowfarm.com). Reservations are a must.

SegTours offers a battery of tours on Segway transporters, spring through fall, from $50 per person; visit segtours.com or call 717-253-7987 or 1-888-4SEGTOURS.

Gettysbike offers morning, evening, and sunset tours that beat the heat. They'll rent you bikes, but you can also pedal your own. Call (717) 752-7752, stop in at 1995 Baltimore Pike, or check gettysbike.com. Closed Sun and winter months.

In the little town of Gettysburg, stop by the restored old train station on Carlisle Street or the nearby **Wills House,** where Lincoln worked on his famous address. Check the website for hours at nps.gov/gett/planyourvisit /david-wills-house.htm.

JANUARY

Mummers Parade

Philadelphia
(215) 599-0776
visitphilly.com
Wake up early on New Year's Day and catch the Mummers Parade, the all-Philadelphia strut of 30,000 costumed "Mummers."

Pennsylvania Farm Show

Harrisburg Farm Show Complex
(717) 787-5373
farmshow.state.pa.us
The Pennsylvania Farm Show has it all. For 10 days each January, the events at the Harrisburg Farm Show Complex attract human and animal competitors from all over the commonwealth. More than 350,000 people attend the show each year, making this century-old slice of Americana the largest indoor agricultural event in the United States. And it's free.

MARCH

Philadelphia International Flower Show

Pennsylvania Convention Center
(215) 988-8899
theflowershow.com
Spring means flowers, but nowhere more so than at the Philadelphia International Flower Show—the largest and most prestigious flower show in the world, with 10 acres of lush gardens and lavish floral settings. There's an admission fee, paid even by the show's judges.

APRIL

Penn Relays

University of Pennsylvania
(215) 898-6145
thepennrelays.com
The venerable Penn Relays are held at the University of Pennsylvania the last weekend of April. This track event attracts the country's fastest runners, from high schoolers to Olympic wannabes to the over-80 Masters. Reserved seating is available for Saturday events, which attract crowds of more than 40,000.

MAY

Devon Horse Show and Country Fair

Devon Fairgrounds
(610) 964-0550
thedevonhorseshow.org
The tony Devon Horse Show and Country Fair, the nation's largest outdoor horse show, creates traffic jams up and down Route 30 for a week at the end of May.

JULY

Blobfest

Phoenixville
(610) 917-1228
thecolonialtheater.com
Do you pride yourself on a truly blood-curdling scream? Test it against others at Phoenixville's Blobfest. The contest is only one of the bizarre features of the town's celebration of the cheesy horror classic *The Blob*, filmed here in 1958. Held the second weekend of July.

Don't forget your own handmade tinfoil hat to ward off evil alien space rays.

AUGUST

Philadelphia Live Arts Festival and Philly Fringe
Philadelphia
(215) 413-9006
fringearts.org
Thousands of artists converge on Philly each August for the wild and wacky art party known as Philadelphia Live Arts Festival and Philly Fringe. For 2 weeks, dancers, actors, playwrights, musicians, visual artists, video-makers, and puppeteers roam the city's streets and fill its performance halls. At night, festival-goers head to the Festival Bar for dancing, drink specials, and visual media installations. Location of the bar is to be determined.

Renaissance Faire
Mount Hope Estate and Winery
Route 72, Cornwall
parenaissancefaire.com
Her Majesty is at the Renaissance Faire, held weekends from late August through mid-October. Watch blacksmiths, taste "roasted turkey legges," and let loose your inner groundling. Held at Mount Hope Estate and Winery, Route 72, 0.5 mile south of Pennsylvania Turnpike exit 266.

SEPTEMBER

World War II Days
The Eisenhower National Historic Site
Gettysburg
(717) 338-9114
nps.gov/eise

Gettysburg hosts all kinds of soldiers' reunions. The Eisenhower National Historic Site, home of the Allied commander, observes World War II Days the third weekend of September, with reenactors, demonstrations, tanks, and talks.

OCTOBER

Dracula Festival
Rosenbach Museum & Library
(215) 732-1600
rosenbach.org
Twilight fan alert: A month-long Dracula Festival brings fans of the vampire novel into the light for theatrical readings, cupcake-decorating workshops, and photo booths equipped with costumes at the Rosenbach Museum & Library, which holds Bram Stoker's original *Dracula* outlines and research notes.

DECEMBER

Reenactment of Washington's Crossing
1112 River Rd., Washington Crossing
(215) 493-4076
ushistory.org/washingtoncrossing
George Washington crossed the Delaware River on December 25, 1776, to launch his attack on the British in Trenton. The Reenactment of Washington's Crossing launches each Christmas Day from Washington Crossing Historic Park in Bucks County, 35 miles north of Philadelphia. The visitor center displays artifacts and provides details.

There are plenty of kitschy attractions in Gettysburg, such as the **Hall of Presidents** (717-334-5717), which features wax reproductions of 36 presidents who relate American history in their own words. For a complete listing of tourist territories, dining, camping, and lodging, stop by the **Gettysburg Convention and Visitors Bureau** at 35 Carlisle St.; call (717) 334-6274; or visit gettysburgcvb.org.

Gettysburg nightlife offers few options except ghost tours. Many of the 51,000 battlefield casualties were carried to homes and buildings in town, and legends of ghostly apparitions have persisted for decades. One place to get into the spirit, so to speak, is **Farnsworth House** (401 Baltimore St.). In addition to selling Civil War memorabilia and books, the house also hosts candlelight evening ghost walks through town and presents the Civil War Mourning Theater, with dramatic and sometimes ghoulish monologues. A dinner theater on the premises offers period music. For details visit farnsworthhouseinn.com, or call (717) 334-8838.

Drive to 900 High St., Hanover, and take a deep breath. Fresh air? No. Fresh Utz (the name rhymes with *huts*) potato chips. Here is the factory of **Utz Quality Foods,** and you're welcome to take a free self-guided tour Mon through Thurs 10 a.m. to 3:30 p.m. Call (800) 367-7629 for details.

As you head west on Route 30 from Gettysburg, you have an opportunity to see the largest herd of elephants in the country. The rolling farms hereabouts are nothing like the savanna, but you can find a plethora of pachyderms at **Mister Ed's Elephant Museum** in Orrtanna. Owner Ed Gotwalt curates a collection of 6,000 specimens, all his: political, plush, Hindu, and other specimens. Tusks and ivory carvings, too. Most of the items fall into the deliciously kitschy category. So do the old-fashioned penny candies and roasted peanuts on sale in the gift store. Open every day from 10 a.m. to 5 p.m. The shop—er, museum—is at 6019 Chambersburg Rd. Call (717) 352-3792 or visit www.mistereds.com.

Hickory Bridge Farm B&B in Orrtanna offers 9 rooms, including cottages, all with private baths. Two rooms have private whirlpools, too. Guest rooms are furnished with Pennsylvania Dutch antiques, and the cottages have wood-burning stoves. It's a genuine farmstead that boasts a red barn-turned-restaurant, a country museum with old farm equipment, a spring-fed swimming pond, and a trout stream surrounded by 50 acres of farmland. In the restaurant you're offered amazing quantities of Pennsylvania Dutch cooking in a designer country setting, Fri and Sat night and Sun noon to 3 p.m. Call (717) 642-5261 or visit hickorybridgefarm.com for more information.

Places to Stay in Southeastern Pennsylvania

CHESTER HEIGHTS (CHADDS FORD)

Hamanassett Bed & Breakfast
PO Box 366
(610) 459-3000
hamanassett.com
A Federalist-style mansion surrounded by Brandywine hunt country.

LANCASTER

Lancaster Arts Hotel
300 Harrisburg Ave.
(717) 299-3000
lancasterartshotel.com
Chic boutique hotel and restaurant in a historic tobacco warehouse near Franklin and Marshall College.

GETTYSBURG

Brafferton Inn
44 York St.
(717) 337-3423
brafferton.com
This brick-front inn in the historic district dates from 1786.

KEMPTON

Hawk Mountain Bed & Breakfast
221 Stony Run Valley Rd.
(610) 756-4224
hawkmountainbb.com
A contemporary inn with swimming pool and mountain views.

PHILADELPHIA

Thomas Bond House
129 S. Second St.
(800) 845-BOND
thomasbondhousebandb.com
In Independence National Historic Park the home of a Revolutionary-era physician is now a restored bed-and-breakfast with views of the Delaware River.

DOYLESTOWN

Highland Farm Bed and Breakfast
70 East Rd.
(215) 345-6767
highlandfarmbb.com
Oscar Hammerstein II raised his family—and wrote "Oklahoma"—at this genteel 1840s estate. Broadway memorabilia abounds.

Places to Eat in Southeastern Pennsylvania

CORNWALL

The Blue Bird Inn
2387 Cornwall Rd.
(717) 273-3000
bluebirdinn.com
Casual pub grub. Late-night entertainment on the tiki-torch deck attracts a young crowd on Fri and Sat nights.

DOYLESTOWN

Paganini Trattoria
81 W. State St.
(215) 348-5922
paganinidoylestown.com
Homemade pasta and more (plus a casual cafe across the street).

GLEN MILLS

Harvest Seasonal Grill
549 Wilmington Pike
(610) 358-1005
harvestseasonalgrill.com
Plenty of salads, veg and vegan dining options. Near Longwood Gardens and the Brandywine Museum.

Jimmy John's
1507 Wilmington-West Chester Pike (Route 202)
(610) 459-3083
jimmyjohns1940.com
A Brandywine hot dog institution. Drop a quarter in the slot to operate the massive model train display.

HARRISBURG

Rubicon
270 North St.
(717) 317-9027
Ambitious and unusual, this is a popular destination for the political crowd, with indoor and outdoor dining.

LEBANON

Trattoria Fratelli
502 E. Lehman St.
(717) 273-1443
tratfrat.com
Voted best in central Pennsylvania for a decade. Upscale innovative Italian cuisine served Tues

through Sat. Try grilled chicken and polenta or crabmeat specials.

LENHARTSVILLE

Deitsch Eck
87 Penn St.
(610) 562-8520
the-eck.com
Pennsylvania Dutch comfort specialties like pig stomach and corn pie are offered weekly.

PHILADELPHIA

The Garden at Cherry Street Pier
121 North Christopher Columbus Blvd.
(215) 839-8031
cherrystgarden.com
This spacious open-air waterfront eatery near Penn's Landing is an

upscale bistro with live entertainment and specials like Taco Tuesdays. Dinner only from 4 p.m.

Pat's King of Steaks
1237 E. Passyunk Ave.
(215) 468-1547
patskingofsteaks.com
Cheesesteaks and hoagies.

Zahav
237 St. James Place
(215) 625-8800
zahavrestaurant.com
A prix fixe tasting menu with an Israeli accent from acclaimed chef Michael Solomonov in Society Hill.

White Dog Cafe
3420 Sansom St.
(215) 386-9224
whitedog.com

A hip eatery and bar on the University of Pennsylvania campus, with Main Line branches in Wayne and Haverford.

READING

Judy's on Cherry
332 Cherry St.
(610) 374-8511
judysoncherry.com
New American–style cuisine and brewpub downtown. Open Tues through Sat.

Red Plate Diner
440 E. Penn Ave.
Wernersville
(610) 678-7721
redplatediner.com
Comfortable, all—American, all-day eatery.

South Central Pennsylvania

As you head west into south central Pennsylvania, you'll see higher highs and lower lows. The mountains loom higher, the valleys get broader, and the attractions can throw you an unexpected curve. Railroad buffs call these peaks of the Alleghenies Railroad City, and **Horseshoe Curve** is the star attraction hereabouts. As the early railroads expanded westward, the Pennsylvania Railroad ran into a major snag at Altoona: mountains. The grade in the Alleghenies was far too steep for a run straight up or down. To circumvent the situation and to connect two sides of Kittanning Point, engineers designed a huge, curving track, which opened to train traffic in 1854. Men used picks, shovels, and horses to carve the curve, which is still considered an engineering marvel. The length of the curve is 2,375 feet; the grade is 1.8 percent; the degree of curvature is 9 degrees, 25 minutes; and the central angle is 220 degrees.

When you come to this spot (using the Seventeenth Street exit off I-99/Route 220) where trains make a U-turn, ride the funicular or walk the 194 steps to the top; a sturdy fence protects your body from the trains but leaves your eyes and ears free to enjoy. To imagine what it's like, think of a football stadium 50 times larger than reality. You are sitting at one end

near the goalpost, two rows down from the top tier. At the topmost level of the stadium, a train approaches from the far end. It chugs on by, wrapping around the curve—and around you—as the engineer waves and toots his whistle. The long train continues on the other side of the stadium so that at one point, an endless iron snake surrounds you. Eventually it disappears around another curve, but you can still hear it, and everyone near you is still smiling. If the weather's nice, you can have a picnic while waiting for a few more of the 60 passenger and freight trains that traverse the curve daily. The curve is open daily in Apr from 11 a.m. to 4 p.m. From May to Oct, it is open 9 a.m. to 6 p.m. Mon through Sat and 11 a.m. to 6 p.m. on Sun. Prior to Thanksgiving, the curve is open weekends only in Nov from 11 a.m. to 4 p.m. From Dec through the end of Mar, the curve is closed. An annual grounds pass to the curve costs $6, but for $10 ($9 for seniors, $8 for children under 12), you can buy a combination pass that also covers a ticket to the **Altoona Railroaders Memorial Museum.** This all-in-one admission can be purchased either at the curve or at the museum, 1300 Ninth Ave. To get to the museum from I-99, take the Seventeenth Street exit, then turn right on Ninth Avenue. It's open daily May through Oct, Mon through Sat 9 a.m. to 5 p.m., and Sun from noon to 5 p.m. The museum is also open weekends from the beginning of Nov until mid-Dec. Open only weekends in Nov, Dec, and Apr; closed Jan 1 through Mar 31. For information on either site, call (814) 946-0834 or visit railroadcity.org.

Leap the Dips, the historic wooden side-friction roller coaster in Altoona's **Lakemont Park,** is a beloved institution. It plans to reopen to riders for the 2022 season. Meanwhile, try the two other roller coasters in the park, the batting cages, and the tiny monster truck rides. To get to the park from I-80, take Route 220 south; after Route 220 becomes I-99, exit at Frankstown Road. Call (814) 949-7275 or (800) 434-8006 or visit lakemontparkfun.com.

AUTHOR'S TOP 10 FAVORITES IN SOUTH CENTRAL PENNSYLVANIA

Carlisle

Chambersburg Heritage Center

Coffee Pot

Gravity Hill

Horseshoe Curve

Millersburg Ferry

National Museum of the American Coverlet

Nature Inn at Bald Eagle State Park

Pike to Bike Trail

Road Kill Cafe

Alongside the park is the new home of the **Altoona Curve,** an Eastern AA League baseball franchise that also throws fastballs and sliders. This is *Bull Durham*–type baseball, laid-back and family-friendly. Check the schedule at (877) 99-CURVE or altoonacurve.com.

You'll find another historic landmark at 3205 Sixth Ave. **Reighard's** claims to be America's oldest gasoline station, offering full service to motorists since 1909.

Just 12 miles west of Altoona off Route 22, visit the **Allegheny Portage Railroad,** now a National Historic Site. At this location in 1834, canal boats were loaded onto railcars, reducing the trip between Philadelphia and Pittsburgh from three weeks by wagon to four days by railroad and canal. At the visitor center you can take a brief history lesson. You can also walk forested trails along the railroad's route or, if you're so inclined, watch a costumed stonecutting demonstration. It's open from 9 a.m. to 5 p.m. from mid-Apr through mid-Nov, closed major holidays. You'll get a weeklong pass for $5. For more information call (814) 886-6150; or visit nps.gov/alpo.

By now, you've got the idea: Railroad buffs love this area. Their hotel of choice is **The Station Inn** in Cresson. It's a little shaky. That's why they like it. The inn's front porch is the perch where enthusiasts can watch 70 trains rumble past each day on the Norfolk Southern line. The trains are just 150 feet from the door of the hotel, built in 1866. Its 7 modest rooms are named for old railroads; the porch is where buffs trade anecdotes and lore. Contact the inn, located at 827 Front St., at (814) 866-4757, or visit stationinnpa.com.

If you head north on Route 220, then north on Route 360 and west on Route 322, you come to **Clearfield,** which originated as the Indian town of Chinklacamoose. A portion of the Old Town Historic District is listed on the National Register of Historic Places. Several stately Victorian homes offer an interesting self-guided walking tour extending 4 blocks along Front Street.

caboose with a view

The New Portage, Allegheny, and Gallitzin railroad tunnels were so strategically important that they were guarded during World War II. The bright-red caboose at tiny **Gallitzin Tunnels Park** tells their story. Call (814) 886-8871 or check gallitzin.info to visit.

West of Altoona, along Route 22, visit the **Mt. Assisi Monastery** and the **Holy House of Father Gallitzin** in Loretto. Father Gallitzin was a Russian prince who gave up his title and inheritance; he became the first priest to receive all the orders in the United States, and he served the community of Loretto. Catholics on a pilgrimage find it refreshing to stop there as well as at the Carmelite Monastery and St. Michael's Church. For more information and to schedule a visit to the sunken gardens—open year-round, dawn to dusk—call (814) 693-2800, or see francis .edu. The monastery is on the campus of St. Francis University. While visiting, stop by its Southern Alleghenies Museum, one of four locations of this regional institution. The permanent collection of American art here includes works by Pennsylvanians Mary Cassatt, Thomas Sully, and John Kane.

Heading northeast from Altoona, you discover the town of **State College,** home of **Pennsylvania State University** (not to be confused with the University of Pennsylvania, which is in Philadelphia). It's a member of the Big Ten football conference, so sports—playing, watching, and wearing blue-and-white outfits—is an important undergraduate major. Penn State was founded in 1855 as the Farmers' High School. It has grown. Beaver Stadium, the fourth-largest stadium in the country, is often packed beyond its 106,572-seat capacity. If you're a sports fan, don't miss the **Penn State All-Sports Museum.** Located at the southwest corner of the stadium opposite the Bryce Jordan Center (look for the blue canopy), it offers a viewpoint for the stadium and exhibits on the university's athletic glories. Stadium viewing times vary, so call ahead to (814) 865-0044. Regular museum hours are Tues–Sat from 10 a.m. to 4 p.m., Sun from noon to 4 p.m. The museum is only open on the weekends. Find out more at gopsusports.com/museum. The State College Spikes, an MLB Draft League team, play their home games at Medlar Field at Lubrano Park on campus.

Penn State's **HUB-Robeson Galleries,** a venture of the university's Paul Robeson Cultural Center, programs lively events from performing arts to animation festivals. The center gives voice to underrepresented student groups; check HUBRobeson on Instagram for the latest.

Penn State's College of Agriculture Sciences has spun off a few beloved attractions. Just to mention two: Don't miss the **Arboretum and H. O. Smith Botanic Gardens,** open for strolling year-round, and the **Berkey Creamery.** Campus cows contribute to the tasty ice creams here. The shop is an absolute must. Visit daily at 447 Curtin Road.

who'sthirsty?

Whether your beverage of choice is a craft brew, cider, dry riesling, or rum, the Alleghenies can fill your cup. A dozen friendly spots await along the **Central Pennsylvania Tasting Trail**, where scenic wineries and funky pubs abound. Find your DD (designated driver) and explore the list at visitpennstate.org.

Off-campus, encourage your children's future genius at the **Discovery Space Children's Science Museum.** Your miniature meteorologist or paleontologist can explore the hands-on STEM activities at 1224 N. Atherton St. It's open Fri through Sun from 10 a.m. to 4 p.m. Admission is $7 per person over age 3. Everyone under 17 must be accompanied by an adult. For more information on special programs, visit mydiscoveryspace.org.

Fourteen miles south of the main campus lies the university's **Shaver's Creek Environmental Center** (3400 Discovery Rd., Petersburg). Located off Route 26 in the Stone Valley Recreation Area, it offers lots of painless education workshops for kids and adults. The facility has a cool Raptor Center, where birds of prey like owls, hawks, and eagles can be studied up close and personal; a bat colony where more than 1,200 brown bats roost nightly; herb and flower gardens; and picnic areas. One popular annual event is the Maple Harvest Festival in late March. For more information on that, go to shaverscreek .org, or call (814) 863-2000.

The small village of **Huntingdon** is worth a detour onto Route 26. See a monument to the town's Native American past here, and glimpse the future in the students at Juniata College. Landscape sculptor Maya Lin created the college's open-air Elizabeth Baker Peace Chapel, open to the public on a serene mountaintop near campus.

The Oneida Nation, who once lived in this region, had a custom of erecting a huge monolithic stone—think *2001: A Space Odyssey*—outside their villages. These "standing stones" bore tribal symbols and history. When the first white settlers arrived in Huntingdon County in 1754, they reported a 14-foot standing stone near the Oneida village. Neighboring Tuscarora Indians somehow stole the stone. War erupted. Though the Oneida regained their stone, they moved west as settlers moved in, and the stone vanished. To commemorate Native American history, Huntingdon created a replica of the standing stone in the historic town center. It's still there, surrounded by well-kept century-old homes and the college. The monument also conferred a name on the cozy café in the center of town: **Standing Stone Coffee Company** at 1229 Mifflin St.

Route 522 runs along the ridgetop near Raystown Lake, a vast man-made reservoir. Seriously huge, it's the largest lake entirely in Pennsylvania—27 miles long—and 200 feet deep in places. Waterskiers love it. So do campers and houseboaters. **Lake Raystown Resort** offers cabins, a lodge, a café, and a marina with boat rentals (visit rvcoutdoors.com/lake-raystown-resort).

Valleys of the Susquehanna

Due north of State College, although there are no direct roads, is **Bellefonte,** meaning "beautiful fountain." It's best known for its **Big Spring,** which gushes 11.5 million gallons of water each day. Find the spring in Talleyrand Park, named for the French diplomat who supposedly suggested the town moniker during a US visit.

This diminutive town bred seven governors of Pennsylvania, according to a marker in front of its Palladian courthouse. The Victorian downtown still has lively little shops and restaurants. The friendly folks at the visitor center—located at 320 W. High St. in the 19th-century rail station by the park—will provide a map for a self-guided walking tour. *The Gamble Mill,* a boutique hotel, microbrewery, and fine restaurant, is the town's 18th-century gristmill. It's a real find (518-727-7026; gamblemillbellefonte.com).

Just 12 miles from Bellefonte on Route 150 is the *Nature Inn at Bald Eagle State Park.* Perched on 5,900 acres of state forest, the cozy inn is emphatically not a resort. It has just 16 rooms, not hundreds; it offers a patio with a fire pit and gas grills instead of a gourmet dining room. But it has a great lakefront location and LEED Gold certification for energy efficiency. Park rangers offer interpretive hikes for guests, each room offers binoculars for bird-watching, and there's a fun playroom for younger kids. It's a secluded getaway for sure, but since it's only 25 miles from State College, it's also a smart choice for lodging during Penn State football weekends, when Happy Valley can overflow. Get the details on the inn, located at 201 Warbler Way, Howard, at (814) 625-2879 or natureinnatbaldeagle.com.

Boalsburg is home to the *Pennsylvania Military Museum,* honoring the women and men of Pennsylvania who served their country in war. From Benjamin Franklin's first military unit—the Associators—through the 20th century, this museum tells the tale of these patriots. The museum is open Mar through Nov Wed through Sat 10 a.m. to 4 p.m., and Sun from noon to 4 p.m. Admission is $6. For information call (814) 466-6263; or visit pamilmuseum.org.

trivia

The Statue of Liberty also lifts her lamp over the Susquehanna River near Dauphin Narrows. As you drive along Route 322, you'll see her 25-foot white replica on an abandoned pier in the middle of the river.

Sail on. Sail on. Sail on and on to see relics and heirlooms of Christopher Columbus at the *Boal Mansion and Columbus Chapel,* just off Business Route 322 at 163 Boal Estate Dr. in Boalsburg. The chapel, which was part of the Columbus family castle in Spain, contains the desk of Christopher Columbus and 2 relics said to be pieces of the true cross of Jesus. The Boals brought the chapel to Boalsburg in 1909. Family scion Pierre Boal was a French flying ace in World War I and later served as a US ambassador. That's why memorabilia from the early days of flight are also collected by the museum. You may visit daily, May through Oct. Guided tours ($10 per adult) depart at 10 a.m. and 2 p.m. Call (814) 466-6210, or visit boalmuseum.com.

The people who live in Juniata and Mifflin Counties strive to uphold their heritage, their small-town way of life, and a standard of living not usually found in rural areas. Visiting here can be like taking a trip back in time, as you meet descendants of the early German settlers, including many Amish and Mennonite clans. Any Wednesday during spring, summer, and fall, drop in on market day in Belleville (on Sale Barn Lane, just off Route 655, due west of Lewistown).

The stellar attraction in Mifflinburg is the **Buggy Museum** (598 Green St.), commemorating passenger carriages, not mosquitoes and bumblebees. The museum shows you where William A. Heiss manufactured horse-drawn vehicles from the late 19th to the early 20th century, employing painters, blacksmiths, carpenters, and wheelwrights. Abruptly, the Heisses shuttered the shop, and half a century passed before it was reopened, good as new. Visit the museum open Sat and Sun from 1 p.m. to 4 p.m. from the first Thurs in Apr through the last Sun in Oct. For more information call (570) 966-1355 or visit buggymuseum.org.

Take a deep breath while driving to **Northumberland,** which has a big spot in history for such a little place. It was the home of Joseph Priestley, who is remembered for his pioneering work in chemistry, most notably the discovery of oxygen. He was also the founder of the Unitarian Church. Priestley's philosophic and scientific writings greatly influenced Thomas Jefferson, who based the curriculum of the University of Virginia on Priestley's ideas.

Visit the grand **Joseph Priestley House** (472 Priestley Ave.), which is open Mar through Nov for tours Sat and Sun at 1, 2, and 3 p.m. Adult admission: $6. Call (570) 473-9474 or go to http://joseph-priestley-house.org.

"A school for how to have fun" is how **Camp Woodward** describes itself. Simply put, it's an extreme-sports paradise, outfitted with runs, ramps, and tramps galore for skateboarders, BMXers, gymnasts, and cheerleaders. Located 25 miles west of State College in **Mifflinburg,** Woodward supplements its kids' summer-camp business with weekend packages Sept through May, and they swear they even get some adult visitors without kids. (If you bring kids, fair warning: The camp requires you to stay and watch their every death-defying move.) With only 11 lodge rooms for adults, accommodations fill quickly, especially during Penn State football season, so always book ahead. For room reservations call (814) 349-5520; for camps, call (814) 349-5633. Or do a double ollie to worldofwoodward.com.

Centralia, a tiny village off Route 61 in Columbia County, has the unique distinction of having been on fire since 1962. That's when an underground blaze erupted in a coal mine under the town. All sorts of engineering marvels were employed to put out the fire; none succeeded, and by 1991 nearly all of the town's residents had been evacuated. The wisps of smoke you see curling up through the ground are evidence that there's still fire down below.

Skeeball. Tilt-A-Whirl. Coasters. Bumper cars. Check, check, check, and check. *Knoebel's Amusement Resort* in Elysburg, 5 miles west of Centralia, is one of those twirled-and-true summer destinations. Some attractions, like the Carousel Museum and the bald eagle exhibit, are free: A day pass for all the coasters runs $43 for adults (book in advance online for discounts). The century-old park is shady and scenic, and parking and picnicking are free every day. You'll love it. See knoebels.com; (800) 487-4386.

Most people driving along the Susquehanna River between *Sunbury* and Harrisburg take Routes 11 and 15 on the west side for speed; but on the east the less-traveled Route 147 gives you lovely glimpses of the river valley and the interesting towns that dot the banks. In *Millersburg* you can ride the *Millersburg Ferry,* one of the last surviving wooden, double-sternwheel paddleboats in the country. It runs a mile back and forth to Liverpool at one of the river's widest points. A National Historic Landmark, the first ferry began operation in 1825, a big step forward for passengers and freight haulers accustomed to using rowboats and pole boats. At the peak of river commerce, four boats made the trips.

Now only the *Falcon* and the *Roaring Bull V* ply the river, which at this spot rarely gets more than 3 feet deep. Each ferry accommodates 4 cars and 50 passengers. To find the pickup point, drive into Millersburg on Route 147 and follow

trivia

Lorenzo DaPonte, Mozart's librettist, lived for a time in Sunbury.

the signs. A passenger car or pick-up costs $10 one way; a horse and buggy, $20. Doublecheck hours on Facebook; ferries run weekends and some weekdays. For more information call (717) 692-2442 or visit millersburgferry.org.

Across from the ferry landing, on the west side of the Susquehanna at *Liverpool,* lies *The Winery at Hunters Valley.* Located on a 150-year-old farm, the winery combines traditional wine-making methods with stainless-steel fermenters and fine filtration. The grapes come from vineyards that were planted in 1982.

In many ways the growing conditions resemble those in parts of France, with full sun, good air circulation, excellent drainage, and temperatures moderated by the river and mountains. You may walk through the vineyards and picnic on the grounds daily; tastings, tours, and, of course, sales are available. Call (717) 444-7211 or go to huntersvalleywines.com.

It's worth crossing the Susquehanna at Lewisburg, home of Bucknell University, to visit *The Fence Drive-In.* Just south of the bridge on the lovely eastern bank, the diner still boasts carhops to take your order. It's open Apr to Oct daily from 11 a.m. to 8:30 p.m., and it's cash only. Located at 1605 State Route 405 in Milton. Call (570) 524-2865. For more information visit fencedrivein.com.

Southern Border

Head south to **Carlisle,** where I-81 connects with the Pennsylvania Turnpike and Route 15. All that concrete stays, thankfully, on the outskirts of this comfortable Cumberland County seat.

Proud, prosperous, and preservation-conscious, the town's still-inhabited log cabins sport screened windows; the cannonball dents in the courthouse (relics of a pre-Gettysburg skirmish on July 3, 1863) are unrepaired. The colonial street plan is unchanged. The farmers' market has been held weekly for a couple of centuries. And how many towns of 19,000 have their own spacious historical society, complete with research library, gift shop, and guidebooks?

To call the town center the traditional meeting place is an understatement. Five Indian paths converged here before white settlement. The pioneer settlers bent on killing western tribes mustered here in 1756. Constitutional and slave riots followed, a century apart; a hot-air balloon ascended in 1843. Geronimo paraded through in 1905, en route to Teddy Roosevelt's inauguration. And every event was carefully documented. As you stroll downtown, look for the illustrated markers that describe three centuries of remarkable events. Do stop by the Cumberland County Historical Society, which provides free handouts for self-guided walking tours. The Society and its library (book research appointments in advance) share a beautiful redbrick building at 21 N. Pitt St. (717-249-7610). The museum is free from Tues through Fri 10 a.m. to 4 p.m. and Sat 10 a.m. to 2 p.m.

trivia

Who knew? The fierce Molly Pitcher, an all-American girl who followed her man (or perhaps men) to Revolutionary War battle and actually got paid for it, is buried in Carlisle, where her statue brandishes a ramrod over the town graveyard. Raise a toast to her at Molly Pitcher Brewing Company on W. High Street.

The historic district's blocks of stately churches and homes also have a modest hippie vibe, thanks in part to downtown Dickinson College. Instead of costumed interpreters, the streets buzz with skateboarders, guitarists, and pub patrons. And as a college town, Carlisle also boasts plenty of pubs and good restaurants. Two to try: Café Bruges, serving Belgian mussels, frites, and beers at 16 N. Pitt St. (cafebruges.com) and Sunrise

Café, offering breakfast and lunch, a covered patio, and fresh baked goods in a 300-year-old home at 231 N. Hanover St. (sunrisecafecarlisle.com).

Carlisle has been a military town since the first British fort of the 1750s. The **US Army War College** (the site of the famous Carlisle Indian School in the 19th century) is located here but is not open to the public. Instead, learn about the soldiers who have defended America for 250 years at the **US Army Heritage and Education Center.** AHEC has 2 stories of indoor exhibit and library space at 950 Soldiers Dr.—including the largest collection of Civil War photography in the world. Outside, an outdoor trail (punctuated by an enormous Vietnam-era Huey helicopter and other period structures) interprets campaigns from the French and Indian War to World War I trenches. Free admission and parking. It's open daily. Call (717) 245-3971 or visit usahec.org.

Near Carlisle is some of the best fly-fishing in the world. The Letort Stream runs right through town. Another blue-ribbon favorite, Yellow Breeches Creek, supposedly derives its name from the British soldiers who crossed the creek during the American Revolution; their white trousers became stained from the yellow tint of the water. Many outfitters guide on the Letort, and because so much of the shoreline belongs to exclusive trout-fishing clubs, it's best to get expert advice on where you can safely throw your line. Check with the tourism folks at visitcumberlandvalley.com.

Civil War history awaits at **Chambersburg,** 32 miles south of Carlisle on Route 11. The Confederates occupied the city, then an important rail junction, three times during the Civil War. The last time, in 1864, 3,000 Confederate soldiers rode into town demanding $100,000 ransom in gold, which Chambersburg couldn't pay. The Confederates burned the town, putting two-thirds of its citizens out of their homes, then rode off to McConnellsburg. Today, Memorial Square at the center of town honors the Union troops. On the corner of Lincoln Way (Route 30) stands a grand bank designed by architect Frank Furness in 1915. The handsome old structure, complete with a large circular vault, is now the **Chambersburg Heritage Center.** It offers great exhibits about the region's history, from the 1730s, when Indian attacks plagued white settlers, through the 19th century. The center offers walking tours by appointment and publishes a nice series of themed driving guides ($2.50 per set). Pick some up to navigate rural Franklin County on your own. Center admission is free Mon through Fri year-round. Visit from 8 a.m. to 5 p.m.

South of Chambersburg, two spots illustrate this valley's early history. Mercersburg was the early home of Pennsylvania's only president, James Buchanan. He was also the only bachelor to serve as president, though ineptly; in his single term from 1856 to 1860, he was unable to bridge the growing divide between north and south. Remarkably, his childhood home at 15 N. Main St. (Route 16) is now a thriving pub and inn called the *James Buchanan Hotel and Restaurant* (717-328-0011; jamesbuchananhotel.com). Across the street is the family home of Harriet Lane. Buchanan's niece, she served as his White House hostess and so was called the first "First Lady."

As homesteaders moved west across Pennsylvania in the mid-18th century, they incurred the wrath of Native Americans furious at the theft of their lands. Stories of kidnapping and massacres on the frontier are told at the *Conoco-cheague Institute,* headquartered in a homestead that dates from 1752 (12995 Bain Rd., Mercersburg; 717-328-3476; cimlg.org). The center on the banks of the creek (pronounced Con-a-ka-CHEEG) is open to the public year-round; stroll the grounds on your own from dawn to dusk, or arrange a tour of the homestead in advance at $5 per person. The staff programs activities on Sat from 10 a.m. to 5 p.m.

Shielded from the interstates by the southern Alleghenies, **Bedford** is easy to miss. It's perched alongside the Raystown branch of the Juniata River along Route 30. But don't pass by this classic redbrick county seat, enfolded by deep-forested mountains.

People have been passing through Bedford for centuries, starting with the Shawnee people, who blazed the first trail west. The British soldiers who followed hacked their way over the mountains on their way to kicking the French out of Pittsburgh. Bedford's buildings reflect these past transients. Forts and log cabins from the 1750s (a few with aluminum siding additions) still stand alongside Federal-era town houses. George Washington stayed in Bedford, while his troops, farther west, quelled the Whiskey Rebellion in 1794. President James Buchanan received the first transatlantic cable at the Bedford Springs Resort (now the Omni Bedford Springs Resort), a mile south of the downtown business district.

Join the Friday afternoon historical walking tours around the town square starting at the visitor's center at 131 Juliana St. The free, easy, 4-block tour includes the 1828 courthouse, the town squares, and the Espy House, where Washington stayed. "This place is operating now as what it was as far back as the 1700s," leaders remind visitors at the tour's end at the *Golden Eagle Inn.* The basement-level tavern used to host muddy boots, smoke, and spurs. Now the 3-story brick hotel and restaurant is nicely restored, furnished with wit, charm, and lots of antiques. Find it at 131 E. Pitt St., Bedford; call (814) 624-0800; or visit bedfordpainn.com.

Also on Pitt Street is the Pitt Theater (showing only 1 movie a night), 3 antiques stores, the Fort Bedford Museum, and Old Bedford Village, a colo-

Renfrew and Redware

A 200-year-old farmstead on Route 16 is home to an impressive collection of redware. Local potter John Bell and his descendants popularized this all-American variety of stoneware pottery during the mid-19th century. Today, authentic redware commands five-figure prices. See the exhibit of original work in the visitors' center at *Renfrew Museum and Park*, 1010 E. Main St., Waynesboro; call (717) 762-4723 or check renfrewmuseum.org.

nial-era re-creation. Another friendly stop is *HeBrews.* Yes, it's a coffee shop, open daily at 103 S. Richard St. (814-623-8600). Worth a quiet stroll is Bedford Memorial Park, a nicely restored 200-year-old cemetery.

The *National Museum of the American Coverlet* sounds like a snooze. It's not. Housed in old Bedford Common School, which dates to 1859, the museum showcases examples of fine handwoven folk designs used to adorn colonial beds. The museum shop offers nice replicas of the textiles for your house, too. It's open daily (for $10 per adult) at 322 S. Juliana St.; call (814) 623-1588; or visit coverletmuseum.org. Right across the street you'll find the *Chancellor's House,* an Italianate mansion restored as a comfortable B&B (341 S. Juliana St.; 866-535-8414; thechancellorshouse.com).

A mile west of town along Route 30, a venerable tavern still serves travelers. The *Jean Bonnet Tavern* is an authentic 1760s inn, with an authentically dim ground-floor dining room with fireplace, a bright upstairs brewpub, and a few guest rooms. This was a Whiskey Rebellion site—farmers irate with the whiskey tax rallied around a liberty pole here in 1794, as the state historic marker relates. These days, the whiskey flows freely, 7 days a week, and the tavern is part of the regional Whiskey Rebellion Trail. Raise a toast to the past at 6048 Lincoln Hwy. Phone (814) 623-2250; jeanbonnettavern.com.

Bedford County has 14 covered bridges, and you can tour them on bike or by car. They are usually named for their original 19th-century builders, and most have been safely rebuilt in recent years. The *Bedford County Visitors Bureau* (800-765-3331; visitbedfordcounty.com) offers a web link and a printed brochure with distances and details. The bureau is open year-round Mon through Fri 9 a.m. to 5 p.m.; May through Oct, the bureau is also open Sat 9 a.m. to 5 p.m. and Sun noon to 5 p.m. To plan a cycling, paddling, or hiking adventure, see thealleghenies.com. Call them at (800) 458-3433.

Breezewood, the self-proclaimed "Town of Motels," is mainly a giant clover-leaf garnished with neon. But for cyclists, it's also a trailhead for a unique thrill ride: the *Pike to Bike Trail.*

Handmade Along the Highway

Whether you prize hand-woven baskets, art glass, vibrant pieced quilts, hand-painted gourds, or "Scherenschnitte"—old-time German papercutting—you'll find a high-quality selection at independent shops. Search "Artistic Byways" at visitpa.com for a list of participating creators and merchants.

The Superhighway Trail, or P2B as it's known hereabouts, became an appendix to the state's main east-west artery in 1968, when the Pennsylvania Turnpike was rerouted through bigger four-lane tunnels. Between the old ones, Sideling Hill and Rays Hill, the discarded stretch of road was relegated to highway researchers and underage boozers. But since the Southern Alleghenies Conservancy took it over in 2001, recreational cyclists—a few hundred each weekend—have reclaimed the roadway. Riding through the pitch-black tunnels (Rays Hill is 0.75 miles, Sideling Hill, 1.3) provides the thrill. In between there's Buchanan State Forest and not much else. Make sure to bring a bike light. The 8.5-mile trail is officially closed, but it's an open secret. For more information, see pike2bike.com. Local outfitter Fat Jimmy's sells and rents outdoor gear from bikes to kayaks to paddleboards at the shop just behind historic Fort Bedford (it shares the space with the *Olde Bedford Brewing Company*, BTW). Go to 109 Railroad St. in Bedford or check fatjimmys.com.

As you explore the peaceful southern Juniata River and its 60-mile Raystown Branch, which flows from Bedford to Saxton, you may need a spot to park your RV or rent a cabin. *Woy Bridge Campground and Cabins* hosts those traveling by road or river at 190 Campground Rd., Everett; 814-730-5054; visitbedfordcounty.com/woybridge.

On silent Route 4016 near New Paris, there's a country road that's downright spooky: *Gravity Hill.* "Stay calm," read the directions in our county-issued brochure. "Keep cool. Put your car in neutral and take your foot off the brake." We did. And then the car began moving. Backwards. Up the hill. On cue, we screamed.

Whatever its explanation, Gravity Hill is one of those certifiably off-the-beaten-path attractions that you can't miss. And once you get there, you'll find a second Gravity Hill three-tenths of a mile past the first. Get the very specific directions from the Bedford County Visitors Bureau.

No cappuccino at the *Coffee Pot.* No latte. Not even cream and sugar. Just a way-larger-than-life-sized coffeepot built in 1925, an example of the

JANUARY

Twelfth Night

Joseph Priestley House, Northumberland
(570) 473-9474
In January the Joseph Priestley House in Northumberland celebrates Twelfth Night, ringing in the New Year as English dissenters (like Unitarian scientist Priestley) did at the close of the 18th century.

MAY

Day in Towne

Boalsburg
(814) 466-6311
Memorial Day was born in Boalsburg in 1864 and declared a national holiday a few years later. The village celebrates annually with a Day in Towne on Memorial Day. From 9 a.m. to 5 p.m., it's crafts, food, music, and a reenactment of a Civil War event. At 6 p.m. everybody walks from the square to the cemetery, where cannons boom, a brass band and bagpipes play, scouts raise and lower the flag, and the VFW plays taps. If you're into Memorial Day, this is the real thing.

DirtRag Dirt Fest

dirtragdirtfest.com
This legendary annual celebration of mountain biking, sponsored by the magazine, takes place in Hesson, at Raystown Lake. More than 36 miles of single-track trails. And beer. Registration is $40; kids under 16 are free.

JULY

4thFest

State College
(814) 466-6124
4thfest.org
Happy Valley lights up with a parade, fireworks, and family activities on the Penn State campus. Free admission.

AUGUST

Vintage Corvettes at Carlisle

Carlisle
carlisleevents.com
Four-wheeled at the Carlisle Fairgrounds is a town tradition. The August Corvette show, in particular, is a winner.

OCTOBER

Fulton Fall Folk Festival

McConnellsburg
(717) 485-4064
fultoncountypa.com
On the third weekend in October, McConnellsburg hosts the Fulton Fall Folk Festival; the annual Grease, Steam & Rust Show (featuring antique machinery); and the Historical Society Open House, all at once.

DECEMBER

Victorian Christmas

Bellefonte
(814) 355-2917
bellefontevictorianchristmas.com
Bellefonte's holiday celebration includes music, theater, and crafts shows and horse-drawn carriage rides.

"programmatic architecture" that dotted the Lincoln Highway, Route 30, aimed at luring tourists and travelers. The pot, located across the street from the entrance to the Bedford County Fairgrounds, has been closed for years. But things may be perking up. The Lincoln Highway Heritage Corridor is trying to preserve the, er, grounds and building for future java lovers. Call (724) 879-4241 or visit lhhc.org for more information.

When you hear the name *Road Kill Cafe,* you just have to go. The cafe is 10 miles south of Bedford in Clearville. The bare-bones, cinder block cafe offers home cooking and cabins and is run by Barb Snyder, whose homemade pies (as well as T-shirts with tasteful slogans like "You Kill It, We Grill It") have made the place a legend. The cafe (814-784-0031), at 633 Crooked Run Rd., is closed Mon and Tues and opens at 8 a.m. other mornings.

Consider a side trip to Rainsburg on Route 326, a community established so long ago that a 19th-century historian wrote, "the memory of man runneth not to the contrary," regarding its existence. The small borough features the *Rainsburg Male and Female Seminary,* incorporated in 1853 to offer secondary education and train teachers. And while you're in the area, stop in Chaneysville, a small town also on Route 326 that sheltered fugitive slaves before the Civil War. For a wonderful look back in time, read David Bradley's excellent novel *The Chaneysville Incident.*

Places to Stay in South Central Pennsylvania

BEDFORD

Golden Eagle Inn
131 E. Pitt St.
(814) 624-0800
bedfordinnpa.com
An authentic inn with spacious rooms and friendly service.

BELLEFONTE

Reynolds Mansion
101 W. Linn St.
(800) 353-8407
reynoldsmansion.com
A grand 1855 home restored as a B&B.

CARLISLE

The Carlisle House
148 S. Hanover St.
(717) 249-0350
thecarlislehouse.com
Within walking distance of Dickinson College campus.

DUBOIS

The Inn at Narrows Creek
44 Narrows Creek Ln.
(814) 371-9394
narrowscreek.com
Eight rooms and suites in a rural setting, with a country store.

MERCERSBURG

Mercersburg Inn
405 S. Main St.
(717) 328-5231
mercersburginn.com

Lavish Greek Revival home near Mercersburg Academy.

STATE COLLEGE

Graduate State College
125 S. Atherton St.
(814) 231-2100
athertonhotel.net
The former Atherton Hotel, now part of the Graduate chain, stands at Penn State's doorstep.

Places to Eat in South Central Pennsylvania

BEDFORD

Jean Bonnet Tavern
6048 Lincoln Hwy.
(814) 623-2250
jeanbonnettavern.com
Historic 1760s inn.

BOILING SPRINGS

Allenberry
(717) 258-3211
allenberry.com
This updated resort along the Yellow Breeches Creek offers a nice choice of dining and activities. Allenberry Playhouse hosts classic live musical comedy year-round.

OSTERBURG

Slick's Ivy Stone Restaurant
8785 William Penn Rd.
(814) 276 3131
slicksivystone.com
Hearty casual meals. Closed Mon and Tues.

Southwestern Pennsylvania

Golden Triangle

East is Philadelphia, and west is **Pittsburgh,** and never the twain shall meet. You'll be surprised how many folks in the former have only the vaguest idea where the latter is (it's 300 miles to the left). The Allegheny Mountains, it turns out, have been a pretty effective barrier to westward movement ever since the British first hacked their way into the wilderness 250 years ago. But easterners—in fact, any visitors—are bowled over by southwestern Pennsylvania's offerings, from high art to high fives (pro sports are big here), once they arrive.

Downtown Pittsburgh used to be called the Golden Triangle, in reference to its location, where the Allegheny and Monongahela Rivers form the Ohio (next stop, via the Mississippi: the Gulf of Mexico). So much water, surrounded by high bluffs with lots of trees, reminds some folks of San Francisco, but with a winter.

All that's gold also glitters. Adding to the scenery is the dazzle of downtown architecture, including Philip Johnson's PPG Place (all glass, of course) and Michael Graves's O'Reilly Theater. Along the waterfront are architect Rafael Viñoly's

swooping convention center and the contemporary Carnegie Science Center. A hard throw from the business district is PNC Park (named for the PNC Financial Services Group). It's the prettiest retro ballpark in America, next door to Heinz Field, the football stadium. The downtown bridges are painted gold, and the Steelers (football), Penguins (hockey), and Pirates (baseball) all have black-and-gold color schemes (colors that appear on the Pittsburgh city crest).

triviatidbits

Between downtown stops, you can ride Pittsburgh's subway train, the T, for no charge.

The identical bridges the city dubs the "Three Sisters" are the Clemente, Warhol, and Carson Bridges across the Allegheny River downtown.

First, let's look back. From about 1870 to 1970, the Pittsburgh region led the nation in producing iron, steel, and glass and in mining bituminous coal. Meanwhile, clouds rolled by on skies of black and gray, not blue, and nights sometimes glowed orange. Rivers flowed brown and green. Initial attempts at controlling smoke and floods were hampered by a couple of world wars and by a boom-and-bust economy. In 1941, the year Pittsburgh had the nation's highest rate of pneumonia, the mayor created a commission to eliminate smoke. Numerous rankings now call Pittsburgh "America's most livable city."

As a burgeoning high tech center, driven by the brainpower of Carnegie Mellon University and the University of Pittsburgh, the city has attracted firms such as Google, Apple, Uber, Duolingo, and Astrobotic. Their workers belie the city's heavy manufacturing image and have, in turn, transformed once down-trodden residential neighborhoods such as Lawrenceville and East Liberty.

It's a place you've got to see for yourself.

AUTHOR'S TOP 10 FAVORITES IN SOUTHWESTERN PENNSYLVANIA

Carrie Furnace

Confluence

Fallingwater

Jimmy Stewart Museum

Kayak Pittsburgh

Mattress Factory

Ohiopyle

St. Anthony's Chapel

Vanka murals

Westmoreland Museum of American Art

Richardson Romanesque

Few architects have an architectural style named after them, but **Henry Hobson Richardson** is one of them. His **Allegheny County Courthouse and Jail**, begun in 1883, is a famous example of the architect's muscular style. Massive stonework, rounded arches, and towers are his signature, shown to great effect in his masterpiece in the heart of Pittsburgh. (Photos show his physique was much like his buildings.) Called Richardson Romanesque because of its similarities to 11th-century European architecture, the architect's style actually draws from a variety of sources.

Richardson stressed theatrical sculptured shapes: deep-set windows, cavernous door openings, and bands of windows. (He devised an arched bridge over Ross Street, between the courthouse and the jail, to allow prisoners to be taken to trial directly from the jail. Hence the local nickname, the Bridge of Sighs.)

Richardson's work can be seen all over the East Coast, and once you see it, you'll always recognize his style. The courthouse is widely considered one of his finest works. He died at age 47 in 1886—just before its completion.

Don't neglect the Cultural District downtown, home to fabulously restored dowager theaters along Penn Avenue. Around the corner, on the side of the Byham Theater, you'll find the inside of an old steel mill—in a fabulous giant mural by Robert Haas. Next door is a subtle light sculpture by Robert Wilson, which is installed across the top of a building (look for the turning triangles). When you come to the corner of Seventh and Penn, facing a hulking Aztec-style pyramid, you've reached two more public art installations. Temporary ones often join the lineup. They're as much fun as the theatrical performances.

After taking in a show, explore the myriad of restaurants in the city. In 2019, local chefs took a collective bow as the BBC magazine proclaimed Pittsburgh as one of the world's top foodie destinations.

Playwright August Wilson grew up and set his famous century cycle of dramas in Pittsburgh's Hill District. His hometown honors his legacy at the **August Wilson Home** at 1727 Bedford Ave., where his work is performed and other African American artists work (augustwilsonhouse.org). The **August Wilson Center for African American Culture** (acc-awc.org) maintains a full schedule of exhibits and performances.

Around Town

If you ask for directions to "the Carnegie Museum" from downtown, you'll be branded a tourist for sure, because there are four. On the city's North Shore, find the **Carnegie Science Center** (1 Allegheny Ave.; 412-237-3400; open daily). Kids love to visit its Earthquake Cafe, which really shakes them up. The museum also salutes Pittsburgh's newest industry with "roboworld," the world's largest robotics exhibit. European visitors—and Pop Art devotees from all over the world—love the nearby **Andy Warhol Museum,** with a cool style that appeals to both kids and adults (117 Sandusky St.; 412-237-8300; closed Mon). The **Carnegie Museum of Art** (4400 Forbes Ave.; 412-622-3131; closed Mon except between the Fourth of July and Labor Day), 2 miles away in the Oakland section, is where old meets new: magnificent casts of architecture and sculpture from antiquity, plus fine impressionist and contemporary art collections. Drop-in tours are offered daily. Look for the bronze *Diplodocus*, nicknamed Dippy, outside the complex; he'll point you toward the **Carnegie Museum of Natural History** (4400 Forbes Ave.), with its nightmare-inducing *Tyrannosaurus rex* and other fossils. The renowned collection is showcased in "Dinosaurs in Their Time" in a vaulting 2-story space. There are wonderful Egyptian mummies and gem collections here, too. For varying admission prices, exhibit information, and hours for all four museums, visit carnegiemuseums.org.

eyeballart, anyone?

Go on a scavenger tour of downtown Pittsburgh's great public art with a guide to more than 80 works, from the eyeball benches at Agnes Katz Plaza to the giant mayor on the steps of the City-County Building. They're mapped in a project from the Pittsburgh Office of Public Art. Download your free copy at opapgh.org.

Cover the Waterfront

Purposeful Pittsburgh used to use its riverbanks only for work: docks and steel mills. But now the city shoreline bustles with the **Three Rivers Heritage Trail,** which connects several paths. Joggers, bicyclers, and e-scooters glide along the Eliza Furnace Trail (since it passes a county jail, it's usually called the Jail Trail). You can connect to the North Shore and skate to a Pirates game at PNC Park or bike across the Hot Metal Bridge (aka South Twenty-ninth Street; it used to carry buckets of molten steel) and head 10 miles south to the city limits. If you want a taste of the trail, borrow a bike through the city's bike share program, POGOH (pogoh.com). See the online map at friendsoftheriverfront.org.

A bucket list item for bikers is completing the well-known Great Allegheny Passage, a trail which extends from the rivers' confluence at Point State Park to the Georgetown waterfront in Washington, DC. The GAP joins the C&O towpath along the Potomac River in Cumberland, Maryland, for a 334.5-mile trail. The scenic route attracted 1.4 million users in 2020.

The Best Front Door in America

Your first words about Pittsburgh are likely to be "Oh, wow!" Called the "Best Front Door in America," the cityscape that bursts upon you as you emerge from the Fort Pitt Tunnel shimmers with rivers and riverboats, skyscrapers, towering hills, and golden bridges. Smoky city? No more.

When planners wanted to raise the guardrails on the Fort Pitt Bridge, local activists raised their voices. They argued that higher barriers would blind incoming motorists to Pittsburgh's signature view. The result: The state highway department bowed to the beautiful and agreed to keep the lower barriers.

The **Pittsburgh Zoo** (1 Wild Place; 412-665-3640 or 800-474-4966; pittsburghzoo.com) nurtures more than 4,000 animals in habitats as diverse as an African savanna, a reptile house, and a glass-bottomed polar bear pool (where visitors walk underneath the ursine swimmers). The zoo is open daily 9:30 a.m. to 6 p.m. Memorial Day through Labor Day, 9 a.m. to 5 p.m. in the fall and spring, and 9 a.m. to 4 p.m. the rest of the year. Closed Thanksgiving, Christmas, and New Year's Day. Admission for adults is $17.95, with reduced rates in cooler seasons.

But, hey, you're here to get off the beaten path, so leave time for other stops. You'll want to stroll **Point State Park** downtown, for its postcard views of the confluence of the three rivers. But detour to the Allegheny riverbank and catch the activity at Allegheny Pop-Up park, directly opposite the stadiums. Here the public streets have been blocked off for street hoops, dancing, food trucks, music, and other free entertainment each summer. Market Square, the city's oldest, hosts farmers' markets, evening concerts, and the city's popular Christmas market.

Pittsburgh's neighborhoods are the soul of the city. Start at the handsome **Senator John Heinz History Center** at 1212 Smallman St., a converted 19th-century brick icehouse. It offers a retrospective of three centuries, starting when Pittsburgh was the country's western frontier. The center, a Smithsonian satellite, includes the Western Pennsylvania Sports Museum. This region's especially proud of its great NFL quarterback tradition. Here's where to pay tribute to Pittsburgh greats like Johnny Unitas, Jim Kelly, Dan Marino, Joe Montana, Joe Namath, and more. The museum is open daily 10 a.m. to 5 p.m. except major holidays; adult admission is $18. Call (412) 454-6000 or visit heinzhistory center.org for more information.

For funky grocery shopping visit **The Strip,** a flat, 20-block stretch along the Allegheny waterfront above the Convention Center. (Better yet, sign up for a taste of the neighborhood through burghfoodtour.com, which offers a menu of a dozen walking tours.)

Continue east on Smallman Street, or on parallel Penn Avenue, for a bustling parade of chefs (pinching melons and grabbing gourmet ingredients) and hipsters (browsing the selection of funky furniture shops, like Hot Haute Hot). The Strip's schizophrenia is part of its charm. Whether you need a whoopee cushion, fresh biscotti, aged cheese, or a full-size inflatable Steeler, this is the place to hit. At **Primanti's** (46 Eighteenth St.; 412-263-2142) get your daily fat quotient in one sitting, with french fries and cole slaw crammed inside your Wonderbread sandwich. Parking's impossible, but walking is a blast.

Mt. Washington is the riverside bluff that looms above the confluence, opposite downtown. A ride to the top on the inclines, the tiny vertical railways that have hauled Pittsburghers up and down the hill for more than a century, is an absolute must for visitors—and cheap, at $5 per round-trip.

trivia

Novelist Michael Chabon set his *Mysteries of Pittsburgh* and *Wonder Boys* here. Like his Pulitzer Prize–winning heroes, Kavalier and Clay, he grew up loving comic books (his favorite hangout was the comic emporium, Eide's Entertainment, at 1121 Penn Ave.). If you, too, still love cartoons, don't miss the Toonseum at 943 Liberty Ave.

Start the journey at water level, at **Station Square,** a grand railroad terminus-turned-entertainment-center that's an easy subway hop from downtown. (This is also the boarding place for the **Gateway Clipper fleet** of paddleboats, which tour the rivers and ferry fans to Pirates and Steelers games.) Hop the **Monongahela Incline,** built in 1869, here (tip: it's pronounced IN-cline). Its partner, the red-sided **Duquesne Incline,** is a mile up East Carson Street. Both offer a steep and silent 4-minute ride to the top.

The aptly named Grandview Avenue, along the crest of Mt. Washington, encourages gawkers with a promenade and viewing platforms. One addition to the Mt. Washington scene, and one more way to view the cityscape below, can be found on the hiking trails of the newly developed **Emerald View Park,** which snakes around Mt. Washington (more information at mwcdc.org) and the adjacent Duquesne Heights neighborhood. It's still a work in progress but worth venturing onto the hilly treks, with recommended loops of between 1 and 2.5 often vertical miles. Most of Grandview's restaurants are special occasion destinations, mostly for their postcard view, so save your appetite for yet another bustling neighborhood below, the **South Side.**

On the southern bank of the Mon, as locals call the Monongahela River, the South Side boasts that it has "both kinds of blue hair"—on the elderly residents of century-old row houses surrounding former steel mills, and atop youthful loft dwellers and students from Duquesne University, CMU, and Pitt. On weekend evenings, East Carson Street belongs to the latter, who flood the bars, coffeehouses, and grills.

Restaurants spring up along the Carson Street sidewalk like crabgrass. One neighborhood secret is the tiny *Dish Osteria and Bar* (128 S. Seventeenth St.; 412-390-2012; dishosteria.com), with small appetizers (such as mixed marinated olives), great pasta, and fresh fish. At *SouthSide Works,* the riverside Hofbrauhaus offers a beer garden with oompah music and a great view of the waterfront scene on weekends.

trivia

Did you love *The Last of the Mohicans*? Each spring re-enactors of the French and Indian War camp at Fort Pitt (now Pittsburgh's Point State Park) don war paint, buckskins, and bonnets. Duck inside the Fort Pitt Museum there (heinzhistorycenter.org) to get the full story of the conflict.

Live—and loud—music is offered at the South Side's many bars, especially on weekends. But at *Club Cafe* (56 S. Twelfth St.; 412-431-4950; clubcafelive .com), you can find great big-name acts and good local bands on a tiny, starry stage, performing for a hundred folks at cozy tables. It's a sixties coffeehouse with a cyber-vibe.

Above the South Side lie the city's oddest streets: steep vertical steps that no cars could climb. To get to the top of the South Side Slopes, you'll need to bring a walking stick. And maybe a cardiologist. With nearly 700 steps just to the crest of the South Side Slopes, the workout is extreme, but it's the panoramic views that are killer.

The Slopes claim 68 step streets, making this slice of the city feel like a European village: a blend of historic piety, cliffside houses, and quiet corkscrewed streets.

"When I walk the steps, I always get the sense of the mill workers from years ago," local steps historian Bob Regan tells me. "They walked down in the morning, and then, 12 hours later, they walked back up."

Start your climb on Eighteenth Street, pause for a breath at Pius Street, and continue to St. Paul's Monastery, a beautiful Bohemian church at the top. Each fall, the community association sponsors a "Step Trek" tour of the neighborhood, but you can book tours with Walk the Burgh (walktheburgh.com) to peek at the Slopes or follow a dozen other themed strolls through town.

From the base of the Slopes, follow Carson Street 10 more miles east and you'll arrive at *Kennywood Park* (Route 837 in West Mifflin; 412-461-0500; kennywood.com). This charming century-old amusement park is a National Historic Landmark. It's an institution so loved by Pittsburghers that they come

But Where are the Steel Mills?

Yes, it's still called by the old nickname of Steel City, but Pittsburgh's moved on. Along the Monongahela River, the Jones and Laughlin steel mills commanding both sides of the Monongahela River have been transformed into the South Side Works, a waterfront retail development, and Hazelwood Green, a huge tech center that's home to regenerative medicine and AI research. US Steel's Edgar Thompson Works, once the largest producer in the world, is now The Waterfront, a sprawling shopping center. But you can revisit steel's heyday through *Rivers of Steel*, a heritage site that preserves the impressively hulking, rusting relics of the industry at sites throughout the Mon Valley. At *Carrie Furnace* in Rankin, a National Historic Landmark since 2008, Rivers of Steel has enthusiastically encouraged the unique artistic possibilities of the 168 acres: theater, graffiti, site-specific sculpture, and more. By all means, visit: walking tours and boat tours are offered year-round. You can even watch drive-in movies here. Check riversofsteel.org.

back every summer, usually with a crowd: the company picnic, the school picnic, or on Nationality Days, a great local ethnic tradition (Italian Day, Croatian Day, etc.). Nationality Days date back to the immigrant steelworkers who flocked to this bank of the Mon. A few miles downstream is the site of US Steel's Homestead Works, formerly one of the largest steel mills in the world and now a vast shopping and entertainment center called the Waterfront.

pittsburghfirsts

Radio station, KDKA

Public television station, WQED, home to *Mister Rogers' Neighborhood*

Polio vaccine

The Ferris wheel

Kennywood's claim to fame is its roller coasters: the wooden Thunderbolt, ranked one of the best in the world by enthusiasts; the Phantom's Revenge, a coaster-in-the-dark; and many more. Hold onto the bar! All-day passes begin at $39.99 for adults, with discounts for shorties (under 46 inches tall) and seniors. Open May through Labor Day. On your way to Kennywood, and adjacent to the Waterfront retail complex, you'll pass Sandcastle, a vast waterpark, sandcastle waterpark.com. To hit those big slides, it'll cost adults $37.99, and those under 48 inches tall, $27.99.

Rising above I-376 near Monroeville is a sight you might expect along the Ganges River, rather than the Monongahela: a huge, wedding-cake-style temple with Indian flourishes. It's the *Sri Venkataswara Temple,* one of only 10 Hindu temples in the United States. It attracts worshipers from all over the East Coast. Remove your shoes and take a tour; temple members welcome anyone who'd like to view the ornate building and appreciate its murals and statuary.

It's located at 1230 S. McCully Dr. in Monroeville; call ahead to (412) 373-3380. The website (svtemple.org) gives details and directions.

Head back to downtown Pittsburgh to the Point and plunge in. *Kayak Pittsburgh,* in the shadow of PNC Park under the Clemente Bridge, offers kayaks and canoes for self-guided tours of the confluence May through Oct. One Federal St.; use the stairway next to the statue of Roberto Clemente at PNC Park on the North Shore. Call (412) 969-9090 or (412) 255-0564 or visit ventureoutdoors.org/kayak-pittsburgh. Kayak racks at PNC Park and the South Side let you "park" for an afternoon.

The 42-story *Cathedral of Learning,* a Gothic Revival skyscraper, dominates the University of Pittsburgh and the surrounding Oakland neighborhood. The Commons Room, on the first floor, is evocative of a medieval cathedral. Around its perimeter are the *Nationality Rooms* (1209 Cathedral of Learning; 412-624-6000; nationalityrooms.pitt.edu). The classrooms are decorated in the style of 26 different nations. Pittsburghers are proud of them; visitors, especially international ones, are crazy about them. The *Stephen Foster Memorial* next door commemorates the country's first pop music composer (412-624-4100; pitt .edu/~amerimus/Museum.htm).

This cathedral, just a few blocks down Fifth Avenue from St. Paul's Roman Catholic Cathedral, is across the street from Schenley Plaza, a simple but inviting grassy expanse between two imposing libraries—the main branch of the Carnegie, and Pitt's Hillman. It regularly attracts students, Frisbees, and summertime concerts while serving as a visual bridge between Pitt's campus and Schenley Park.

Schenley Park, just off Forbes Avenue, has amenities galore. A student favorite is the city's popular disc-golf course (where 18 holes means tossing a Frisbee into 18 baskets). The park's most popular attraction is the shiny carousel at Schenley Plaza, a great public space with outdoor cafes and performances, near an 18-hole public course. The glass onion just over the hill is the *Phipps Conservatory,* a Victorian wonderland of exotic flowers and fountains. The indoor tropical forest overlooks a dramatic ravine.

All exhibits are wheelchair accessible. Price of admission is $12 for adults and $9 for children aged 2 to 18. Open daily from 9:30 a.m. to 5 p.m., till 10 p.m.

pittsburgh zombies

One of the most beloved movies ever made in Pittsburgh was George Romero's *Night of the Living Dead.* The 1968 classic has inspired an annual pre-Halloween Zombie Walk, where gruesomely costumed participants stagger with arms outstretched through the Monroeville Mall moaning, "Brains . . . must . . . have . . . brains."

George Washington Swam Here

Why is it called **Washington's Landing**? Easy. In December 1753 a young George Washington narrowly escaped drowning as he paddled across the Allegheny River where the Washington's Crossing Bridge now stands. Thankfully, he landed safely— in what's now called Lawrenceville.

Washington crisscrossed western Pennsylvania frequently, often in the company of Christopher Gist, a friend and guide. (You'll even find a marker showing his footsteps through Kennywood Park!) In fact, when he first set eyes on Pittsburgh, he made a note to himself: "fine place for a fort."

He was right.

Fri, at 700 Frank Curto Dr. Call (412) 622-6914 or check phipps.conservatory .org. Overlooking the Steve Faloon Trail (voted one of America's top 20 urban running trails by *Runner's World* magazine) is the park's visitor center, a charmingly restored coffeehouse. Get details and directions at pittsburghparks.org or (412) 682-PARK. A high-energy race through the park's hairpin-turn roads, the **Pittsburgh Vintage Grand Prix** (pvgp.org) brings hundreds of classic race cars and thousands of classic car lovers to town each July; it's one of the few international races held on real city roads with spectators nearby.

Lawrenceville, running from Sixteenth to Sixty-second Streets along the Allegheny River, is a chic district of galleries, cafes, and design boutiques that reminds some visitors of Brooklyn's Park Slope. **Allegheny Cemetery** (4734 Butler St.; alleghenycemetery.com) is the peaceful public park that welcomes strollers.

The shopping district anchored by the World War I Doughboy statue has plenty of antiques shops; try Pittsburgh Furniture Company at 4312 Butler St. For women's apparel and killer shoes, try Pavement at 3629 (412-621-6400). Check out the Thunderbird Cafe at 4023 (thunderbirdmusichall.com) for nightlife, Poulet Blue at 3801 (412-622-0111) for chic Parisian eats, and Spirit (spiritpgh.com), a funky converted Moose Lodge, on the corner of 51st St. The Arsenal School is named for the site where 78 young workers, mainly women, were killed in an explosion at a Union munitions plant in 1862.

Nearby **Clayton** (7227 Reynolds St.; 412-371-0600; thefrickpittsburgh .org) is the grand former home of Henry Clay Frick, where you can see how Pittsburgh's millionaires lived at the dawn of the 20th century. Don't miss the working orchestrion, a room-size mechanical orchestra that was the home theater of its day. The greenhouse, the fab art museum, and the car museum are free. The cafe is award-winning gourmet; its afternoon teas are white-glove. For house tour tickets and hours, check online.

North Side

In the historic Mexican War Streets section north of the Allegheny is the **Mattress Factory** (500 Sampsonia Way; 412-231-3169; mattress.org), a fascinating display of contemporary art. The factory, which is, indeed, a converted factory, commissions, exhibits, and collects site-specific installations; it also provides living and working space for artists from around the world. The permanent collection includes visionary contemporary artists such as James Turrell, Yayoi Kusama, and Greer Lankton; your fellow visitors are likely to be overseas art lovers who've come to Pittsburgh expressly because of the Mattress Factory's world-class reputation for cutting-edge programming. (Check out the basement.)

Down Sampsonia Way from the Mattress Factory is another unique cultural community, the brilliantly decorated rowhouses associated with Pittsburgh's

> ## trivia
>
> "Pittsburgh is undoubtedly the cockeyedest city in the United States," complained journalist Ernie Pyle in 1937. "Physically, it is absolutely irrational. It must have been laid out by a mountain goat. . . . And then the steps—oh, Lord, the steps!"

City of Asylum @ Alphabet City. Exiled authors and artists from around the world have found refuge through the program and celebrate their freedom by painting and adorning the exterior of their homes. The program offers readings, workshops, jazz performances, a restaurant and bar, and a bookstore at the restored Masonic Temple nearby at 40 North Ave.

The motto of the **Pittsburgh Children's Museum** is "play with real stuff." So go ahead. Squirt water. Take things apart in The Garage. Get muddy in The Backyard. The award-winning renovation of this combination of two grand old buildings is a treat. It's at 10 Children's Way; call (412) 322-5058 or visit pittsburghkids.org. Make a play date Wed through Sun 10 a.m. to 5 p.m. Timed admission is $16 for adults, $14 for others, with discounts for early birds. Just a few steps away, in the Victorian park called Allegheny Commons, lie the kid-friendly **National Aviary and Lake Elizabeth.** The Aviary gives a perch to more than 600 species in a lovely old-fashioned glass conservatory; it's open daily except Christmas. Adult admission is $13.

Other North Side gems: **Photo Antiquities** (531 E. Ohio St.; 412-231-7881; photoantiquities.org), a collection of rarities from the 19th century, including fine Civil War–era images (soldiers loved the newfangled invention). Closed

They Came from Pittsburgh

- Stephen Foster, *composer*
- Billy Eckstine, *musician*
- Rachel Carson, *conservationist*
- George S. Kaufman and August Wilson, *playwrights*
- Gene Kelly, *actor and dancer*
- David McCullough, *historian*
- Gertrude Stein, *author*
- Fred Rogers, *TV pioneer*
- Mary Cassatt, *artist*
- Henry Mancini, *composer*
- Perry Como, *singer*
- Michael Keaton, *actor*
- Wiz Khalifa, *rapper*
- Christina Aguilera, *singer*

Tues and Sun. Open 10 a.m. to 4 p.m. every other day of the week. Admission is $10. And don't miss **St. Anthony's Chapel,** said to be the largest collection of Catholic relics from saints and popes. In the 1890s St. Anthony's was a sort of mini-Lourdes, where the faithful flocked to be blessed by the church's pastor (who collected most of the 4,200 bones, skulls, and other relics). Even in a city of churches (see pghshrines.org for examples), this one is completely unique. The ornate European-style chapel, at 1704 Harpster St. in Troy Hill, is open afternoons for tours 1 p.m. to 4 p.m. except Fri. Check (412) 231-2994 or saintanthonyschapel.org for details.

Just a few blocks off one of the busiest bike trails on the North Shore is **Bicycle Heaven** (see bicycleheaven.org or call 412-734-4034), which bills itself as the world's largest bicycle museum and shop. It's open seven days a week from 10 a.m. to 7 p.m. at 1800 Preble Ave. It's an actual bike repair and sales shop surrounded by literally thousands of bikes on display from Schwinn Sting-Rays to rare Bowden Spacelanders.

Allegheny River Valley

Heading north from Pittsburgh on Route 28, the gritty post-industrial town of **Millvale** appears to have spent all its treasures. In fact, the hillside church of St. Nicholas hosts one of the most unusual mural collections in the country.

Between 1937 and 1941, Croatian artist **Maxo Vanka** created a searing series of religious murals in the interior of the Catholic church. Depicting the struggles of Croatians and other ethnic groups then arriving in southwestern Pennsylvania, the images combine social realism with elements of Byzantine church decoration and Croatian folk art. As the church raises funds to protect and restore the murals, it welcomes visitors. One-hour tours are offered Sat at 11 a.m., noon, 1 p.m., and 2 p.m. The church is located at 24 Maryland Ave. Visit vankamurals.org.

It's easy to miss **Aspinwall**—but don't. This old-fashioned cutie of a riverside town has a nicely restored riverfront park, bookstores, gift shops, and cafes along Brilliant Ave., and great architecture.

Audubon at Beechwood, a property of the Western Pennsylvania Conservancy, has varied walking trails. Stop by the Audubon Society; the reserve is great for wildflowers, birds, and photography. Eight marked, named footpaths range in length and ease of terrain. The Pine Hollow path smells best. Weekly guided nature walks are scheduled year-round. To get to the reserve from

Pittsburgh Rocks

The view from the choir loft is impressive: a huge nave swelling with music, with wisps of smoke wafting from the sanctuary. The upturned faces of the young congregation seem transported. But then a snarling guitar chord rips rudely through the congregation, and the crowd at the former St. Ann's Church erupts. The liturgy being celebrated in this century-old house of worship isn't High Mass, but a gig at Pittsburgh's church of rock 'n' roll.

Let us play.

Clubs like **Mr. Small's**—the desanctified Catholic church a few miles upriver from downtown in Millvale—the **Roxian** in McKees Rocks, **Spirit** in Lawrenceville, and **Gooski's** on Polish Hill attract some of the city's best local bands. Touring bands regularly hit the Thunderbird (thunderbirdmusichall.com).

Rock comes downtown too. Check **Stage AE,** an indoor/outdoor venue on the North Shore, and the **Byham Theater.** The **Three Rivers Arts Festival** also offers free outdoor concerts during its run each June.

Route 28, take the Fox Chapel Road exit north and go about a mile. Turn left on Squaw Run Road, then right on Dorseyville Road. Beechwood Farms is almost 2 miles on the left. Phone (412) 963-6100; or go to aswp.org.

On a warm evening there's no hotter ticket than the free concerts at **Hartwood Acres** (215 Saxonburg Blvd.). This county park cradles a band shell at the bottom of a 10-acre meadow and hosts free summer concerts. In the winter there are hayrides. Year-round there are tours of the original manor house. Call (412) 767-9200 or visit alleghenycounty.us/parks for more information.

Talk about the sound of music: The **Bayernhof Museum** in Pittsburgh's North Hills turns up the volume. This suburban home, with a bizarre rococo-Bavarian theme that includes gnome statues and an indoor pool and grotto, houses a large collection of music boxes and other kitschy contraptions. Check out the serinettes (musical bird boxes), Wurlitzer band organs, player pianos, and more. It's at 225 St. Charles Place in a quiet residential neighborhood overlooking the Allegheny River. Tours (for those over the age of 5) are available by appointment for groups of no more than 12 people; call ahead—at least a week in advance if possible. Admission is $10. The phone number is (412) 782-4231; the web address, bayernhofmuseum.com.

trivia

The Nickelodeon, the earliest form of public film exhibition, opened on Smithfield Street in Pittsburgh in 1905. The Harris Theater, which screens films around the corner, is named for the nickelodeon's inventor.

Coal lies under most of the mountains in western Pennsylvania. To get an up-close look at the history of coal mining, go underground at Tarentum's **Tour-Ed Mine** (748 Bull Creek Rd.; 724-224-4720; tour-edmine.com). Take a tour 150 feet below the surface on a specially modified train. Don't worry; it's perfectly safe. The mine is just off exit 48 (Allegheny Valley) of the Pennsylvania Turnpike. It's open Memorial Day through Labor Day; limited hours through Oct. Admission is $12 for adults and $11 for children 12 and under.

Above ground, the Tour-Ed Mine and the Allegheny-Kiski Historical Society get support from the **Fleatique,** a popular seasonal flea market. A $3-per-car charge supports the nonprofits, and shoppers and swappers get to browse several acres of Hawaiian shirts, vintage glassware, and other finds. The outdoor market is held on the third Sun of the month May through Oct. See the schedule at akvhs.org or call (724) 224-7666.

You can appreciate history on a trip to **Old Economy Village** at **Ambridge,** less than an hour northwest of Pittsburgh. Old Economy is the preserved third and final home of the Old Harmony Society. One of the many pious and industrious German sects to settle in Pennsylvania, they arrived in 1804. Because they expected the Second Coming of Christ to happen at any moment, they adopted celibacy to purify themselves for Christ's thousand-year reign on earth. Religion came first in their lives— they celebrated the Last Supper six times a year—but their communal lifestyle was not austere. Harmonites ate well, adorned their furniture, played music, planted flower gardens, and made money for the community. By 1825 they had built cotton and wool factories powered and heated by steam engines, a steam laundry, and a dairy. They constructed shops for blacksmiths, hatters, wagonmakers, and linen weavers. Their canny business sense produced fine furniture, sturdy buildings, beautiful grounds, and many beneficial investments in the nearby towns. The community lasted until 1905.

trivia

The Pittsburgh Pirates are the second-oldest professional athletic team in the country. Originally called the Alleghenies, they changed their name when other teams accused them of "pirating" players from their rosters.

Your hour-long tour takes in the community kitchen, the cabinet and blacksmith shops, granary, wine cellar, tailor shop, store, great house, and gardens. The village and its gift shop are open Apr 1 through Dec, Fri through Sun 10 a.m. to 4 p.m. Admission is $10 for adults; call (724) 266-4500; or visit oldeconomyvillage.org. To get there follow I-79 to Sewickley, then go north on Route 65 along the Ohio River until you see the white picket fence.

If you're looking for a gentle adventure, consider hot-air ballooning over western Pennsylvania. Balloonist Tim Meteney flies daily in warm weather at dawn and dusk. You'll lift off from the tiny *Beaver County Airport* off Route 51 at the speed of the wind. That means the experience is gentle; the gondola barely sways as the green hills pass smoothly, 1,000 feet below. Schedule your adventure ($300 per person) in advance but remember that weather conditions can rearrange your plans. Call (724) 336-2300 or visit balloonpa-ohio.com.

trivia

Dancer Gene Kelly and composer Billy Strayhorn grew up in Pittsburgh's East Liberty neighborhood. They are remembered there at the Kelly-Strayhorn Theater, 5941 Penn Ave., offering concerts and performances year-round.

Ride 'em Shovelers!

The annual *Beaver County Snow Shovel Riding Championship* in *Ambridge* is a classic community event, with minimal equipment required. "The key to winning," says organizer Jack Hilfinger, "is to remember that the shovel doesn't have to touch the ground." That means you can customize your ride with a snow tube, skis, or anything else that slides. The fun takes place the third Saturday of January, snow permitting.

Westsylvania

Passionate collectors create great museums. One little gem in Butler, easily reached from Pittsburgh via I-79 or Route 8, is the *Maridon Museum.* Named for its founders, Mary and Donald Phillips, it's the only museum in the region devoted to Asian art. Jade, ivory, and Meissen figurines are specialties in this collection of pieces from Japan and China. It's open Wed through Sat from 11 a.m. to 4 p.m. or by special appointment at 322 N. McKean St.; admission for adults is $4 (724-282-0123; maridon.org).

Slightly farther north you'll find *McConnell's Mill State Park,* which appeals to historians, geologists, rock climbers, birders, botanists, hunters, anglers, rafters, and, of course, picnickers. The park gets its name from a restored gristmill, open seasonally, which you can reach by parking in a lot near the top of the hill and following a footpath down. Through the park runs Slippery Rock Creek and its adjacent walking trail. Be sure to venture toward *Slippery Rock Gorge,* 20,000 years old and 400 feet deep. Take I-79 to the Route 422 exit and go almost 2 miles west on Route 422. A sign indicates a left turn for the park.

Want your own fishing cabin on a peaceful lake? At *Moraine State Park,* on the opposite (eastern) side of I-79 from McConnell's Mill, rent a nice one (for about $62 a night during peak season, if you're a state resident), and fish Lake Arthur to your heart's content. The only powerboats allowed on the 3,200-acre lake are the putt-putt pontoon type, so it's blissfully quiet. Off Lakeview Beach, one of two sandy swimming areas, windsurfers abound. To windsurf you'll need a state park launching permit from the Crescent Bay boat rental office on the south shore, which offers canoes and paddleboats (get details at 724-368-9955 or moraineboatrentals.com). A 7-mile paved bike path winds along the lake. It's easy enough for youngsters and there's a rental concession in the northwest corner of the park. For more information visit dcnr.state.pa.us /stateparks/findapark/moraine/index.htm.

The town of **Slippery Rock**—home of the former Slippery Rock State Teachers College, now **Slippery Rock University**—resembles most college towns, with music stores and coffee shops. One resident said the addition of a McDonald's made the place "big time." Then came Burger King. If the town's name sounds familiar, it's because many football stadiums in the country used to announce the Slippery Rock scores at the end of their games. Enough people were titillated by the term to generate some funny stories about its origin.

trivia

Early white settlers in the Allegheny Valley attracted the ire of local Seneca and Munsee tribes. Travel alongside their hunting grounds by the historic Buffalo Creek, now the Butler-Freeport Community Trail.

Between Erie and Pittsburgh, I-79 is largely rural, scenic, and lightly traveled. Roughly halfway between these cities, it's worth taking some time to go both east and west on Route 208. Near the intersection of I-79 and I-80, the easterly road goes to Grove City, where signs direct you to **Wendell August Forge** (1605 S. Center St.). The forge is a self-contained industry in the middle of a quiet community, one of the few remaining forges in the country that still fabricates aluminum, pewter, bronze, and sterling-silver pieces by hand, without any production machinery.

Today the forge is operated by the Knecht family, who rebuilt after a 2010 fire. On weekdays, you can walk through part of the forge to witness the entire process and ask the craftspeople questions. All items produced at the forge are for sale in the showroom (open Mon through Sat) for prices ranging from a few dollars to a few thousand. Call (800) 923-4438 or visit wendellaugust.com.

Going west on Route 208 from I-79 takes you to **Volant,** about 10 miles from Grove City, and 4 miles farther, to **New Wilmington,** the historic home of Westminster College. This is the heart of an authentic Amish area. The handsome college overlooks Brittan Lake, and the carillon in Old Main peals for special town events. Amish craftsmen bring their buggies to Wilson's Lumber to pick up supplies, so there are often as many horses on the street as there are cars. Stop for a cup of coffee at Mugsies (that's all that's served here; the town is dry), and drink in the quiet.

As you pass the giant Premium Outlets at Grove City, where I-80 meets I-79, you'll swear the mall is being invaded by paratroopers. Wrong. Those parachutists are landing at an airfield just behind the shops, at **Skydive Pennsylvania** (496 Old Ash Rd., Mercer; 800-909-JUMP; skydivepa.com). Experienced instructors there, with a perfect safety record, will get you up and back to earth in just a day. Your jumping companions might be fraternity brothers, members of a wedding party, or an 80-year-old grandma. Explains former owner Jeff Reckard, "The goal is to land safely with an open parachute over your head." (Duh.) Or stop for an hour, stretch out on the patio, and watch others land.

trivia

Hot Mass: an idea, an event, a big non-liturgical celebration with techno, funk, and dance for Pittsburgh's LGBTQ+ community and everyone else. Check the schedule on social media.

Golf, anyone? You might think that Atlanta and Palm Springs have the best golf courses. And, indeed, they might. But the nation's *first* golf course, or at least the oldest course in continuous use, is near where you are at this very moment: in Foxburg. In 1887 Fox built a five-hole course for the enjoyment of his neighbors, with greens of sand and one-quart tomato cans serving as cups. Three holes were added, then one more, bringing the modern total to nine. Since its inception the course has seen continuous play and is now the **Foxburg Country Club.** Weekday fees are $23 for 9 holes, $29 for 18 holes with a cart; on weekends, $25 for 9 holes, $35 for a full round. Senior discounts are offered Mon and Wed. Fore!

The nostalgic log clubhouse contains the **American Golf Hall of Fame** and the Tri-State P.G.A. Hall of Fame. The museum and library chronicle 400 years of golf. The museum, golf course, and clubhouse are open daily, Apr through Oct. For more information and tee times, call (724) 659-3196 during the season. You might want to overnight at the Foxburg Inn (foxburginn.com) and dine at the Allegheny Grille (alleghenygrille.com), both on the picturesque riverfront on Main St. Foxburg is located just minutes south of I-80 (exit 45).

Three miles from Foxburg, the wild and scenic Allegheny River runs through a spectacular and densely forested valley. Quaint Victorian homes lie just across the river in Emlenton (near I-80 exit 42). At the corner of Main and Second Streets stands America's first steam-powered gristmill. Built in 1875, the refurbished **Old Emlenton Mill** serves as a central point for the annual Christmas in Oil Country celebration.

Built on the banks of the Mingo Creek, and now mostly known as the intersection of I-70 and I-79, is the town of **Washington,** the county seat of Washington County and one with a charming downtown. Make sure to stop at the **Whiskey Rebellion Education and Visitor Center** (whiskeyrebellion center.org) on Main St. for an excellent introduction to local history; Apr through Nov, from 10 a.m. to 4 p.m. on Wed, Thurs, and Sat. The Center helps organize the Whiskey Rebellion Festival each July. Around the corner at 49 E. Maiden St. you can visit the **LeMoyne House Historical Museum** (49 E. Maiden St.; wchspa.org), Pennsylvania's first National Historic Landmark of the

Whiskey and Rebellion

Western Pennsylvania has a historic yen for rye whiskey. As you head south from **Beaver County**, you're entering Whiskey Rebellion country. Local farmers grew rye grain, distilled it, and traded it for all kinds of 18th-century supplies, and went ballistic when the federal government asserted its right to tax the proceeds. The **Oliver Miller Homestead**, in Allegheny County's South Park, is the home of one of the instigators, shot in August 1794 when he joined an angry mob that surrounded nearby **Woodville Plantation**, the home of General John Neville. Both sites, though modest, are open seasonally to the public: visit olivermillerhomestead.org and woodville-experience.org. Thirteen thousand federal troops, led by President George Washington, mustered to put down the insurrection.

A few years back, local distillers joined forces with history buffs to celebrate the birthplace of American whiskey. The **Whiskey Rebellion Trail** (whiskeyrebelliontrail.com) is the brilliant result. Like Kentucky's Bourbon Trail, the effort links craft distillers and rebel landmarks. Around Pittsburgh, visit award-winning **Wigle Whiskey** (wiglewhiskey.com) at its Strip District distillery and restaurant. In Washington, just around the corner from the Whiskey Rebellion Education Center, take a tipple at **Liberty Pole Spirits** (libertypolespirits.com).

Throughout the region, to Philadelphia, Baltimore, and beyond, you'll find a dozen related historic sites and craft distilleries where you can raise a toast. You can even buy your own liberty cap, the red knitted beanie worn by the rebels. Make your plan at whiskeyrebelliontrail.com.

Underground Railroad. In the handsome house, built in 1812, you can learn about life before the Civil War and local abolitionist activity.

Just outside, the garden contains medicinal herbs that LeMoyne used in his medical practice, plus culinary herbs and fragrant and flowering herbs for pleasure. Volunteers tend the garden, changing plants and shrubs frequently. You can take a self-guided tour of the garden and see, in addition to mint, foxglove, and brown-eyed susans, a Native American grinding stone and mile markers from the old National Highway. Tours run year-round Tues through Fri 11 a.m. to 4 p.m.; group tours only on Sat. Admission is $5 per adult. Call (724) 225-6740 or visit wchspa.org for details. While you're at LeMoyne House, peek at the guns and uniforms in the **Southwest Pennsylvania Military Museum,** a repository of memorabilia from all of America's wars. The book and gift shop offers an array of history-inspired products. Appropriately, the Washington County Historical Society also operates from the LeMoyne House.

Also in Washington, tour **Bradford House** (175 S. Main St.), once the home of David Bradford, a leader in the Whiskey Rebellion of 1794. The home is furnished in period antiques and is open for tours ($5 adults, $4 seniors)

Albert Who?

At the three forks of the Missouri River, Lewis and Clark came to an agreement about names for them. They were to be the Jefferson, Madison, and Gallatin Rivers. Uh—Gallatin?

Albert Gallatin—the statesman, diplomat, financier, historian, ethnologist, industrialist, and farmer—is remembered today, at least by a few, at *Friendship Hill,* his frontier home near Point Marion (223 New Geneva Rd.; 724-329-2501; nps.gov/frhi/index.htm). Overlooking the Monongahela, the estate (which Gallatin left in 1825) is a monument to the savvy financier, who paid for the Louisiana Purchase and oversaw the beginnings of a national transportation system. The next time you hear his name on "Jeopardy!," you'll be an expert. Take a self-guided tour with your cell phone and stay till sunset to wander the trails. Open daily 9 a.m. to 5 p.m., except federal holidays; free admission.

Apr through Nov on Wed from 11 a.m. to 3 p.m., or throughout the year by appointment; call (724) 222-3604 or visit bradfordhouse.org.

Get prehistoric at the *Meadowcroft Rockshelter and Historic Village,* about 20 miles northwest of Washington. (Go north on Route 844, then west on Route 50.) People have lived and worked on the land at Meadowcroft for 19,000 years—longer than at any other documented site in North America. Archaeologists continue to excavate the Meadowcroft rock shelter, but it's also open to the public. Here you can see how Native Americans, frontier settlers, farmers, and lumbermen shaped the history of western Pennsylvania. Learn to throw an atlatl like a caveman, or watch a blacksmith forge red-hot iron. Meadowcroft is open Memorial Day through Labor Day, Wed through Sun 10 a.m. to 4 p.m.; special hours in May, Sept, and Oct. Buy adult admission tickets online at $15 each; kids 6–17 enter free. For information call (724) 587-3412 or visit meadowcroftmuseum.org.

Here in Greene County, a soggy summer day is always a cause for celebration. Back in 1978, locals noticed that it always seemed to rain on July 29. So, ever since then, the town has thrown an annual free party on High Street, with food, music, crafts, and umbrellas. Get details on the *Waynesburg Rain Day* celebration at raindayfestival.com, or call the borough office at (724) 627-8111.

Three miles east of Waynesburg (take exit 3 off I-79) the *Greene County Historical Museum,* a mid-Victorian mansion, features period antiques, a country store, and collections of pottery, glass, quilts, and Indian and early-American artifacts—more than 10,000 items in all. The site, at 918 Rolling Meadows Rd., once housed the county poor farm. Little is known about the operation of the poor farm except that after an extremely unfavorable review of the home by the *Atlantic Monthly* in 1886, a reform campaign was launched to improve the conditions. From mid-Apr through mid-Oct, the museum is open Tues through Sat from 10 a.m. to 3 p.m. Adult admission is $10. Call (724) 627-3204 or visit greenecountyhistory.org.

A sculpted Mingo Indian seems ready to pounce at **Bushy Run Battlefield** (Route 993, Jeannette; 724-527-5584; bushyrunbattlefield.com). The statue stands in a museum that marks the site of a fierce battle where Chief Pontiac's warriors fought 400 British soldiers during Pontiac's Rebellion in August 1763. Check out the site's visitor center, open Apr through Oct, Fri and Sat 9 a.m. to 5 p.m. and Sun noon to 5 p.m. Admission is $5 for adults.

Five miles east lie the crossroads of **Hanna's Town.** Homesteaders built a thriving village here between 1758 and 1773, when it became the county seat. When word of the battles of Lexington and Concord reached these western settlers two years later, they protested British authority by issuing the Hanna's Town Resolves, which foreshadowed the Declaration of Independence. They even created their own flag, with a rattlesnake and the "don't tread on me" motto. An interpretive center is planned for the hilltop overlooking the settlement. Visit the site and its interpretive center Thurs through Sun; reserve group tours in advance. Learn more at westmorelandhistory.org or call (724) 836-1800.

> ## trivia
>
> The Underground Railroad, the system used to help free Southern slaves, traversed Pennsylvania. See historic markers in Sugar Run, Rummerfield, Towanda, Ulster, and elsewhere.

The 104-mile Western Division of the Pennsylvania Mainline Canal ran through Saltsburg before connecting with Johnstown and Pittsburgh. Beginning in 1829, it was the town's lifeblood for nearly 30 years. Nearly two centuries later the village on the Kiskiminetas River remains mostly unchanged. To see it, shoot for Canal Days, held the first weekend of every June. Or paddle the local waterways in a kayak or canoe. And be sure to visit the **Rebecca B. Hadden Stone House Museum** (105 Point St., Saltsburg; 724-639-9003). Hours are Wed from 10 a.m. to 2 p.m. and most Sundays from 1 to 5 p.m. They suggest a $2 donation. Call for tour information.

Punxsutawney

Remember the movie *Groundhog Day,* in which Bill Murray plays a grumpy TV weatherman who has a really bad day—over and over and over again? Check out the scene for yourself in **Punxsutawney.**

In Punxsutawney (rhymes with chunks-soo-SAW-me), Punxsutawney Phil, the groundhog, officially does or does not see his shadow at dawn on February 2, determining whether we will or will not have six more weeks of winter. The televised event takes place on **Gobbler's Knob,** a mythical, magical area, before an audience of media and more than 35,000 people. The town sits where Route 119 crosses Route 36. For more information call (814) 938-7700 or (800) 752-7445 or go to punxsutawney.com.

The groundhog tradition stems from beliefs associated with Candlemas Day and the days of early Christians in Europe. According to an old English song:

If Candlemas be fair and bright,
Come, Winter, have another flight;
If Candlemas brings clouds and rain,
Go, Winter, and come not again.

In Europe hedgehogs emerged in spring; in western Pennsylvania a groundhog had to do.

There's only one way to see Phil up close and personal on his big day: Get there early, around 2:30 a.m. That's when shuttle buses depart from six downtown locations for the music, fireworks, food, and mindless hilarity until 7:25 a.m., when Phil usually debuts. Visitors can't drive to the Knob and can't bring alcohol or illegal substances. But they can and do wear groundhog hats, suits, and T-shirts; carry banners ("Free Phil"); and cheer insanely when the Seer of Seers finally appears.

This is a once-in-a-lifetime must-do. But since the town has only one hotel, accommodations are scarce. The town sponsors overnight "crash pads" in public buildings, and there are a handful of motels within a half-hour drive. (One solution for partiers: Bring your own RV, park at the town campsite, and shuttle to the Knob.) At the conclusion of the festivities, linger to enjoy church-sponsored pancake breakfasts and small-town charm.

Up Close & Personal with Phil

My sons will never forget their first Groundhog Day in Punxsutawney. Unprepared for the crowds, we didn't reach the Knob in time for Phil's official pronouncement. But when we finally arrived, the mob had thinned out to reveal Phil himself—fat, sleek, and toothy. His top-hatted handler kindly let James and Bill pet the 15-pound prognosticator—a thrill they remember fondly each February 2. They also remember that we found a five-dollar bill lying in the snow.

Many of Punxsutawney's nostalgic Main Street building facades have been renovated, including the grand old post office that's now the **Punxsutawney Weather Discovery Center.** Kids can learn weather basics, deliver their own TV weather reports, and climb and slide through the exhibits. It's open Thurs through Sun, 10 a.m. to 4 p.m. Admission is $7 per person over 3 years old; visit weatherdiscoverycenter.org or call (814) 938-1000.

Even if groundhogs are the animals with the biggest reputation in metropolitan Punxsutawney, they're not the biggest animals. Bison are. At **Nature's Comeback Bison Ranch,** the Hineman family raises the large mammals. They may end up on your table, but they're happy, well-fed, free-range bison during their lifetime. "Many people are amazed at how playful bison actually are," says owner Brian Hineman. "They have been seen throwing logs that weigh over 500 pounds several feet in the air and bouncing around like little lambs. Bison can run up to 45 miles an hour—amazingly fast for their massive size." The breeder bull, who weighs over a ton, is called Hercules. To produce more healthful meat with lower fat content, Nature's Comeback feeds the bison only hay and grass. The meat, says Hineman, "tastes like your best cuts of beef without the waste of trimming the fat." The ranch, which has been in the family for over 150 years, will give you a warm-weather tour or sell you some tasty meat; call ahead (814) 590-6965 to make a tour reservation at this off-the-beaten-path attraction. (Watch where you step as you get up close and personal with large animals.) Visit buffalobrian.tripod.com. Take I-80, exit 97, 1 mile off Route 119 south.

trivia

In 1868, in the Jacks (Oak Hall) School in Porter Township, Clarion County became the home of a chapter of the Anti-Horse Thief Association. Although there is no record of a horse being stolen for many decades, the association holds an annual dinner. In 1956, when Dwight D. Eisenhower and Arthur Godfrey belonged, it cost $1 to become a life member.

A trip to nearby **Smicksburg** is an enjoyable drive, particularly at harvest time. Home of the largest Amish settlement in western Pennsylvania, Smicksburg has a lovely rolling landscape freckled with farms. Motorized vehicles share the winding roads with horses and buggies, and you find fine craftsmanship and craft shops at every turn. Because of the strong religious faith, many shops close on Sunday.

Off Route 219, 4 miles north of Grampian, you will find **Bilger's Rocks,** a phenomenon of massive, ancient sandstone formations, called "rock city," covering some 20 acres. One 500-ton boulder rests on a smaller one in perfect balance. Visited for centuries, these giant sandstone formations tower 30 to 50 feet.

From groundhogs to bison to rabbits. Or at least invisible rabbits. Okay, one invisible rabbit. You know, Harvey, the bunny only Jimmy Stewart could see in the movie *Harvey*. Stewart's life and films are alive and well and entertaining everyone at the *Jimmy Stewart Museum* in Indiana, Pennsylvania. Sit back in a 1930s-style movie theater and watch *Mr. Smith Goes to Washington* and *It's a Wonderful Life*. The small museum occupies the third floor of the public library, and it's dedicated to the homeboy who catapulted from his family's hardware store to the heart of Tinseltown. Admission costs $8 per adult, and the museum is open from 10 a.m. to 4 p.m. Mon through Sat and noon to 4 p.m. Sun and holidays. The library is at 845 Philadelphia St., and the mailing address is Box One, Indiana 15701. Call (724) 349-6112 or (800) 83-JIMMY (that's really 800-835-4669) or visit Harvey and the gang at jimmy.org.

The *Ghost Town Trail* threads through 16 miles of abandoned mining towns along the Black Lick Creek. At the midpoint of its run from Dilltown in Indiana County to Nanty Glo in Cambria County is *Eliza Furnace,* one of the best-preserved iron furnaces in the United States—and the source of haunted tales. Some say that owner David Ritter's wife ran off with a man named George Rodgers, or that Ritter's son fell into the furnace and was killed. Either way, he was so distraught that he hanged himself. His ghost can supposedly be seen hanging in the furnace's entrance.

coalinthem tharhills

As you pedal the Ghost Town Trail, look beside you: Near Vintondale you'll spy an exposed coal seam in a rock face alongside the trail, shining like dark icing in a stone layer cake. That's why Cambria County is still coal-mining country.

But don't let the tall tales keep you away. The Ghost Town bike trail features masses of rhododendrons in the spring (and some wild water colors where mine subsidence still fouls the creek). For directions call the Cambria County Conservation and Recreation Authority at (814) 472-2110; for details go to indianacountyparks.org.

Noah weathered a flood, but he heeded the warning. The town of *Johnstown* did not. Late in May 1889 it started raining. The neglected South Fork Dam, upriver from Johnstown, gave way May 31, and a wall of water moved 14 miles downstream, plucking chairs, doors, walls, and complete houses out of their rightful places. The water immersed and erased the industrialized city in 10 minutes, killing more than 2,200 people. The *Johnstown Flood Museum* (304 Washington St.) re-creates this shocking episode—the catastrophe of death and homelessness, followed by the triumph of the human spirit that allowed the town to rebuild. (So does David McCullough's masterful 1987 history of the tragedy.) Every hour the museum shows *The Johnstown Flood*, which won the 1989 Academy Award for best short-subject documentary. One survivor expresses the drama: "My boyhood home was crushed like an eggshell before my eyes, and I saw it disappear." See the flood in 3-D, in books, and in souvenirs at the museum.

The flood is only one of the stories told in town, and the Johnstown Discovery Network links them all. Around the time of the flood, thousands of immigrants from southern and eastern Europe, lured by ready jobs in its steel mills, came to Johnstown to build a better life. Experience their stories first-hand at the **Heritage Discovery Center** at 201 Sixth Ave. You'll be handed an immigrant "identity card" that allows you to assume the role of one of eight characters, from a Bohemian farmhand to a Russian peasant, in the interactive exhibits. The **Wagner-Ritter House,** open for guided tours only, depicts a typical 19th-century German immigrant's household. The **Stone Bridge** over the Conemaugh River downtown, which survived the flood, sparkles with colored lights each evening, **Peoples Gas Natural Park** offers pedestrian paths, and the **Johnstown Children's Museum** offers a kid-sized tower dubbed "the Inclimber," with a rooftop garden with river views. Admission to all of these attractions is as easy as tapping your cell phone. The Johnstown Heritage online pass gives users a 20 percent discount to visit the whole bunch over several days. An adult pass is $30, with discounts for seniors and children. Hours for all are Tues to Sat 10 a.m. to 5 p.m. and noon to 5 p.m. on Sun. Just go to jaha.org.

Two years after the flood, the Cambria Iron Company (a predecessor of Bethlehem Steel Corporation) began building houses in the community of Westmont, 500 feet up Yoder Hill from downtown Johnstown. Since no roads existed, the company assembled a vertical commuter system, which remains today as the **Inclined Plane,** rising at a grade of 71 percent. It's scheduled to reopen after repairs in 2023. The *Guinness Book of World Records* ranked it the steepest vehicular inclined plane in the world. Originally designed to carry people and their horses and wagons, it now accommodates people and their cars. The wheels, rails, and other parts came from standard railway equipment (and, in fact, the cars are duplicates of those that hauled cargo boats over the Allegheny Portage railroad). The Inclined Plane is composed of two sets of tracks implanted in the side of the hill; two cars run simultaneously, one going up and the other going down. The cables are 2 inches in diameter and 1,130 feet long. They can safely carry 337,000 pounds, or 167 tons. For more information call (814) 536-1816 or (814) 535-5526 or visit inclinedplane.org.

At the top of the Inclined Plane is **Westmont,** originally called Tiptop. Locals say the town has always been divided in two parts: the more affluent southern section with single-family homes, called the "dinner" side, and the less affluent northern section with twin homes and smaller singles, called the "supper" section. Westmont attracts naturalists, too: Lucerne Street contains the longest municipally owned stand of American elm trees east of the Mississippi (even small towns like a claim to fame). Although half of all American elms were killed by Dutch elm disease, this beautiful, stately "cathedral arch" of elms is maintained. The borough now has nine trees that qualify as historic elms, which means they measure at least 10 feet in circumference at chest height.

Can you scutch? To learn how, follow Route 219 south to **Somerset** and visit the **Somerset Historical Center,** which portrays rural life in southwestern Pennsylvania, where making linen from flax included that skill. On its 150 acres you can see utensils, machinery, and restored buildings from different periods of Pennsylvania history. The Center also maintains extensive genealogical records of the county, so if your people settled here, you may find some roots in the records. From May through Oct, it's open 10 a.m. to 4 p.m. Wed through Sat. On first Fridays, you're invited for live music and casual dining from local food trucks. Admission is $6 for adults, with discounts for seniors and military families.

Shanksville, 6 miles from Somerset, will forever be remembered in world history as the first resistance to the war on terrorism. On September 11, 2001, United Airlines Flight 93 crashed here after passengers attempted to wrest the plane away from terrorists. Forty innocent people lost their lives. The National Park Service's **Flight 93 National Memorial** opened on this peaceful field in 2011. To get to the site from Route 30, take Lambertville Road south for 1.7 miles to Skyline Drive and follow it 0.8 mile to the parking area. The grounds are open from dawn to dusk year-round. The Visitors Center is open from 9 a.m. to 5 p.m. daily except federal holidays. Visit nps.gov/flni.

Laurel Highlands

Everyone who visits—or lives in—Pennsylvania should see **Fallingwater,** the summer retreat that architect Frank Lloyd Wright designed for the Pittsburgh department-store owner Edgar J. Kaufmann. The house, completed in 1939, was constructed of sandstone quarried on the property and built by local craftsmen. It's the only remaining Wright house where the original setting, furnishings, and artwork remain intact. Fallingwater reflects Wright's genius, which allows the house to merge with its environment outside and to echo nature in its stone and wood interior. The house, appearing to grow out of the boulders and rocks, extends over a natural waterfall of Bear Run. You can't see or hear the water from inside, but you can do both from any balcony or from a stairwell down from the living room. A gray sandstone 4-story chimney at the core of the house anchors it into the stone cliff. Wright built a desk in every bedroom and placed all headboards on eastern walls so that no one would be awakened by the sun. Genius. The home retains a feeling of seclusion and oneness with the natural environment, even though many people visit. It's open for guided tours (no wandering on your own) from mid-Mar through Nov, daily except Mon, 9 a.m. to 4 p.m. In Dec and early Mar it's open only weekends, and it's closed Jan and Feb. Reservations are required, especially during July, Aug, and Oct, the busiest months. Try to visit midweek and bring comfortable walking shoes. And a camera. Standard exterior tours are $18 for adults. More in-depth tours range up to $150. For more information call (724) 329-8501; or visit fallingwater.org.

Fallingwater is on Route 381 between the villages of Mill Run and Ohiopyle (pronounce it Ohio-PILE) about 90 minutes southeast of Pittsburgh. Children under age 6 may not tour Fallingwater, but they can play at its Family Room, and there's a nice little cafe on-site.

Other Wright-designed homes are close by. West of Ohiopyle, 7 miles along a scenic mountain road, lies **Kentuck Knob,** a smaller, simpler 1950s home that Wright designed for the Hagan family of Uniontown. (It was originally known as the I. N. Hagan House.) The house is hexagonal, with hexagonal accents, all made of native fieldstone and tidewater red cypress. It hides in—rather than sits on—the mountain it occupies, so you're practically at the front door before you see it. On the grounds behind the visitor center is an oversize apple core by artist Claes Oldenburg and other large-scale contemporary sculpture. In Jan and Feb you're invited to cross-country ski the grounds after your house tour. The house is open for tours on weekends in early Mar and most of Dec; from Apr to Nov, it's open 10 a.m. to 4 p.m., with limited hours on Tues. Admission is $25 for adults if you reserve early. Book tickets online at kentuckknob.com.

If you've ever wanted to spend the night in a Wright creation, here's your chance. North of the Pennsylvania Turnpike in Acme—no relation to Wile E. Coyote's famous products—is Polymath Park. Two of Wright's ultra-practical Usonian homes have been moved to this property, flanked by two similar homes designed by Wright disciple Peter Berndtson. No tours during the winter. From Mar, $26 tours can be arranged any day except Wed from 11 a.m. to 3 p.m. There are many other options for brunch, lunch, and dinner tours that include dining at TreeTops, the property's cozy restaurant on the mountaintop. Get all the details at polymathpark.com.

Now is a perfect time to stop for a walk or a picnic along the Youghiogheny River at **Ohiopyle State Park,** almost 18,500 acres of wilderness delight. It's been named the best state park in the country—see why. The

The Slides

I love the scenic waterfalls at Ohiopyle State Park—especially the Slides, where our family always ends the day with a ride down the slick limestone boulders. The stream varies from gentle to intense, depending on recent rainfall. If it's early in the summer, or there have been lots of thunderstorms, you'll move at top speed (and the water will be colder). Watch your step—Band-Aids may be required.

Youghiogheny Gorge, carved 1,700 feet into the Laurel Ridge by the river, takes your breath away. Totally contained within the state park is the borough of Ohiopyle, almost 2 whole blocks long. Fifty-four people live here, and commercial establishments include a grocery store with a few small cafes, a gas station, and, in season, a Dairy Queen and a pizza parlor. One ultra-casual spot, perfect for beer-drinking in soggy post-river attire, is the *Falls City Restaurant and Pub* (112 Garrett St.; 724-329-3000; fallscitypub .com). Owner Eric Martin also owns Wilderness Voyagers next door. The tavern's hours vary seasonally, so call ahead.

"The name of the town, Ohiopyle, is subject to fact and fiction depending on who you're talking to," says Mark McCarty, mayor and manager of an outfitter. The state park's interpretation is something like "white frothing water," but if you study the early settlers' writings, it's more like "peaceful river." The water in this case is the Yough, Youghiogheny being a Native American word for "flowing in a roundabout course." Yes, it's off the beaten path, says Jim Greenbaum, manager of *White Water Adventurers.* "On the other hand, there are two interstate highways within a half hour of here." Ohiopyle has lured tourists since the early 1900s, when people came by train from Pittsburgh and Washington to swim in the river and hike on Fern Cliff. Once three large hotels dominated the borough. Then "the railroads went away," as Greenbaum puts it. In the early 1960s a new industry—white-water rafting—was born. The

Yurt, Anyone?

Pennsylvania has 11 state parks that offer Mongolian-style accommodations in addition to cabins, and Ohiopyle has more yurts than any other. The round-framed, fabric-covered structures have floors and even decks (but in typical nomadic fashion, no indoor plumbing).

The cost is between $17 and $90 a day, and $102 to $400 weekly, depending on the season. Western-style cabin rules apply: no pets, no alcohol, check in at 3 p.m., check out at 10 a.m. To reserve, go to visitpaparks.com or call (888) 727-2757.

season for rafting runs Mar through Oct, with the bulk of tours scheduled from mid-May until mid-Sept.

The Middle Yough, says Greenbaum, is the easy section, great for kids over 5 or first-time adult rafters. The Lower Yough is rated intermediate, recommended for people age 12 and older. The Yough sections called Pure Screaming Hell, Bastard, and Double Pencil Sharpener are recommended for rafters with the most technical expertise—but then, so is Cheeseburger Falls. If you'd like to try a rafting trip, call one of the four Ohiopyle outfitters with state concessions:

White Water Adventurers, (724) 329-8850 or (800) 992-7238; wwaraft.com.

Laurel Highlands River Tours, (724) 329-8531 or (800) 472-3846; laurel highlands.com.

Ohiopyle Trading Post, 4 Negley St., (724) 329-1450 or (888) 644-6795; ohiopyletradingpost.com.

Wilderness Voyageurs, 103 Garrett St., (724) 329-1000 or (800) 272-4141; wilderness-voyageurs.com.

The Great Allegheny Passage is a 150-mile trail from Pittsburgh to Cumberland, Maryland. Biking fanatics have worked for two decades to clear this gorgeous non-motorized path along the Youghiogheny and Casselman Rivers. The result is a flat, scenic route right through to the 185-mile Chesapeake and Ohio Canal towpath, which ends in Washington, DC. (My husband and I did the full trip in five days. But believe me, you should take seven.) The trail traverses Big Savage tunnel, a spooky passage through a mountain on the Pennsylvania-Maryland border. (The Western Maryland Railroad used to travel this right-of-way, hence the name rails-to-trails.) Meanwhile, you can explore as much or as little as you like. Map your trip at gaptrail.org.

In addition to Ohiopyle, where the river outfitters also offer cheap bike and e-bike rentals, seek out the other charming villages along the trail. Confluence, some 12 miles south of Ohiopyle, has three rivers (hence the name), a few coffee shops and luncheonettes and the *Confluence Cyclery,* which rents and repairs the bikes seen everywhere here. The *River's Edge Cafe* (203 Yough St.; 814-395-5059; riversedgecafebnb.com) has a comfy Victorian porch for lingering over dinner in the twilight. Next door is the *Parker House* (213 Yough St.; 814-395-9616; theparkerhousecountryinn.com), a beautifully restored guest house, great for groups. In Rockwood, another 18 miles south, you'll find a few more B&Bs, a real opera house (now shops and a cafe), and the Rock City Cafe, a beer 'n' wings spot.

JANUARY

Beaver County Snow Shovel Riding Championship

Economy Park
(724) 846-5600

This annual race is held in Economy Park on the third Saturday in January, unless there's too little snow. Call (724) 846-5600 or (800) 342-8192 for more information.

FEBRUARY

Groundhog Day

Punxsutawney

There's only one place to be on February 2: Punxsutawney. The savvy little town has turned Groundhog Day into a multiday extravaganza with food fests, weddings performed by the mayor, music, and hilarity (when the holiday falls next to a weekend, look out).

MAY

National Road Festival

National Road Heritage Park
(724) 437-9877
nationalroadpa.org

In mid-May the National Road Festival celebrates the historic national road, US Route 40. Food, fun, and entertainment stretch for 90 miles along the National Road Heritage Park.

JULY

Big Butler Fair

(724) 865-2400

The Big Butler Fair is a 150-year-old institution with plenty of noise—demolition derbies, tractor pulls, and more. It's held over the Fourth of July.

AUGUST

Antique Flea Market

Somerset
(814) 445-6431

The Antique Flea Market is held in Somerset the second Saturday in August.

Flood City Music Festival

(814) 539-1889
jaha.org

Accordions. Trombones. Blues. Balkan bop. It's all at the Flood City Music Festival, held in Johnstown each August. More than 70 hours of nationally known acts are programmed each year. Everything takes place at the downtown festival park.

North Washington Rodeo

(724) 894-2064
nwfd.com/rodeo

Saddle up yer bronco, or at least your sport-utility vehicle, and head to the North Washington Rodeo, on Route 38, 16 miles north in Washington County, during the third week in August. Daily performances at 8 p.m. feature men doing saddle bronc, bareback, and calf roping, and women running barrel races. There's always something at intermission for the kids and raffles for the grown-ups. You might win a registered colt or a steer that the rodeo organizers have purchased from the local 4-H group.

SEPTEMBER

Flax Scutching Festival
Monticue's Grove, Stahlstown
(724) 238-9244

During the second weekend in September, there's a Flax Scutching Festival at Monticue's Grove in Stahlstown. If the town's not off the beaten path enough for you, the event surely is. Here you can see how craftspeople used to take the flax plant and scutch it—in other words, break down the tough fibers to make linen. To learn more about scutching or the second-oldest flax-scutching festival in the world, call (724) 238-9244.

Peanut Butter Festival
Gumtown Memorial Park, New Bethlehem
(814) 275-3929
redbankchamber.com

New Bethlehem initiated its annual Peanut Butter Festival in 1996 to promote the Smucker's peanut butter plant. If you think toast and jelly are naked without p.b., visit Gumtown Memorial Park on Water Street on a weekend in mid-September.

OCTOBER

Pumpkinfest
Confluence
visitconfluence.org

The tiny Youghiogheny River town of Confluence proves it has more gourds than people each October at Pumpkinfest. There's a Pumpkinfest Queen, a tough-guy tractor pull, live bands, and more.

Step Trek
Pittsburgh
(412) 488-0486
steptrek.org

Get a cardio workout and a great view of downtown Pittsburgh during Step Trek, the South Side Slopes Association's open house along the steepest step streets in Pittsburgh. The October event benefits the neighborhood association.

DECEMBER

First Night
Pittsburgh
(412) 471-6070
firstnightpgh.com

December 31, celebrate First Night (it's really Last Night, isn't it?) throughout downtown Pittsburgh.

As you pedal along, you'll see a few anglers (trout fishing is big here), maybe a few black bears way down in the ravines, and lots of families also pedaling around Ohiopyle, especially on the weekends. Other than that, you'll have the Laurel Highlands to yourself—on the level.

For super-easy, one-click planning, including accommodations and meals, log on to gaptrail.org, or contact the Great Allegheny Passage at (888) 282-2453.

If the rustic simplicity of Fallingwater makes you pine for an upscale night or two, consider **Nemacolin Woodlands Resort and Spa** in Farmington. With French food, French paintings, and a par-72 golf course, its motto could be "extravagance R us." Elegantly appointed guest rooms include marble baths and plush terry-cloth robes. Entertainment for kids, a shopping mall, a ski slope, a wild animal park, a golf course, skeet shooting, stables, a polo field and a climbing wall are on the premises. Dining? Choose among four elegant restaurants, including Lautrec, the only western Pennsylvania recipient of AAA's Five Diamond rating. The place is named for a western Delaware Indian named Nemacolin who, in 1740, carved a trail through the Laurel Mountains between what is now Cumberland, Maryland, and Brownsville, Pennsylvania. When Congress established the National Highway in the mid-1800s, the highway incorporated Nemacolin's trail. For resort reservations log on to nemacolin .com, or call (724) 329-8555 or (866) 344-6957.

Near the popular ski resorts of Seven Springs and Hidden Valley lies the old-money charm of **Ligonier,** founded as a British fort in 1758. The **Fort Ligonier Museum** has re-created the redcoats' armaments, used against the French and the Indians, in authentic detail. Its treasures include jaw-dropping portraits of the British leaders of the 1750s by Joshua Reynolds, Allan Ramsay, and others. There's also a comprehensive, 300-artifact exhibit on the Seven Years' War, the worldwide European conflict that touched North America as the French and Indian War. It's open seasonally at 200 S. Market St. Call (724) 238-9701 or visit fortligonier.org.

Ligonier's central "diamond" has a Victorian bandstand and pleasant shopping—good restaurants, too. And just on the edge of town lies **Idlewild,** an amusement park with low prices, low temperatures, and a laid-back feel. Its biggest coaster isn't the Mauler, but the Wild Mouse. Even the shyest toddlers will love Idlewild's Storybook Forest, where they can meet the Billy Goats Gruff (played by real billies, but minus the trolls). Older kids can holler on the Tarzan vines and water chutes. A miniature railway runs over Loyalhanna Creek, and the towering trees keep pathways cool. Don't miss the restored pastel merry-go-round. Idlewild is open from Memorial Day weekend through Labor Day on Route 30, Ligonier. Admission prices vary. Call (724) 238-3666 or visit idlewild.com for details.

On Route 381 in nearby Cook Township lies **Powdermill Nature Reserve,** a field research station of the Carnegie Museum of Natural History. Here kids and adults can spy on wildflowers, trees, songbirds, butterflies, and salamanders with eyes and ears (the kids, not the salamanders), magnifying glass, or camera. Youngsters can sign up for weeklong nature classes during the summer, and individuals and families can attend other free programs. The nature reserve is open year-round Wed through Sat 9 a.m. to 4:30 p.m. and Sun noon to 4:30 p.m. It is also open Tues 9 a.m. to 4:30 p.m. from Apr through mid-Nov. For hours and program information, call (724) 593-6105, or visit powdermill.org.

Compared to Ligonier, the Westmoreland County seat of Greensburg is a big city. Here's where you'll find the **Westmoreland Museum of American Art.** A bequest of masterworks from the estate of millionaire Richard Scaife extended an already-impressive three-century collection. Open Wed through Sun; admission is free. It's at 221 N. Main Street. Call (724) 837-1500 or browse online at thewestmoreland.org.

If you love close encounters of the third kind, make your way a few miles east of Greensburg. On December 9, 1965, the tiny hamlet of Kecksburg saw a gigantic fireball streak into nearby woods. Witnesses who saw it—before members of the military swooped in and took it away—say it was not a meteor but a craft of some kind from somewhere. Today the town memorializes the event with a huge sculpture of the mysterious acorn-shaped missile outside the Kecksburg Fire Club, which happens to be the location of the **Kecksburg UFO Museum.** Explained one beer-drinking patron, as we trooped through the firemen's bar to the closet-sized "museum": "We're the aliens." Find it at 5128 Water St., Mt. Pleasant. Open Mon through Thurs 11 a.m. to 11 p.m., Fri 11 a.m. to 1 a.m., Sat noon to 1 a.m., and Sun noon to 11 p.m. Call (724) 423-9540 for more information. The **Cigar Box Guitar Museum** decorates Speal's Tavern, which has been dubbed "New Alexandria's homemade Hard Rock Café" (spealstavern.com).

All these hills, all these valleys: Sounds like a perfect place for mountain biking, and there are some gnarly opportunities on the **PW&S Trails** in Forbes State Forest. "When I ride here in the evening, I see grouse, deer, and bear," says Gates Watson, a local enthusiast. There are 5 loops here, carved from an old logging railroad; like ski trails, they vary in length and difficulty. For details call (724) 238-7560 or pick up a map at the Forbes State Forest office on Route 30 outside Laughlintown.

Route 669 leads you straight to (well, not really straight, but toward) **Mt. Davis** in the Forbes State Forest—at 3,213 feet above sea level, the highest elevation in the state.

If you're into gallows humor, pop up Route 281, nearly to I-70, and go to the courthouse in Somerset. The building served as the county jail from 1856 to 1981, and the double hanging gallows is still intact: a warning, perhaps, to tardy employees.

Places to Stay in Southwestern Pennsylvania

FARMINGTON

Summit Inn
101 Skyline Drive 9 (just off Rt. 40)
(724) 438-8594
summitinnresort.com
A century-old inn with killer views atop Laurel Caverns, the largest cave in PA.

INDUSTRY

Willows Inn
1830 Midland Beaver Rd.
(724) 643-4500
willowsinnpa.com
Just off Route 60, a short drive from Beaver business district.

PITTSBURGH

The Priory Hotel
614 Pressley St.
(412) 231-3338
thepriory.com
Formerly a monastery, now a popular North Shore boutique hotel.

Renaissance Pittsburgh
107 6th St.
(412) 562-1200
renaissancepittsburgh.com

A jewel amid the theaters of the downtown Cultural District, and right across the Clemente Bridge from PNC Park.

TRYP by Wyndham
147 40th St.
(412) 567-0555
wyndham.hotels.com
Cheeky hotel, fun nabe: this Lawrenceville spot has an airy rooftop bar atop rooms in a former trade school.

PUNXSUTAWNEY

Jackson Run Bed and Breakfast
363 Jackson Run Rd.
(814) 938-2315
jacksonrun.com
Farmhouse accommodations in an apple orchard.

VOLANT

Candleford Inn Bed and Breakfast
225 Mercer St.
(724) 533-4497
candlefordinn.com
Open year-round in Mercer County's Amish country.

Places to Eat in Southwestern Pennsylvania

BEAVER

Cafe Kolache
402 Third St.
(724) 775-8102
cafekolache.com
A friendly Main Street coffeehouse with delicious filled Czech pastries. Closed Sun.

Wooden Angel
308 Leopard Ln.
(724) 774-7880
woodenangel.com
Award-winning American wine cellar.

BROOKVILLE

Courthouse Grill and Pub
209 Main St.
(814) 849-2557
Open daily for casual lunches and dinners.

FARMINGTON

Stone House Inn
3023 National Pike
(724) 329-8876
stonehouseinn.com
Casual fine dining year-round.

FOX CHAPEL

Alta Via
46 Fox Chapel Rd.
(412) 408-3816
Fresh Italian food, done to perfection in a suburban trattoria. Closed Mon.

MERCER

Iron Bridge Inn
1438 Perry Hwy.
(724) 748-3626
springfields.com/iron-bridge-inn/
Famous for prime rib and Sunday brunch.

PITTSBURGH

Church Brew Works
3525 Liberty Ave.
(412) 688-8200
churchbrew.com
Brewpub in the former St. John the Baptist Church in Bloomfield.

Apteka
4606 Penn Ave.
(412) 251-0189
aptekapgh.com
An unusual combo—Eastern European vegan cuisine—that just works. Lawrenceville.

Gaucho Parrilla Argentina
146 Sixth St.
(412) 709-6622
eatgaucho.com
This carnivores' delight features a wood-fired grill and rooftop dining.

Pamela's P&G Diner
(Various locations)
pamelasdiner.com
A Pittsburgh tradition in a half-dozen venues; crepe-style pancakes make the city's morning. President Barack Obama is among the many fans.

The Warhol Cafe
Andy Warhol Museum
117 Sandusky St.
(412) 237-8300
warhol.org
Open Tues through Sun 10 a.m. to 4 p.m. (Fri to 9 p.m.). Seasonal light meals, wines, and microbrews.

WASHINGTON

The Springhouse
1531 PA Rt. 136
(724) 228-3339
Baked goods, hot meals, home-smoked hams, ice cream from the family farm, and room for kids to roam the fields. Open daily.

Northwestern Pennsylvania

The Lake District

The Erie area is Pennsylvania's beach. Ohio, Lake Erie, and New York State form the western, northern, and eastern borders of Erie County, respectively, and getting to *Erie* from anywhere in Pennsylvania means driving through miles and miles and miles of scenic woodland and uninhabited terrain.

People here are fiercely proud of the pristine natural environment, from wildlife refuges to forest wilderness to rushing streams to The Lake.

A few decades ago, Lake Erie was pronounced dead. But it wasn't really dead—the problem was actually too much of the wrong kinds of life. Nutrients such as phosphates and nitrates, especially plentiful in agricultural runoff, encouraged excessive growth of algae, which grew so fast that it choked out other forms of plants and fish. The process is called eutrophication. In water where no oxygen can reach the bottom, the only fish that can live are small panfish. As Lake Erie deteriorated, only the panfish survived. A massive combined effort by area manufacturing companies, local colleges, state and federal governments, and concerned citizens turned things around. The City

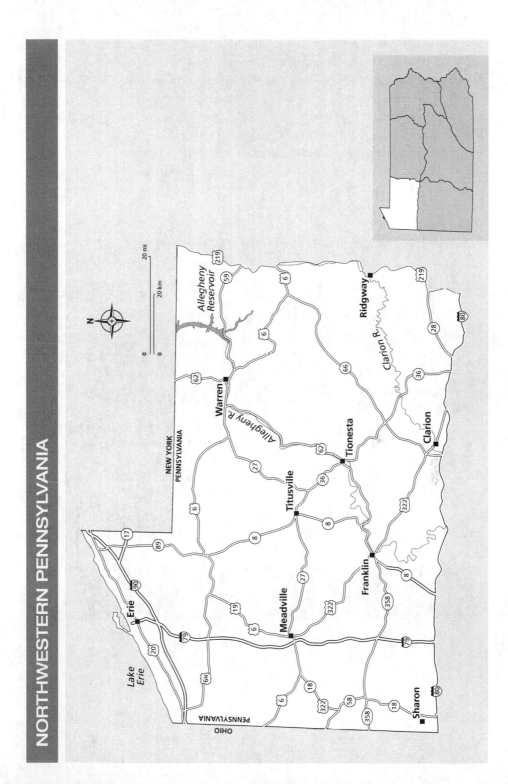

of Erie improved its sewage disposal system. The Department of Health now tests regularly for harmful bacteria. Industries treat their wastes so that they won't hurt the lake. Colleges run ecology projects, continuously monitoring the state of the water. At least one Erie councilman pilots his boat, at cost, for the monitoring teams. Game fish have returned. In fact, the city celebrated when the first coho salmon was caught after a long dry spell.

The resurgence of other species is no fish story. Every fall, hundreds of Pennsylvania anglers descend on the Lake Erie tributaries—Elk and Walnut Creeks and the mouths of Trout and Godfrey Runs—for the annual steelhead spawning runs. These whoppers are reputed to swim right up to the boat and can almost be scooped up by hand. They're most plentiful when the water temperature hovers around 55 degrees.

Part of the success story comes from the central role that Lake Erie plays in the lives of the people who live here. Hundreds of people go to the public dock in the city every day, if not to fish, at least to check out conditions. Adults who've lived here all their lives talk about having gone out fishing every morning before school or every evening after school. These stories help explain the spirit of the lakeshore. The passion is contagious. Among the most ardent users are the Benedictine Sisters of Erie, whose main house is on East Lake Road. The sisters live a life of prayer, promoting peace and justice—but they're also avid anglers.

The best place to learn about Erie and the lake is ***Presque Isle State Park*** (rhymes with press-TILE). One of the most remarkable places in Pennsylvania, it offers enough outdoor recreation to keep you busy for weeks. It's a 3,200-acre peninsula extending from the City of Erie (just 4 miles west of downtown) into Lake Erie. Although in French Presque Isle means "almost an island," this area has been a real island several times. Storm waves have broken through the neck of land, isolating the distant portion at least four times since 1819. One

AUTHOR'S TOP 10 FAVORITES IN NORTHWESTERN PENNSYLVANIA

Dan Rice Days in Girard	Indian God Rock
Flagship *Niagara*	Lawrence Park Dinor
French Creek	Meadville Market House
Glass Growers Gallery	Pennsylvania Firefly Festival
Hickory Creek Wilderness	Quaker Steak & Lube

gap remained open for 32 years. Interestingly, the combined effects of erosion on one side and sand deposits on the other change the peninsula's shape and location noticeably, not in thousands of years, but in just a few. Geologists call it a recurving sand spit and estimate that the peninsula has moved about 0.5 mile east in the past hundred years. The Stull Interpretive Center, located at the beginning of the park near Barracks Beach, displays maps showing the changes. If you avoid the peak summer swimming season, it's possible to walk for hours along the beaches and in the woods without seeing another human being.

The diverse nature of Presque Isle is astounding. It has six distinct ecological zones, each with a unique plant and animal community. Due to the peninsula's location along the Atlantic flyway (that's the celestial interstate system for migratory birds), more than 320 species of birds have been recorded here. They usually visit in April, while heading north, and again in November, because Presque Isle offers one of the best avian bed-and-breakfast systems around. At the tip of the peninsula, Gull Point is designated a restricted, protected, fragile ecosystem. You may not enter this area between April 1 and November 30.

The big glass lighthouse shape just outside the park entrance is the ***Tom Ridge Environmental Center,*** named for the Erie native son who served as Pennsylvania's governor and the first director of the US Office of Homeland Security. Admission to its exhibits about the wonders of Presque Isle is free. The center is open daily except Thanksgiving, Christmas, and New Year's Day at 301 Peninsula Dr. Call (814) 833-7424 or check presqueislesp@state.pa.us.

Children will probably want to skip the center and head for the beaches, where the surf is usually high enough to be interesting without getting rough enough to be dangerous. Sadly, some beaches are closed when water contaminants rise, so call ahead: (814) 833-7424. Near Grave Yard Pond you can rent rowboats, canoes, and motorboats, but stay tuned to Channel 16 for boating conditions.

Presque Isle also offers bliss for bladers: a superb 13.5-mile recreation trail, beautifully leveled and paved, along the shoreline loop. Park at the first lot inside the park entrance off Route 832, strap on your in-line skates, and go.

Discoveries on Presque Isle

Jerry McWilliams has been birding on Presque Isle since he was 5. As we hiked the secluded 1-mile trail to Gull Point, he talked excitedly about recent rare sightings: a white-morphed gyrfalcon from Greenland, the first ever seen at Presque Isle, and a boreal owl, a northern Canadian native not seen here since 1893. "They live in forests so deep that if they saw a human, they'd allow you to touch them. They don't know fear," explains McWilliams.

Kids will also love **Waldameer Park and Water World,** the kind of old-fashioned amusement park that summer vacations are all about. Its wooden Ravine Flyer coaster swoops over the park's entrance road. It's located at 220 Peninsula Dr., the road into the park (814-838-3591; waldameer .com). Waldameer's competition is **Splash Lagoon,** a year-round indoor water park with laser tag, located off I-90, exit 24; call (866) 3-SPLASH or visit splashlagoon.com.

Another way to cover the waterfront is aboard the **Lady Kate.** The 110-passenger cruiser makes frequent trips around Presque Isle from its moorings by the Perry Monument (on East Fisher Drive). From mid-June through Labor Day, there are 5 90-minute narrated tours each day, from 11 a.m. to sunset. From mid-May to mid-June and again from Labor Day through the end of Sept, there are 3 sailings a day on weekends only. Reservations are suggested. Fares for adults are $16; $9 for children 5 through 12; children under 5 are free. Call (814) 836-0201, or visit piboattours.com.

For boating on a grander scale, visit the restored **Flagship** Niagara in Erie. The ship, captained by Oliver Hazard Perry during the War of 1812, captured a famous victory on September 10, 1813, when nine American ships triumphed over the British fleet on Lake Erie—the first time in naval history that a British squadron was defeated and captured. The *Niagara* and Perry gave the world the famous line: "We have met the enemy, and they are ours." (See the *Niagara* on special Pennsylvania license tags with a retro sepia image.) The beautifully restored *Niagara* is one of only four remaining ships in the world from that era; the USS *Constitution* and *Constellation* and Britain's HMS *Victory,* all built at the end of the 18th century, are the others. But the *Niagara* is the only one seaworthy enough for regular cruises (usually through the Great Lakes, but every four years, along the Atlantic Coast). During warm-weather months lucky landlubbers are welcome aboard for day cruises—but you must apply in advance for this thrill. Demand far exceeds available space on the summer weekends the *Niagara* boards guests. Schedules change each season. Get details at sailfnl.org. You can also call (814) 452-2744.

When the *Niagara* is berthed dockside at the Erie Maritime Museum, you can take 1-hour tours (make reservations) above and below deck. In the days when its crew numbered 140, quarters on board were extremely tight, what with all those cannon, furled sails, and the manger of live animals. Watch your head below deck—the ceiling is 5 feet tall. By contrast, the tops of the masts tower 12 and 10 stories above deck.

Though the *Niagara* is often off hobnobbing with other tall ships, the Flagship Niagara League also offers sails (daily in summer) from the same location

Three Erie Lighthouses

Presque Isle, residence of park superintendent. Exterior viewing daily 8 a.m. to sunset.

Erie Land Lighthouse, first built in 1818, replaced in 1856; no light since Christmas Eve 1899. Exterior viewing daily.

North Pier, located at the south entrance of the channel. Viewing daily.

on a restored 1893 fishing schooner, the **Lettie G. Howard.** Adults may board the 90-minute cruise for $25 each; children over 33 pounds sail for $15.

The *Erie Maritime Museum,* by the way, is well worth a visit. Inside a former power-generating plant, its creative exhibits give an overview of the War of 1812 and a glimpse of the human side of the conflict and its heroes. Did you know that a quarter of Commodore Perry's men were African Americans? A short video takes you through the battle of September 10, 1813. It's open year-round, but hours vary. Admission is $10 for adults. Call (814) 452-2744, extension 223, or visit sailfnl.org.

For an action-oriented display visit the *Firefighters Historical Museum* (428 Chestnut St.), which is in the old #4 Erie Firehouse. It contains more than 1,300 items of fire department memorabilia, including old uniforms and equipment and an 1830 hand pump. The museum is open June through Aug from noon to 4 p.m. Sat. Admission is $4. Call (814) 456-5969 or visit firefighters historicalmuseum.com for more information.

Kids in Erie love the *ExpERIEnce Children's Museum* (420 French St., 2 blocks from the waterfront), where they can paint their faces, dance on a stage, and learn what owls eat for dinner. Kids age 1 and under enter free, and others pay $8. The museum is open Wed through Sat 10 a.m. to 5 p.m. and Sun 1 to 5 p.m. Call (814) 453-3743 or visit eriechildrensmuseum.org.

That's Dinor to You

Don't ask me why diners in northwestern Pennsylvania are called "dinors." But they are, and one of the funkiest is the **Lawrence Park Dinor** in Erie. *Diners of Pennsylvania,* the definitive study by Brian Butko and Kevin Patrick, calls it a classic—a tiny, trailer-shaped, 1948 Silk City model with room for 2 dozen diners (or dinors). Try the special Greek sauce, a spicy ground-meat gravy that tops everything from burgers to french fries. Located at 4019 Main St., outside the General Electric factory entrance; open Tues through Sun, 8 a.m. to 2 p.m.; (814) 899-4390.

In the same complex, called Discovery Square, are two other museums. The **Erie County History Center** (419 State St.) focuses on county history. Phone the center at (814) 454-1813; fax (814) 452-1744; or check eriehistory.org. The **Erie Art Museum** (411 State St.) has a small permanent collection and changing exhibits of fine art. Phone (814) 459-5477 or visit erieartmuseum.org.

To shop for contemporary American jewelry, studio pottery, carvings, and textiles, stop at the **Glass Growers Gallery** (10 E. Fifth St.; 814-453-3758; glass growersgallery.com). Upstairs are the creations of local and regional artists.

You've been through town, yet you haven't heard a word about the barges filled with lumber, coal, and hay. Where, oh where, is the **Erie Canal,** you wonder. Answer: It *used* to be in New York. It carried barges to the Hudson River, thus linking the Great Lakes and the Atlantic Ocean. The canal opened in 1844 and began to lose business to the railroads as early as the 1850s. The Erie Extension Canal connected to the longer canalway through northwestern Pennsylvania. A small plaque in Hartstown, Crawford County, marks a remaining section.

Elk Creek, the birthplace of the Erie Canal near Presque Isle, flows through the town of Girard, which has a unique place in American history: Dan Rice lived there. Dan *who?* Dan Rice, the circus owner whose carnival spent summers in Girard. Dan Rice, whose flag-waving clown costume included a top hat and balloon pants. Dan Rice, whom Thomas Nast, an artist from *Harper's Weekly,* caricatured—and whose image became known as "Uncle Sam." *That* Dan Rice.

Wine Country

From Erie continue east on Route 5 to visit the local wine region, which stretches about 100 miles along the coast yet extends only 5 miles inland. Wine grapes flourish here because the lake creates a microclimate in which cold spring winds blow in from the lake, keeping the plants from budding too early and becoming vulnerable to frost. In the summer lake breezes cool the vineyards and keep the air circulating; in the fall the stored summer warmth from the lake delays frost. Because the lake once was much larger and has receded, the soils along the shore are especially fertile. Hence, fine wine. (Let's drink to that.)

Hold on, say craft brewers. Don't forget that the Erie region has more than a dozen micro-breweries, too. The Lake Erie Ale Trail maps out all the locations and libations at lakeeriealetrail.com.

In **North East** stop at the **Hornby School Museum** (10000 Colt Station Rd., Route 430), a restored one-room schoolhouse, built in the 1870s. With a reservation you can arrange to experience the kind of lessons that would have been part of a typical school day. The school is open Sun from June through Oct, 1 to 5 p.m. and by appointment. Call (814) 323-4404 for more information or check hornybyschool.org. It's free.

More fun than school, perhaps, **Lake Shore Railway Museum** (31 Wall St.) also has a lot to teach. Two children cried all the way there one morning because they hate museums, but at 4 p.m. attendants had to chase them out of the train cars to close up. The museum displays historical railroad items from the 19th and 20th centuries, ranging from dining car china to signaling devices. Outside the museum, which is in a station house by the tracks, you may tour a caboose and railroad cars on the siding—a Pullman sleeping car, diner, freight car, coach, and baggage car. The wooden caboose looks like one from the olden days, complete with a stove and cooking area. In front of the station is a steamless locomotive, built in Erie in 1937. The schedule of the museum varies with the season and includes some special holiday events, so call (814) 725-1911, or visit lakeshorerailway .com for specific details.

trivia

So many fish are being fed at the Linesville Spillway, on Route 6 west of Meadville, that ducks can walk on the fishes' backs to compete for bread. It's part of the 17,088-acre Pymatuning Reservoir, the largest lake in Pennsylvania.

Mosey a half hour south of North East and you're in the land of biodiversity, home to **French Creek** and a national wildlife refuge. French Creek, named by George Washington for the former residents of this region between Meadville and Franklin, has recently been rediscovered as a stream of astounding diversity. The creek's glacial history and outstanding water quality make it a haven for all kinds of creatures, including peaceable humans.

Petroglyphs on the Allegheny

For more than 300 years people have pondered the engraved graffiti on *Indian God Rock,* 9 miles south of Belmar along the Allegheny River. In 1889 a local newsman proposed that the strange runes were actually made by Norse explorers. More recent experts said that the animals, weapons, and other shapes were definitely made by Native Americans sometime before 1650. To protect the boulder from further vandalism—many 18th- and 19th-century visitors had added their names—the rock was placed on the National Register of Historic Places in 1984. There's a viewing platform near the 22-foot-high stone so you can look but not touch. If you're hiking or biking, take the Sandy Creek Trail.

French Creek and the Allegheny River used to flow north, as part of the St. Lawrence River system. However, the glaciers of the last ice age, which ended about 15,000 years ago, forced the creek to run south. As a result, 117-mile French Creek eventually began emptying into the Allegheny River. Today the creek retains species from the northern waterway as well as the Allegheny. It's home to 80 kinds of fish (an angler's dream), 2 dozen types of mussels, and a giant, very shy, rarely seen salamander—the Eastern hellbender, which some locals call a "mudpuppy." The hellbender can grow up to 29 inches long and live up to 29 years, long enough to savor its status as Pennsylvania's official amphibian.

Canoeing is the perfect way to savor the beauty of the area, and there are plenty of launching spots. If you'd like to rent canoes, kayaks, paddleboards, or bikes for day or overnight trips contact Outdoor Allegheny River Services at 250 Elk St. in Franklin; (814) 388-9122; oarsontheallegheny.com.

As you drive toward the **Erie National Wildlife Refuge**—located in a marsh near Guys Mills, south of the lake—be on the lookout for bald eagles, which find good hunting in the wetlands. This federal site, one of two in the state, offers nearly 9,000 acres for hiking, hunting, fishing, and, of course, bird-watching. A new indoor bird observation area gives you binoculars, bird books, and even microphones to eavesdrop on 237 different species. Enter the refuge 10 miles east of Meadville on Highway 198. The five nature trails are open daily until a half hour before sunset every day, and the visitor center is open weekdays from 8:30 a.m. to 4:30 p.m. at 11296 Wood Duck Ln., Guys Mills 16327; call (814) 789-3585; or visit erie.fws.gov.

Did you know that John Brown slept here? The abolitionist rabble-rouser lived in New Richmond, 13 miles north of Meadville, from 1826 to 1835, long before his Harpers Ferry raid. The farm was a "depot" on the Underground Railroad, helping some 2,500 slaves to freedom. You can't see the tannery where he worked, but you can visit the small **John Brown Farm Museum** near his home (if and only if you call ahead) Apr 15 to Oct 15; in winter, view interpretive displays at the tannery site. The site is located at the intersection of Routes 77 and 1033 at 17620 John Brown Rd. For information call (814) 720-2873.

Oil Country

Sharon is a very small town with some giant-sized attractions: in **Daffin's Chocolate Kingdom,** the world's largest candy store; and in **Quaker Steak & Lube,** the self-proclaimed best hot wings in the USA.

Daffin's (496 E. State St.; 724-342-2892; daffins.com) boasts a chocolate menagerie that includes a 400-pound turtle and a 125-pound reindeer. It's open Mon through Sat from 10 a.m. to 6 p.m., Sun from 11 a.m. to 5 p.m.

Frozen

For fans of extreme recreation, iceboating should be your next adventure. Iceboats are sailboats with sled rails and can glide up to 70 miles per hour across frozen surfaces—like northwest Pennsylvania's largest lakes. Check out this sport in Moraine, Pymatuning, and Presque Isle state parks, but remember that state launch permits are required. Another resource to consider contacting is the *Erie Yacht Club*, which is a great place for beginners. Contact the Erie Yacht Club for more information: erieyacht club.org or (814) 453-4931.

Quaker Steak & Lube is, of course, a play on both the Quaker State and locally made Quaker State Motor Oil, and it carries the automotive theme to fantastic extremes, with real cars as overhead art. People come for the wings, but you can get all sorts of pub-style choices too. Insert your oil joke here. The original location of the regional chain of eateries is open from lunch to at least 9 p.m. 7 days a week at 101 Chestnut Ave.; check thelube.com or call (724) 981-WING.

In the grand Richardson Romanesque style (seen also in downtown Pittsburgh) is the *Buhl Mansion Guesthouse and Spa* at 422 E. State St. Built in 1890 for a wealthy local couple, it's been restored to glory by owners Donna and Jim Winner (he invented the anti-theft device The Club). Visit buhlmansion .com, or call (724) 346-3046.

Lake Erie's not the only swimming spot in northwestern Pennsylvania. Generations of families love *Conneaut Lake,* with its grand old hotel and amusement park. The amusement park has teetered on the edge of bankruptcy but still manages to reopen each season. The park's old-fashioned roller coasters, pony rides, and miniature golf course are classics, and admission to its beach is free. Plan a summer visit by calling (814) 382-5115 or visit new conneautlakepark.com. It's at 12382 Center St. in Conneaut Lake.

Let Meadville lure you off the interstate (off I-79, to be precise). Keep an eye out for a funky monument to the city as you enter along Route 6/322. That's where a bunch of *Allegheny College* students have created a 1,200-foot mural made entirely of recycled highway signs. "Read Between the Signs" is a light-hearted interpretation of local landmarks, including the Allegheny Mountains and French Creek. The state highway department provided the raw materials. The students figured out how to turn them into moving artwork—the mural even includes components powered by sunlight and wind.

Allegheny College, one of the oldest colleges west of the Alleghenies, has a good collection of Abraham Lincoln memorabilia in the Pelletier Library. Ida Tarbell, one of the college's first female students, majored in biology because she hoped to find God with what she could learn through a microscope. After

BEST ANNUAL EVENTS IN NORTHWESTERN PENNSYLVANIA

MAY

Edinboro Art and Music Festival
Edinboro
edinboroartandmusic.com
Each May fans of traditional Appalachian finger-picking, stomping, and crafts flock to the Edinboro Art and Music Festival. The free 3-day event, held the third weekend of the month, happens all over town, with jam sessions, artisan exhibits, and everyone's-welcome workshops in the old-time arts of dulcimer, mandolin, and flat-foot dancing.

JUNE

Thurston Classic
thurstonclassic.com
Meadville's hot-air balloon weekend, with the simultaneous launch of more than 30 balloons, honors the town's long history of aeronauts.

JULY

Presque Isle Triathalon
(814) 838-5138
discoverpi.com
You don't have to paddle to Canada to enjoy Lake Erie. You can bike, run, and swim across Presque Isle each June. Get the details from the Presque Isle Partnership.

AUGUST

Celebrate Erie
Erie
(814) 870-1234
celebrateerie.com
Mid-August brings a 4-day family-friendly street fair to the downtown's Perry Square that concludes with massive fireworks over the lake.

Dan Rice Days
Girard
(814) 774-3535
danricedays.com
A stilt-walking Uncle Sam leads the parade at the annual Dan Rice Days in Girard. Held the first weekend in August, the festival includes games, food, crafts, and such.

SEPTEMBER

Pennsylvania State Championship Fishing Tournament
Tidioute
(814) 484-3585
tidioute.org
During the last full weekend of September in Tidioute (rhymes with "pretty suit"), you can participate in the Pennsylvania State Championship Fishing Tournament on the Allegheny River.

Uncorked
North East
(814) 725-4262
nechamber.org
If you've always wanted to do some grape-stomping, the town of North East will give you the chance each September at its wine festival. You can also sample wines by the glass and try a few champagnes—a local specialty.

OCTOBER

Autumn Leaf Festival
Clarion
(814) 226-9161
clarionpa.com
A Tournament of Leaves parade, an antique tractor pull, and foliage along a wild river? Sign me up.

graduating, she became one of the muckrakers famous at the turn of the 20th century: journalists who tried to expose the abuses of businesses and the corruption of politics. Tarbell wrote an extensive biography of the Lincolns and later donated the papers to her alma mater. The library also has many interesting papers, books, and artifacts related to Tarbell. Two college buildings, Bentley Hall and Ruter Hall, are listed on the National Register of Historic Places.

Meadville's downtown includes more than a dozen historic buildings that should interest those who care about old architecture. You can pick up a free self-guided tour to bygone Meadville at the **Market House** (910 Market St.). On the ground floor a farmers' market flourishes, as it has for more than a hundred years. You can eat at the lunch counter and shop for produce, flowers, baked goods, handicrafts, cheese, ceramics, and collectibles in the marketplace. Market House is open year-round (meadvillemarkethouse.org) except Sun.

A handy 15-minute drive from Meadville's college population is **Sprague Farm and Brew Works** (22043 US Hwy. 6 & 19, Venango). This microbrewery offers a half-dozen varieties. They'll fill up your growler, give you a tour, or put you up for the night. Call (814) 398-2885 or visit spraguefarm.com.

Approximately 30 miles east of Meadville, you can get a glimpse of the early influence of oil, before Texans thought of liquid gold. Start at Titusville with the **Drake Well Park and Museum** (814-827-2797; drakewell.org), site of the world's first successful oil well and an 1860s boomtown. The well is topped by a replica of the derrick. The museum details the early oil days and the continuing impact of fossil fuels. In the library are thousands of photographs and papers of Titusville native Ida Tarbell related to her famous exposé of the Standard Oil Company. Though the museum won't hold their interest, kids may enjoy dipping into "the pits." These are slight depressions in the ground, near the banks of Oil Creek, where Indians scooped oil off the surface of the water—tipping off white settlers to what lay 38 feet below. The oil still seeps to the surface in warm weather. The museum is open Wed through Sun in summer, with reduced hours in the off season, and is closed on major holidays. Admission is $10 per adult.

A short drive southeast on Route 27, then south on Route 227, brings you to Plumer. Go 1.5 miles farther south to the ghost town of **Pithole,** which was an oil boomtown in the late 1860s and was abandoned when the oil business fell off. Now it's part of the Drake Well Park and Museum family, along with McClintock's well. In Pithole, the visitor center contains a pictorial history and artifacts of the town. Only a few ghost streets remain. McClintock's Well was drilled the hard way: Using leg power, the owners "kicked down" the well until it struck oil at a depth of 620 feet—and still produces a few drops each day. Open June through Labor Day. Get details from Drake Well Museum.

Another way to see oil country and its history is to ride the ***Oil Creek and Titusville Railroad,*** sponsored by the Oil Creek Railway Historical Society. The 2-hour trip runs from Titusville to Rynd Farm, 4 miles north of Oil City, passing through the sites of several boomtowns and some lovely countryside in warm weather months. You can board a train at the Drake Well Museum, at the Perry Street Station in Titusville, or at Rynd Farm. The schedule of north-bound and southbound trains is complicated, may change without notice, and includes additional trains scheduled for special celebration weeks in the sum-mer; moreover, you need advance tickets to guarantee a place on the train. If that doesn't deter you, call (814) 676-1733, or visit octrr.org. Tickets are $30 per adult, or $50 for a family of four.

If you'd like to make part of the same trip on bicycle, try the 10-mile paved trail alongside Oil Creek from Petroleum Center to Drake Well Park. The trail is open from 8 a.m. to dark. Whichever route you choose, you're still invited to spend the night on the tracks at ***The Caboose Motel.*** The 21 rooms—er, cars—have all the modern conveniences—heating, AC, phones, and TVs. Book reservations at (800) 827-0690 or get details at octrr.org.

Enjoy a more amusing kind of history at the ***DeBence Antique Music World Museum*** (1261 Liberty St.), not far away on Route 8, Franklin. The museum has more than a hundred antique music machines from the Gay Nine-ties and the Roaring Twenties. Hear the nickelodeons, band organs, orches-trions, and music boxes. The museum is open Apr 1 through Oct 31, Tues through Sat 11 a.m. to 4 p.m. and Sun 12:30 to 4 p.m.; Nov 1 through Mar 31, it's open by appointment only. Call (814) 432-8350 or visit debencemusicworld .com for details. Admission is $8 per adult. Sounds great!

The town of Franklin dates to 1753, when the French established Fort Machault here. Seven years later the British built Fort Venango. But, as with so much of this part of Pennsylvania, striking oil was what really gave life to the community. If you're on Twelfth and Elk Streets on Sat, you can browse through the local farmers' market and peek at the grand courthouse. Wander around town or request a self-guided walking tour at the Franklin Area Cham-ber of Commerce (1327 Liberty St.). For further information phone (814) 432-5823 or go to franklinareachamber.org.

Rolling Along the River

One not-to-be-missed country road is Route 62, which hugs the bank of the Alleghe-ny River between Warren to the north and Tionesta and Franklin to the south. Those three towns, plus the vacation cabins scattered along the shoreline, are just about the only signs of human habitation you'll see as you drive through the forest, passing magnificent vistas as the river widens and contracts.

Festive Fireflies

In 2011, a group of campers near Tionesta saw fireflies flashing in perfect unison around their campsite. Researchers confirmed that the rare Photinus carolinus, or synchronous firefly, and 14 other firefly species light up the skies hereabouts, from the summer solstice to mid-July each year. The PA Firefly Festival celebrates the rare phenomenon annually on the last weekend in June—but also promotes conservation and science to protect the critters year-round. If that sparks your curiosity, visit pafireflyevents.com.

Allegheny National Forest

The 500,000-acre *Allegheny National Forest* is one of 15 national forests in the eastern United States and the only national forest in Pennsylvania. Hardwoods—black cherry, yellow poplar, white ash, red maple, and sugar maple—make up most of the timber. More than 65 million board feet of timber, especially black cherry, are harvested each year. The black cherry is used for fine furniture; much of the rest is used for pulpwood. *Hearts Content,* one comparatively small area of the forestland, has some of the oldest tracts of virgin beech and hemlock trees in the eastern United States.

You can access the forest from many points along Route 6 and Route 62 for some truly off-the-beaten-path travel. Just past East Hickory, at Endeavor, turn right on Route 666, heading into the forest.

From here, turn around and drive back about a quarter mile, where you see a dirt Forest Service road just before Mayburg. Turn left here, on Robbs Creek Road, also known as Forest Road 116. Drive on to Hearts Road (though the signs often disappear) and turn left again. In about 2 miles you'll come to *Hearts Content Recreation Area* in the Allegheny National Forest. From Hearts Content you can hike, camp, and picnic—you know, to your heart's content. Whatever you do, you must take the scenic walk marked by signs. It is short and easy, and it seems to invite meditation. Creeks make light music. The old deciduous trees arch high above, letting through just enough blue sky and sunlight to nurture the carpet of ferns, which reach your knees. Pines and hemlocks, nature's original incense, perfume the air. The forest floor, softened with pine needles and leaves, absorbs enough sound to make the surroundings seem as quiet as a cathedral. A 6-year-old child walking through the area for the first time captured its mystery by asking, "Are we inside or outside?"

The *Hickory Creek Wilderness,* all 8,570 acres of it, is next to the campground. No motorized equipment is allowed. An 11-mile hiking loop takes you through rolling terrain. You will probably see deer, small wildlife, and all kinds of birds.

You can find a smaller—much smaller—peaceful, tranquil natural area in *Clear Creek State Park* by heading north from Sigel on Route 36, then north on Route 949. Call (814) 752-2368 to reach the park office. Scenically located in Jefferson County's Clear Creek Valley, the park encompasses 1,200 acres, with another 10,000 acres of natural resources in adjacent Kittanning State Forest. A highlight of the park is the outstanding self-guided Ox Shoe Trail, which depicts logging practices of earlier years. The area is noted for its abundant wildlife, its hunting and fishing, and the breathtaking beauty of its mountain laurel, which blooms from mid-June to early July, peaking in late June. See if you—or your kids—can identify some mountain laurel, the state flower. The plant grows from 3 to 6 feet high on rocky, wooded slopes. Look for petals that form a nearly perfect pink or white pentagon.

You're quite near *Cook Forest State Park.* One of the finest stands of virgin timber in the eastern part of the United States is located here, and the area has been designated a National Natural Landmark. The trees in this ancient forest are hundreds of years old, measuring up to 5 feet in diameter and towering nearly 200 feet. During a recent old-growth forest conference, three of the tallest trees in the East were identified here in Cook Forest. The old Cook sawmill, home to the Sawmill Center for the Arts, features summer theater, festivals, and craft markets and draws artisans to instruct classes in traditional arts and crafts; check sawmill.org. Much of the area exists almost as it was in the days of William Penn, when it was known as the Black Forest. Cecil B. DeMille used the park in his 1947 film *Unconquered,* starring Gary Cooper and Paulette Goddard.

waterydepths

The icy fresh waters of the Great Lakes preserve a number of shipwrecks, from 19th-century schooners to steamers and scows. Professional divers Georgann and Mike Wachter have mapped the sites where a number of these historic vessels have been found. See the results at eriewrecks.com.

Silver Stallion Stables, just north of the Cooksburg Bridge, offers 1- and 2-hour trail jaunts through old-growth forests daily in the summer for riders as young as 6 years old (summer forest temperatures hover from the mid-60s to mid-70s). No matter how dumb you might feel in the saddle, the stables' owners, Mark and Lori Mills, say, don't worry, the horses are smart. "We're particular to Appaloosa and paint, for their intelligence, their stamina, and their beauty," he notes. Riders with disabilities or other special needs are welcome. Check ride prices at Silver Stallion by calling (814) 927-6636 and look online for additional information at silverstallionstable.com.

Cook Forest Scenic Rides and Dude Ranch, off Clarion-Miola Road, offers "dude packages" with lodging, meals, and private and group rides (patrailride.com). Call (814) 856-2081 for details.

In these parts you may hear a clarion call to slow down and smell the roses—or look at leaves. *Clarion,* calling itself the autumn-leaf capital of the known world, boasts the rugged beauty of untamed natural resources and the nostalgia of an old-fashioned Main Street. It is unmistakably off the beaten path. Stop in the Free Library, on Main Street next to the post office, in downtown Clarion to pick up a booklet outlining a historical and architectural tour of the town, noting 40 structures of interest. Enjoy the old-fashioned streetlights and nostalgic building facades as you stroll downtown. A parasol would be nice.

Places to Stay in Northwestern Pennsylvania

CLARK

Tara
2844 Lake Rd.
Clark
(724) 962-3535
tara-inn.com
Dedicated to "the greatest movie of all time, *Gone With the Wind,*" with rooms called "Rhett's Room" and "Belle's Boudoir." Tours by costumed guides, dining rooms, a spa, and a lake.

CONNEAUT

Hotel Conneaut
12241 Lake St.
(814) 573-7747
thehotelconneaut.com
This refurbished 140-year-old wooden dowager commands the waterfront in Conneaut Lake Park.

COOKSBURG

Gateway Lodge
Cook Forest, Box 125
Route 36
(814) 744-8017
gatewaylodge.com
Rough-hewn log inn with a welcoming stone hearth, modern suites, and a spa. Dinner and music, too.

VENANGO

Sleeping Leaf Lodge
2212 US Hwy. 6 & 19
spraguefarm.com
(814) 398-2885
Cozy farmhouse offered by Sprague Farm & Brew Works next door.

Places to Eat in Northwestern Pennsylvania

ERIE

Smuggler's Wharf
3 State St.
(814) 459-4273
smugglerswharfinc.com

Arrive at this casual Lake Erie eatery by land or sea.

MEADVILLE

Meadville Market House Grille
910 Market St.
(814) 807-0820
Open daily except Sun in the historic Market House; till 7:30 p.m. Wed–Fri.

SHARON

Quaker Steak & Lube
101 Chestnut St.
(724) 981-7221 or
(800) 468-9464
quakersteakandlube.com/sharon_pa
Located in a former gas station. Your dining companions are a 1936 Chevrolet on a grease rack and a Corvette suspended from the ceiling. Hot wings and cool cars.

North Central Pennsylvania

Getting Your Kicks on Route 6

One of the best ways to see what Pennsylvanians call the "northern tier" is by jumping on **Route 6** and following it east through Warren, McKean, Potter, and Tioga Counties. This pleasant, rolling two-laner stretches all the way to Pike County, home of the **Delaware Water Gap.** Running through the Brokenstraw Valley, with mountains on either side, the road is an easy (and in some cases, the only) way to get through this neck of the woods, connecting most of the county seats. Motorcyclists nearly weep when describing their rides here. It's also one of the state's designated bike routes.

With such dense forests, it's no surprise that fall is a popular time to visit the area. But the upper Allegheny River offers plenty of summer fun, too, and on a crystal-clear winter morning, the vistas from a snowmobile are glorious. And you're welcome anytime.

National Geographic called Route 6 "one of America's most scenic drives." (But don't neglect Route 126, the Bucktail Byway, that offers Route 6 some competition.) Get ideas at paroute6.com.

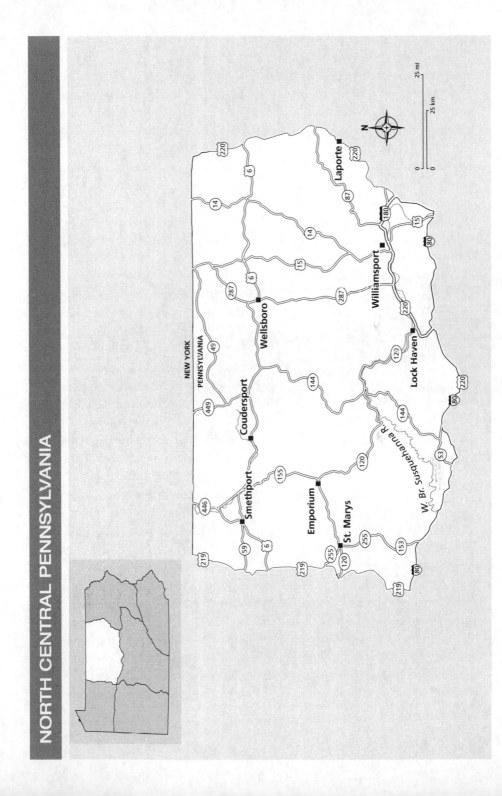

NORTH CENTRAL PENNSYLVANIA

Wild Country

Start your wild-country trek with a fiery sightseeing experience—by visiting the *Zippo/Case Visitors Center* (1932 Zippo Dr.) in *Bradford,* off Route 219 just below the New York border. Zippo is the company that first made windproof lighters. (Legend has it that zippers had recently been invented, and the inventor liked the name, so he copied it.) Your visit includes the museum, which opened in 1994, the repair clinic, and the gift shop (though not the factory). Since Zippos include a lifetime guarantee, and since the repair shop receives about 400 lighters daily, there's always something to watch. The center is open Mon through Fri 9 a.m. to 5 p.m. and Sun from 11 a.m. to 4 p.m. Look for streetlights shaped like giant lighters. Call (814) 368-1932 or (888) 442-1932, or flick zippo.com.

Nearby the Lodge at *Glendorn* is the opposite of utilitarian. It's a plush inn and 4-star restaurant that's the grandest hostelry around, with room rates starting around $550 a night. For that price, you get elegance to the max. The Relais and Châteaux–approved property, nestled in the mountains outside of Bradford, offers skeet, tennis, fishing, and other outdoor activities year-round. Choose the Big House or the cabins; they're equally luxurious. Owner Holbrook Lawson is a member of the Dorn clan, which built this retreat in the 1920s. It's at 1000 Glendorn Dr. in Bradford. Call (800) 843-8568, or reserve rooms or meals online at glendorn.com.

trivia

In Austin, just south of Route 6 on Route 872, a dam broke in 1911, leveling two towns and killing 89 people. The site is listed on the National Register of Historic Places. The town puts on the Austin Dam Show each summer.

For a completely different dining experience, you might drive through the Bradford McDonald's on Main Street. There may have been billions of burgers served at the chain worldwide, but this is the only location that serves them with a side of real oil. Cline Oil #1 in the parking lot pumps dozens of gallons of Pennsylvania Crude each day, just as it has since the 1870s. You'll see other private wells dotting front yards throughout the region.

Pop up to *Singer's Country Store* (814-368-6151) at the crossroads that is Custer City, just off the intersection of Routes 219 and 770 West. For less than a buck you can pluck a fresh pickle out of the briny barrel and browse two stores with everything from wood-crafted furniture to retro candies. See singerscountrystore.com.

Between Bradford and Smethport, make a vertigo-inducing stop at Kinzua Bridge State Park. The wooden railroad bridge built here in 1883—a trestle that

AUTHOR'S TOP 10 FAVORITES IN
NORTH CENTRAL PENNSYLVANIA

Cherry Springs State Park	Little League Baseball World Series
Elk	Route 6
elk burgers	Squatchfest
Frenchville	Wellsboro
Grand Canyon of Pennsylvania	Woolrich Company Store

stood higher than the Brooklyn Bridge—was once called the eighth wonder of the world. The view over a 2,000-foot gorge is still spectacular, but the bridge was felled by a tornado in 2003. Now a pedestrian walkway, similar to that on the rim of the Grand Canyon, includes a glassed-in floor that allows visitors to admire the view. There's a 1-mile hiking loop through the forest. The Skywalk is free and open daily. Enter the park 4 miles from Route 6; it's 1721 Lindholm Dr., Mount Jewett. Details at anf.com/kinzua-state-park-sky-walk.

Ride on to **Smethport,** a picture-perfect country town and county seat. Main Street boasts a solid core of restored Victorian homes and pleasant sidewalks for strolling. The McKean County Courthouse exudes stability, right down to the Civil War statue out front: He's a Bucktail, the local regiment of volunteers who formed the core of the Union Army's Forty-second Pennsylvania Regiment. The fact that every soldier decorated his cap with a deer's tail gives you a hint about the local wildlife—and the sharpshooting skills that made the regiment's reputation.

Main Street is home to a mini-millionaires' row of superb mansions. It's also the address of the Smethport Diner, also known as the Route 6 Diner, and the Hub, a gas/convenience store that refers to the Hubbers, the local high school nickname.

With over a century and a half of history, Smethport is home to the **McKean County Historical Museum** (814-887-5142) in the 1872 jail, open a few afternoons each week right behind the courthouse. Residents have also created the wonderful Planet Smethport website (smethporthistory.org). You can tour local landmarks by clicking up and down streets and learn (lots) about former residents. It's almost like peeking through their windows.

Head east on Route 6, through Coudersport. Across from Denton Hill State Park at Galeton, you reach the **Pennsylvania Lumber Museum,** an outdoor gallery that depicts the history and technology of Pennsylvania's prosperous

Running in God's Country

The God's Country Marathon in Potter County has been named one of the "10 toughest marathons" and one of the "best small marathons" in the US by *Runner's World* magazine. Sometimes it doesn't feel like you are in a race because you're surrounded by the stunning scenery.

Held in early June, the point-to-point course runs west on scenic US Route 6 from the small community of Galeton (elevation 1,300 ft.) through the heart of the Susquehannock State Forest, to the town of Coudersport (elevation 1,400 ft.).

Mile 14 marks the beginning of a 3-mile climb up the fiendish Denton Hill, which traverses the eastern continental divide topping out at an elevation of 2,424 ft. Then it's all downhill to the finish line. Get dates and register online at visitpottercounty.org.

lumbering activities. Two of the world's largest sawmills were located in Austin (24 miles southwest of the museum) and Galeton (11 miles southeast). The museum displays more than 3,000 artifacts related to the logging industry. Walk among the old buildings of the logging camp, the sawmill, and a logging pond, all surrounded by Appalachian Mountain wilderness. The visit re-creates the tough life of "wood hicks" in the days of lumbering. The men worked six days a week, from 5 a.m. to 9 p.m. (no, that's not a typo!), with time off for extended periods of downpour, though rarely for cold or snow. In about 1910 the workweek was reduced to six 10-hour days, and in 1920 to five 8-hour days. Lice and dirt were everywhere. Bathing facilities were nowhere.

sunrisetosunset

Every sunny day you can catch a perfect sunrise from Colton Point State Park. Enjoy the sunset from Leonard Harrison State Park. Both times, you luxuriate in a view of the Grand Canyon of Pennsylvania.

Even though the workers' conditions weren't pristine, the forests and trees were, and the giant white pines were in great demand. Wood hicks felled the trees, tied them onto rafts, and floated them down the Susquehanna River and into the Chesapeake Bay, where they were exported to England to be made into ships. The Lumber Museum, administered by the Pennsylvania Historical and Museum Commission, is open 9 a.m. to 5 p.m. daily, Wed through Sun, plus some holidays. Admission is $8 per adult. Phone (814) 435-2652. Find it at 5660 Rte. 6, Galeton 16922; or visit lumbermuseum.org for more information.

The most dramatic aspect of this section of the state is the mountainous and wooded **Pine Creek Gorge,** commonly known as the **Grand Canyon of Pennsylvania.** The gorge, comprising mostly state parks and wilderness, is 50 miles long and 1,000 feet deep, covering 300,000 acres of state forest. You can access the canyon by driving south on Route 660, midway between Galeton and Wellsboro.

Before the pharaohs built the pyramids, the headwaters of Pine Creek, near Ansonia, flowed to the northeast. Then came glaciers. As the glacial ice melted, it left a dam of gravel, sand, and clay, which blocked the creek's path. It forced Pine Creek to reverse direction and flow south. Thus formed the Grand Canyon, with land formations dating back more than 350 million years. In 1968 the National Park Service declared a 12-mile section a National Natural Landmark.

At two state parks—***Leonard Harrison State Park*** on the east rim of the canyon and ***Colton Point State Park*** on the west (570-724-3061 reaches both park offices)—you can stop at lookouts and pick up short hiking trails that don't require safari gear. Leonard Harrison State Park has a nature center (open spring through fall) and a relatively easy trail along the rim that gives you an orientation to the canyon. If you follow Turkey Path about a mile down to Pine Creek, you'll encounter more ambitious hikes that take in creeks and waterfalls. The area is noted for ferns, songbirds, and superb scenery in any season. In Colton Point State Park, you can hike an easy mile-long loop through a hardwood forest rich in wildflowers and fragrant mountain laurel, the state flower.

trivia

Guidebooks say the name Tioga comes from an old Native American word, but they disagree on what that word meant. Some say it meant "the meeting of two rivers," and others say it meant "gateway" or "place to enter." Either way, Tioga County is a hunter's paradise, serving as home to many species of white-tailed deer, bear, cottontail rabbits, wild turkey, ruffed grouse, and ducks.

What Can You See in the Dark?

Rural **Cherry Springs State Park**, off Route 44 south of Galeton, is one of the darkest spots in the country, making it a perfect spot for stargazing. It's Pennsylvania's first Dark Sky Park, and its hilltop Astronomy Field has a spectacular panoramic view of the nucleus of the Milky Way. Park at the nearby airport and walk to the field (if you've brought your own telescope or laptop, the field has power sources and concrete pads for setup). You can even rent one of four small (3- to 4-person) observatories for $10 per night. Public "star parties" are held several times a year, and there's entertainment at the family-friendly "Music and Stars" shows. A "clear sky clock" on the park's website, dcnr.state.pa.us/stateparks/parks/cherrysprings.aspx, forecasts the best times to visit. There's a modest entrance fee. Call (814) 435-1037.

The Tower That Traveled

The **Lookout Tower** in Leonard Harrison State Park affords views for 100 miles with the naked eye. I remember climbing it where it originally stood, atop Mount Joy, in Valley Forge, where George Washington and his troops spent the winter of 1776 and 1777. The tower was a birders' haven from 1908 to 1988, when surrounding trees grew too tall for its use as an observation tower. At that time, it traveled 240 miles to its current home. Visit the tower daily, sunrise to sunset, weather permitting. Climb 125 steps to reach the top.

One of the state's most spectacular rails-to-trails projects is the **Pine Creek Trail,** which runs 61 miles from Wellsboro Junction to Jersey Shore. This level crushed-limestone path, closed to motor traffic, lets you explore by bike, horse, or foot. If you're a hardbody, you might want to bike in with a tent and backpack and camp overnight at Harrison State Park; if not, there are 10 trailheads where you can exit the trail, and there are motels and inns at both ends where you can actually sleep in a bed. Hot water, too. For a map or information, contact the Tioga County Visitors Bureau at (888) 846-4228, visittiogapa .com. **Wellsboro,** the Tioga County seat, is a beautiful little town, with old trees and gaslights lining the streets. In the public square, called the Green, a fountain splashes over a statue of Wynken, Blynken, and Nod in their wooden shoe. When Wellsboro was incorporated in 1830, it had 250 residents. In the 1990 census, it had grown to 3,400, with another 5,000 within a 5-mile radius and 5,000 more within 10 miles. Don't miss the fabulous lobby décor of the Penn Wells Hotel, an 1869 gem, where Groucho Marx and other celebrities vacationed.

lincolndoor house

So what if Abe Lincoln didn't sleep in Wellsboro? That's no reason not to claim his presence. Or presents. At 140 Main St. is the Lincoln Door House. Abraham Lincoln gave the door—now bright red—to Dr. and Mrs. J. H. Shearer when they bought the house in 1858. Mrs. Shearer and Mrs. Lincoln were friends in Springfield, Illinois.

Lots of cars in town sport bike racks, a clue to the popularity of the nearby trail, and CS Sports, a popular outfitter (81 Main St.; 570-724-3858), rents bikes right in town.

One person who fell in love with Wellsboro's slow pace is Nelle Rounsaville-Prevost, who moved here after 20 years as a flight attendant. "It's just a wonderful Victorian town," she says fondly. She owns the **Wellsboro Diner,** a classic 1939 eatery. Aside from being entirely made of porcelain, the Wellsboro Diner has another claim to fame: It was the subject of a "Zippy the Pinhead" cartoon by Bill Griffith. It serves breakfast all day, has daily specials, and is open daily until 8 p.m. at 19 Main St. Call (570) 724-3992.

Get more from the Wellsboro Chamber of Commerce, 114 Main St., Wellsboro 16901. Phone (570) 724-1926 or go to wellsboropa.com.

The End of the World

Another near-wilderness park is **World's End State Park,** as remote as it sounds. To get there take Route 220 to Eagles Mere, which is about midpoint between Route 6 and I-80 in Sullivan County, then go west on Route 154. Part of the lure of World's End is its primitive quality and its ideal position for picnicking, fishing, swimming, and boating. The park phone number is (570) 924-3287.

The town of **Eagles Mere** is the cosmopolitan village you turn to after exploring World's End. Eagles Mere, which used to call itself "the town that time forgot," is so earnest and simple that it might have inspired Norman Rockwell. In the 1800s wealthy folk from Philadelphia's Main Line visited the 2,100-foot-high mountain area, fell in love with the clean air and clear water, and set about causing development to happen. They built Victorian "cottages," similar to the gargantuan dwellings of Newport, Rhode Island. In 1892, with 90 rental cottages, the town had a summer population of 2,500. Since the roads were not paved, boardwalks covered the streets to protect the ladies' white dresses from dirt.

> trivia
>
> Pennsylvania leads the nation in producing mushrooms and potato chips.

While the geology is a nature photographer's utopia, one human-made element also stands out. It's the **Slide,** a toboggan run built in 1904. When the first intrepid rider, sitting on a big iron shovel, tested the grooved, planed, wooden course, he whizzed so fast that he burned the seat off his pants. Today the slide is a 120-ton, 1,200-foot-long channel of ice, down which you can ride in relative safety at 45 miles per hour. An hour-long pass for five riders costs $25. Get the schedule from the Eagles Mere Slide Association at (570) 525-3244 or online at eaglesmeretobogganslide.com.

To relax after this thrilling plummet, treat yourself to dinner at the **Eagles Mere Inn,** the last remaining full-service inn from the 19th century. Its cozy guest rooms make you yearn for the days before cell phones. In the dining room, innkeeper Toby Diltz's menu changes daily. If you prefer vegetarian

trivia

Bald eagles were once so rare that they were considered an endangered species. In 1980 Pennsylvania counted only three. Thanks to the national ban on DDT (in 1972) and the state Game Commission's introduction of eagles from Saskatchewan, Canada, by spring 1998 eagles were spotted in 27 nests. Eagle populations grow slowly, because pairs rear only one to three young each year, and it takes five years for the young to mature.

or other special diets, call ahead to (570) 525-3273 or (800) 426-3273, or visit eaglesmereinn.com, and they'll try to honor your request. Find the inn at 1 Mary Ave., Eagles Mere.

Like hot dogs? Like peanuts and Cracker Jacks? Every August, **Williamsport** hosts the Little League World Series, attracting thousands of spectators and some of the best 12-year-old baseball players in the world. (Bonus: Tickets are free.) The thwack (or, perhaps, the ping) of the bat and the shouts of the kids remind you why the sport is the national pastime. The Peter J. McGovern **Little League Museum** (570-326-3607; little league.org) honors Tom Selleck, Dan Quayle, George Will, Bill Bradley, Kareem Abdul-Jabbar, Nolan Ryan, and Mike Schmidt, to name a few. Admission costs $5 per adult. It's open 9 a.m. to 5 p.m. daily except holidays. It's located at 525 Montgomery Pike (US Rte. 15), Williamsport.

Little Lock Haven is home to a 5,000-student state university; a recently restored movie theater, the Roxy; and levee-topping riverwalk with pretty views of the Susquehanna and a music amphitheater. It's also home to the **Piper Aviation Museum** (1 Piper Way; 570-748-8283; pipermuseum.com), on the site where the dauntless Piper Cub airplane was manufactured until 1984.

Just north of Route 220, between Lock Haven and Williamsport, is the town of Woolrich. If the name sounds familiar, look inside the neckband of your

trivia

In 1892 the first lighted nighttime football game was played at Mansfield University, Mansfield.

hunting jacket. The company of **Woolrich,** in the town of Woolrich, makes sportswear and outerwear under both its own brand and that of other companies, including L. L. Bean and Lands' End. John Rich built his first woolen mill on Plum Run in 1830, and the rest, as they say, is red buffalo plaid. The actors in *The Horse Whisperer* wore Woolrich garb. Visit the original factory outlet store in Woolrich (570-769-7401; woolrich.com) from 10 a.m. to 5 p.m. Mon through Sat, and noon to 5 p.m. Sun.

In **Laporte,** the bustling little historical society can help you find local relatives. "Genealogy is very important in small towns," explains museum curator

Melanie Norton. "Here we have 6,000 people, if everyone and their dog stays home. There are so many shared family names and so many shirt-tail relations." The museum can help you sift through 150 years of records on births, deaths, marriages, and other details. The complex includes the main brick structure, the Baldwin House (with authentic details like garden plants, outhouse, and playhouse intact), and two barns. The museum can also point you to Celestia, a mountaintop settlement 1.5 miles out of town. That's where a fervent 1850s Christian named Peter Armstrong and his followers planned a town, with a lot reserved for God himself. The museum shows his original street grid and offers a brochure for a self-guided tour. The **Sullivan County Historical Society Museum** is open mid-June through Labor Day, Tues through Thurs from 1 to 5 p.m. But whenever you see the "open" sign in the window on Meylert Street next to the county courthouse, says Melanie, just come on by. Admission is free. Call (570) 946-5020.

One treasure in this neck of the northern woods is the 23,000-acre **Bucktail State Park,** which extends southeast—and downstream—from Emporium to Lock Haven. Route 120, a good road between the mountains, essentially parallels the park, as does the Susquehanna River for half the distance. This pleasant, scenic drive takes you through state forests, parks, and wilderness areas. If you're in the mood for a more active experience, hike a trail or choose a private clearing for a view and a picnic. Almost always, you can count on being alone.

West of Emporium is **St. Marys,** a town with a frothy claim to fame— **Straub Brewery** (303 Sorg St.). Straub's is one of the smallest independent

Elk Lore

- May is the most popular month for elk to have babies.

- Female elk, or cows, usually hang out with the other ladies, disappearing for privacy a few days before childbirth. Mommy and baby remain solitary for about three weeks.

- In late summer the bull elk's antlers are usually white and ivory; they darken later as the animal rubs against shrubs and trees covered with juices and sap.

- Elk antlers, which can grow a half-inch a day, are among the fastest-growing animal tissues.

- Elk, like many humans, dislike thunderstorms.

- During the rutting season, males mate with as many cows as possible, show off to shoo other males, and feed and rest very little. They may lose a hundred pounds in a month. That's serious rutting.

breweries left in the United States. "Of course, that depends on how you define 'small,'" says owner Terry Straub. "A microbrewery makes fewer than 15,000 barrels per year and sells it only on the premises. We average over 36,000 barrels a year, and we distribute it in Pennsylvania and Ohio. So it's okay to call us '*one* of the smallest.'" Bottoms up. Straub produces beer made of water, malt, grains, and hops; no sugar, syrup, or additives. The *Connoisseur's Guide to Beer* dubbed Straub's one of the five best-tasting beers in the country. The company distributes only within a 150-mile radius, which means that to taste the beer, you must either visit the area or convince a friend to send you a six-pack. St. Marys is where Routes 255 and 120 intersect. Hours are

trivia

Pennsylvania has the nation's fourth-largest highway system—more than 44,000 miles of highways under state control. And the Keystone State has the eighth-highest count of highway miles—nearly 119,000 miles. Bottom line: Hit the road.

Mon through Fri 9 a.m. to 4:30 p.m. (Sat hours vary) for free tours (for those 12 and over) and free tastings from Straub's "eternal tap." Be a good guest—wash out your own glass at the sink. To be sure you catch the brewery in operation, call (814) 834-2875 and hope to be placed on hold: The recording plays the sound of a tinkling brook, a subtle reminder of the all-fresh ingredients. Visit the website at straubbeer.com.

If you want to see some strikingly singular celebrities, head to Route 555, and keep your eyes peeled for elk. The 700-head herd of wild, free-roaming elk is one of the largest in the East. The St. Marys airport and the village of Benezette are prime viewing spots.

Elk are huge in Pennsylvania these days. Actually, they're always huge—bulls weigh nearly a ton, with antlers up to 5 feet long. But this state is big on

Best Baked Goods?

If you live in Montgomery, Alabama; Madras, Oregon; or anywhere in between, Pennsylvania has an effect on your cookies. The packages of saltines, chocolate-chip cookies, and buttered biscuits that you buy near home may be marked REG. PENNA. DEPT. AGRICULTURE even if they were made in Madrid, Spain, or Minneapolis, Minnesota. Why? Because the Pennsylvania Department of Agriculture has the strictest standards in the country for packaged baked goods. The department inspects all Pennsylvania bakeries and requires copies of inspection reports for out-of-state and out-of-country bakeries that want to sell to Pennsylvanians. REG. PENNA. DEPT. AGRICULTURE indicates to oatmeal-cookie lovers everywhere that the package comes from a sanitary, safe facility.

the prospect of big game, and the herd roaming Elk County provides a target of opportunity for both tourists who stay at a safe distance and hunters who dream of getting close enough for a shot. Elk don't outnumber people here—yet. But their population boom over the past 20 years has brought a steady increase in fall visitors. (In summer, elk, like humans, hang out in the shade.)

Above the tiny village of Benezette (population 237), the state-built viewing area at **Winslow Hill** overlooks meadows and magnificent hillsides. When fall colors explode through the Allegheny Mountains, the elk graze, gallop, and occasionally clash during the annual rut. The unearthly mating call of the bull elk is called a bugle. It sounds like a cross between a hyena's cry and a rusty hinge, and it is eerie and absolutely unmistakable. Making their most predictable appearances at dawn and dusk, the elk are the subject of a video at the Winslow Hill amphitheater that boasts of the state's success in reintroducing the animals.

Elk were hunted here until 1931, when they became protected by law. By the mid-1970s, their numbers had dwindled to only 38.

In the intervening years, north-central Pennsylvania dug deep into its hills for coal and lumber ("House Coal: Hard or Soft" signs still line the main road). But when those economic engines sputtered, a new one emerged. It turned out to be the elk. Coal strip mines, replanted with tasty grasses, provided a habitat that allowed elk to thrive. Ditto clearcut forest, streams, and farms, all of which dot the local hills. The state lent encouragement

trivia

Pennsylvania was the first state to issue "vanity," or personalized, license plates—in 1931.

by sowing food plots and cleaning polluted creeks. The resulting rebound gave Elk County its signature attraction.

It may seem a contradiction that the state now allows fall hunts to thin the herd, but hunters are thrilled at the prospect. (The viewing area around Winslow Hill is, of course, a no-hunting zone.) In 2014, more than 26,000 hunters entered the lottery for 108 elk tags, or licenses.

Frenchville used to be a place where you could go to *parler français,* but no longer. Mary Kay Royer, a seventh-generation Frenchviller, tells the story. Early in the 1800s a Philadelphia lawyer acquired a tract of land in upstate Pennsylvania. He advertised it in French newspapers at the bargain rate of 12 acres free with each 50 paid. And he found buyers. "You'll notice," says Royer, "that everyone came from within about 20 miles of one another, from Normandy and Picardy in France." Many were aristocrats fleeing the French Revolution: In the early 19th century, many settled in northern Pennsylvania and New York State. Men pioneered, she says, apparently walking overland

BEST ANNUAL EVENTS IN NORTH CENTRAL PENNSYLVANIA

FEBRUARY AND MARCH

Ridgway Rendezvous
Ridgway
(814) 772-0400
chainsawrendezvous.org
In late winter Ridgway hosts the Ridgway Rendezvous, where you can view chainsaw creations of ice and wood sculptures. Many of the results are auctioned off; all proceeds go to charity.

Winter JazzFest
Wellsboro
(570) 787-7800
endlessmountains.org
The final weekend of February brings jazz artists to the Penn Wells Hotel for performances and open jam sessions.

MAY

Upper Pine Creek Trout Tournament
(570) 724-1926
pagrandcanyonsnowmobileclub.com
Everyone's welcome at this weekend fishing event, which offers cash prizes.

JUNE

Pennsylvania State Laurel Festival
Wellsboro
(570) 724-1926
The third Saturday in June, Wellsboro holds the Pennsylvania State Laurel Festival.

JULY

Endless Mountains Music Festival
(570) 787-7800
endlessmountains.org
This 2-week festival of classical and popular music takes places at open-air pavilions and theaters from Wellsboro to Elmira, New York.

Squatchfest
Kane
(814) 837-9760
The Kane Family Drive-In Theater is the venue for this light-hearted July celebration of The Big Guy with food, music, and Bigfoot-calling competitions.

from the ports of Baltimore and New York. When they signed their purchase agreements, they didn't understand that they were buying isolated land inaccessible by normal transport. Clearfield, which was just developing, was the closest town, and Bellefonte was next closest—yet neither of those was (or is) a thriving metropolis. Eventually the men sent home for their wives and children.

Even the inscriptions on tombstones are in French, though misspelled and grammatically incorrect. As new inventions came along—automobile, radio, television—the villagers incorporated English words into their speech. People in Frenchville who are still fluent in French speak a classically pure French, without an American accent and *sans* the slang of contemporary French streets. But few French-speakers remain. Royer's father spoke French at home as a child but was prohibited from speaking it once he got to school, as were others of his generation. He's lost the French he once knew. Royer's parents grew up in French-

AUGUST

Little League Baseball World Series
Williamsport
(570) 326-3607
llbws.org
Watch the Little League Baseball World Series in Williamsport during the last full week of August that does not include the Saturday before Labor Day. You'll see the eight top US teams (from the East, Central, West, and South regions) compete against the eight best international teams (from Canada, Latin America, the Far East, and Europe). The stadium is built into a hillside, so the other 30,000 or 40,000 spectators without tickets spend the day picnicking on the hill and watching from afar. For free tickets write in January to the Little League Museum, PO Box 3485, Williamsport 17701. (No, you can't do it online, though the website answers some FAQs.) Mark the envelope "World Series Tickets."

SEPTEMBER

1890s Weekend
Mansfield
(570) 662-3442
1890sweekend.com
1890s Weekend is held the last weekend in September in Mansfield. The Victorian-themed event always includes a re-enactment of the world's first night football game, played by Mansfield University in Smythe Park on September 28, 1892. Call the Mansfield Chamber of Commerce at (570) 662-3442.

DECEMBER

Dickens of a Christmas
Wellsboro
(570) 724-1926
The first Saturday in December, catch costumed actors and carolers bringing "A Christmas Carol" to life. Main Street is lit by gaslight and lined with food and craft vendors.

ville—"almost everybody is related somehow. And we don't get many newcomers. You can live here 10 years and still be the new person on the block."

The village of several hundred people hides in a pocket of hills and rugged woodlands in Clearfield County. The trip over pitted blacktop roads winds through the remains of played-out strip mines, some of them growing scraggly conifers planted as part of reclamation projects. The heart of the community, as always, is St. Mary's Church, a parish established in 1840. Its first home was a log cabin, where the cemetery now stands. The current building, of native hand-cut stone, was occupied in 1870, the year the town's picnic originated. It was a ceremony of thanks for the construction of the church, and it continues annually, during the third weekend in July, in recognition of that heritage. For more information about Frenchville, St. Mary's, or the Frenchville picnic, e-mail rectory@iqnetsys.net, or phone the rectory at (814) 263-4354.

Places to Stay in North Central Pennsylvania

COUDERSPORT

Millstream Inn
918 E. Second St.
(814) 274-9900
millstreaminn.com
There are 34 rooms, or choose 1 of the 6 suites for extra living and kitchen space.

RIDGWAY

Towers Victorian Inn
330 South St.
(814) 772-7657
towersinn.com
A 19th-century lumber baron's home.

ST. MARYS

Towne House Inn
138 Center St.
(814) 781-1556
A small-town gem on the National Historic Registry.

WELLSBORO

Penn Wells Hotel
62 Main St.
(570) 724-3463
pennwells.com

The classic 100-year-old hotel you always hoped to find. Member, Historic Hotels of America.

Penn Wells Lodge
4 Main St.
The younger refined sibling of the hotel, just down the block, with the same contacts.

Places to Eat in North Central Pennsylvania

BRADFORD TOWNSHIP

Glendorn
1000 Glendorn Dr.
(814) 362-6511
glendorn.com
Gourmet dining at a 1,200-acre estate that welcomes overnight guests.

COUDERSPORT

Sweden Valley Inn
1305 E. 2nd St.
(814) 274-7057
swedenvalleyinn.com
Country pub that goes upscale on the weekend dinner menu. Eleven miles from the Dark Sky Park at Cherry Springs.

MANSFIELD

Lambs Creek Food & Spirits
200 Gateway Dr.
570-662-3222
lambscreek.com
Upscale dining near the Mansfield University campus, accented by a hand-carved European bar, stone fireplaces, and outdoor dining.

SLATE RUN

Wolfe's General Store
PA Rte. 414
(570) 753-8551
Part of the Slate Run Tackle Shop, serving the Pine Creek area, this friendly deli is open daily in summer.

WELLSBORO

Steak House
27 Main St.
(570) 724-9092
Dinner only, closed Sun. Luscious desserts.

WILLIAMSPORT

Bullfrog Brewery
231 W. Fourth St.
(570) 326-4700
bullfrogbrewery.com
Live music and a dozen microbrews on tap. Try the Billtown Blonde.

Northeastern Pennsylvania

Promised Land State Park—the name suggests a biblical desert, but it's actually a scenic wooded spot in Pike County, home of the Poconos. The good news is, it won't take 40 years to wind your way through this region of mountains and gorges, with heavenly panoramas, pre-Revolutionary history, and plenty of anthracite underfoot. The region's two major roads, I-80 and I-81, can get you from point to point fairly easily. When you reach water—the Susquehanna, Lehigh, or Delaware River—stop and enjoy the view.

Hard-Coal Country

To understand northeastern Pennsylvania, you need to understand coal mining. Legend says that in 1791 in the quiet village of Summit Hill, in western Carbon County, Pennsylvania, a major discovery altered American history. While tracking game, a hardy backwoodsman named Philip Ginder accidentally kicked a piece of shiny black rock. He pocketed the stone and took it to Revolutionary War veteran Colonel Jacob Weiss, who took it to his colleagues in Philadelphia. Turns out, Ginder had

discovered anthracite coal, often called "black diamonds" because of its value in the marketplace.

To recap your fourth-grade lesson, coal is a fuel substance composed of plants. You can inspect the raw material if you fail to rake leaves in your backyard for a few thousand years. The two primary types of coal are anthracite, or hard coal, and bituminous, or soft coal. Anthracite is more valuable because it has more carbon content and less moisture, thus it burns cleaner.

In the coal region some stretches of roadway through the hills are lovely, though the landscape has been marred by mining. The working mines aren't especially aesthetically pleasing, but the area is historically rich in details that let us see how people there used to live and work.

Nowhere is the legacy of coal mining more obvious than in Scranton. In downtown Scranton, on Cedar Avenue between Lackawanna Avenue and Moosic Street, the *Anthracite Heritage Museum* describes the lives and work of the ethnic communities in the region. Exhibits survey activities related to canals, railroads, silk mills, factories, and, of course, coal. The museum is on Bald Mountain Road in McDade Park. Take the North Scranton Expressway to the Keyser Avenue exit. Follow Keyser Avenue and signs to McDade Park. The museum is open year-round, 10 a.m. to 5 p.m. Fri through Sun; closed major holidays. Admission is $7 per adult. Call (570) 963-4804 or visit anthracite museum.org for details.

Also for viewing at the museum complex are the *Scranton Iron Furnaces,* open daily from 8 a.m. to dusk. These four huge blast-furnace stacks, built by the Scranton brothers between 1841 and 1857, are remnants of the iron industry around which Scranton grew, with coal mining and railroads falling into place as companion industries. Admission is free.

McDade Park has picnic tables and barbecues, so you can grab a bite before going on to the *Lackawanna Coal Mine* tour, which begins next to

AUTHOR'S TOP 10 FAVORITES IN NORTHEASTERN PENNSYLVANIA

Boulder Field at Hickory Run State Park	Hotel Fauchère
	Inn at Jim Thorpe
Delaware Water Gap National Recreation Area	Peepsfest
Hawk Mountain Sanctuary	Roebling Bridge
Historic Bethlehem walking tours	Upper Mill

the Heritage Museum. The tour takes you down into an abandoned slope mine to see what the miners did and what conditions were like. An electrical powered coal car lowers you from the loading platform to the mine interior. The big yellow car and hoist were designed especially for this purpose.

Inside the mine a retired miner or teacher takes you on a 600-foot tour along a wooden walkway, explaining the sights and answering questions. In the spacious underground area, mannequins in mining clothes and a life-size stuffed mule seem to say, "Hi." Although the mine isn't really dirty, it is underground, and coal can leave its marks, so consider blue jeans and walking shoes. The hour-long tours leave hourly Apr through Nov, more frequently during busy times. More exhibits and artifacts are housed aboveground in a building called Shifting Shanty. The box office opens at 10 a.m.; tours run from 11 a.m. to 3 p.m., but make sure you're there by 2:45 for the last tour of the day. Admission is $10 for adults. Call (570) 963-6463, or visit lackawannacounty.org/attractions.

Within walking distance of the mine is the **Steamtown National Historic Site,** the only place in the national park system that tells the story of steam railroading. The Steamtown Yard is open to the public. Visit the museum, which showcases coal-fired steam locomotives, restored cabooses, freight cars, and railroad coaches, offering a nostalgic journey to a period in American history when industry was on the move. The sights, sounds, smells, and even tastes of that era are brought to life in the presence of some of the most powerful machines ever built. It's located in the original Delaware, Lackawanna & Western Railroad Yard, which operated continuously from 1851 to 1963. The site boasts active locomotive and restoration shops, and a complex that includes a visitor center, history and technology museums, a 250-seat theater, and an operating roundhouse and turntable—the device that was invented to let trains turn around and start over again in the other direction. It's open daily except Thanksgiving, Christmas, and New Year's Day. The park is open daily from 9 a.m. to 5 p.m. (9 a.m. to 4 p.m. Jan through Mar). Adults pay $7 for the museum and additional fees for excursions. Although the entrance to the park is on Lackawanna Avenue, the mailing address is 150 S. Washington Ave., Scranton 18503. For more details visit nps.gov/stea/; call (570) 340-5200 or (888) 693-9391.

Scranton has seen better days, but offers a nostalgic journey to a period in American history when industry was on the move. Each evening a wonderful Art Deco sign high above Linden Street, by the county courthouse, proclaims Scranton's status as "the Electric City" because in 1880, it was the first US city to have a factory lit with electric wiring, and followed that feat with the first electric steetcars in the nation in 1886. Now rewired with white LED lights, the sign gleams proudly.

Harry Houdini, Skeptic

Despite the annual Halloween séances in which people have tried to communicate with the ghost of Harry Houdini, the magician's spirit has been a no-show—perhaps not surprising for a man who delighted in exposing charlatans and fake mediums. After 10 years of trying, Houdini's wife, Bess, wasn't concerned. She wrote to friends that Houdini's permanent eternal silence "struck a mighty worldwide blow at superstition."

Magician Harry Houdini performed in Scranton, where the **Houdini Museum** (1433 N. Main) honors his memory. Ehrich (or Erik) Weiss (or Weisz)—who, abracadabra, became Harry Houdini—was born in 1874 in Budapest and moved to the United States when he was 4. He lived for years in Appleton, Wisconsin, of which he later said: "The greatest escape I ever made was when I left Appleton." In 1918, at the Hippodrome in New York City, Houdini first made an elephant disappear on stage. He performed underwater stunts, for which he practiced by holding his breath in the bathtub. In the museum you'll see Houdini's explanation of how he escaped from the incredible predicaments in which he put himself: "My brain is the key that sets me free." Since his parents spoke Yiddish, Hungarian, and German, his brain was probably also the key that taught him English.

The Houdini Museum also catalogs the history of Scranton and its coal and railroading industries. One exhibit, for instance, says that the Lackawanna Railroad created the image of Phoebe Snow, a delicate woman in a white dress, to foster the idea that riding coal-run trains was a clean event, hence the white dress. "Nothing could be further from the truth," it says. The old steam engines blew soot onto passengers riding the trains with open windows on warm days. Evening mystery events, too (reserve separately at 570-383-9297). Call (570) 342-1821, or go to houdini.org. Admission is $20 for adults.

Near Scranton is the **Dorflinger-Suydam Wildlife Sanctuary,** a 600-acre nature preserve and unique museum. The Dorflingers manufactured glass until the 1920s, and eight US presidents owned some of it. Today the museum of cut glass is open May 1 through Oct 31, 10 a.m. to 4 p.m. Wed through Sat, and 1 to 4 p.m. Sun (weekends only in Nov); admission $3. On summer weekends the Wildflower Music Festival hosts open-air concerts. It's located on Route 6, midway between Hawley and Honesdale; the town is called White Mills, and the location is the intersection of Long Ridge Road and Elizabeth Street. Write to PO Box 356, White Mills 18473; call (570) 253-1185 or go to dorflinger.org for more information.

They Flip for Pizza

There are about 10,000 people in *Old Forge,* 5 miles south of Scranton, and they have one thing in common: They love pizza. In fact, they proudly dub the town the Pizza Capital of the World. There are at least a dozen pizza cafes on Main Street alone. Most of the pizza makers' ancestors hailed from the village of Felitto, near Naples, and most shops are still mom and pop businesses. While there are endless variations on ingredients, the rectangular pies served here, say the locals, are all "the best."

Speaking of great fortunes, try to win yours at *Mohegan Sun at Pocono Downs.* The Wilkes-Barre casino has plenty of excitement, with 82 live gaming tables and 2,300 slot machines, harness racing, and shopping, too. It also offers a huge hotel and Spa Sapphire, which welcomes men and women alike. Visit mohegansunpocono.com.

Ricketts Glen

Knowledgeable outdoorspeople consider *Ricketts Glen* the most spectacular of Pennsylvania's state parks. Its more than 13,000 acres of mountains, streams, waterfalls, and lakes spread through Sullivan, Columbia, and Luzerne Counties. The glen has 22 named waterfalls and a virgin hemlock forest with trees more than 500 years old. The only activity permitted in the natural area is walking. No picnics, campfires, camping, mountain biking, whining, or picking wildflowers. Just hiking. You'll find bass, a swimming beach, and a summer-only concession stand on Lake Jean. The park has 23 miles of hiking trails, some strictly for the physically fit and some shorter loops that are less strenuous. The Falls Trail along the gorge gives you a view of all the falls in the glen and is breathtakingly close to the edge. It is possible to find deserted hiking trails almost any time and wander into the woods feeling that you're the only person in the forest primeval.

The hills are alive with the sound of RVs. You can rent cabins at Ricketts Glen (though not in the natural areas), and the park has good camping for recreational vehicles and tents. Reservations are recommended for overnight visits, especially on weekends during high season, which often lasts through October. Drive to Ricketts Glen via Route 487 or Route 118 north, depending on which side of the park you wish to enter. The grade is so steep that large vehicles should take Route 220, then turn north on Route 487 at Dushore. The park phone number is (570) 477-5675.

Working Valleys

From Scranton you can get to Hazleton quickly on I-81 or cross over to Route 11 and drive down along the Susquehanna River. From about Wilkes-Barre the drive becomes especially hilly in the narrow river valley. Almost any time you tire of it, you can pick up a short road back to the interstate to Hazleton, another formerly thriving coal burgh that was founded in 1837. Whether you follow the highway or your own way, you'll pass some little river towns—not the picturesque, renovated towns of shelter magazines, but real working towns inhabited by laboring folks. You may still see women wearing babushkas (head scarves), kids scuffing their shoes on the sidewalks, and town merchants sitting in front of their stores during idle moments.

Coal country continues west. *Centralia,* a tiny village off Route 61 in Columbia County, has the unique distinction of having been on fire since 1962. That's when an underground blaze erupted in a coal mine under the town. All sorts of engineering marvels were employed to put out the fire; none succeeded, and by 1991 nearly all of the town's residents had been evacuated. The wisps of smoke you see curling up through the ground are evidence that there's still fire down below.

Skeeball. Tilt-A-Whirl. Coasters. Bumper cars. Check, check, check, and check. *Knoebel's Amusement Resort* in Elysburg, between Centralia and Danville, is one of those twirled-and-true summer destinations. Some attractions, like the Carousel Museum and the bald eagle exhibit, are free: a day pass for all the coasters runs $43 for adults (book in advance online for discounts). The century-old park is shady and scenic, and parking and picnicking are free every day. You'll love it. See knoebels.com; (800) 487-4386.

Yuengling Brewery, in Pottsville, started brewing in 1829. During Prohibition the factory switched to nonalcoholic items—ice cream and dairy products. Four daughters in the fifth generation of Yuenglings (pronounced ying-LING) now run the firm.

The writer John O'Hara lived in a mansion once owned by the Yuenglings from 1916 to 1928. The National Historic Site is at 606 Mahatongo St. O'Hara set some of his major works in Pottsville. Thinly disguised as Gibbsville, the town is the backdrop for *Appointment in Samarra, Ten North Frederick, From the Terrace, Butterfield Eight,* and *The Big Laugh.*

Each fall 18,000 raptors get a bird's eye view of *Hawk Mountain Sanctuary,* just south of Pottsville. On routes that can begin at Hudson's Bay and end in Argentina, they soar down the Kittatinny Ridge, the southernmost ridge

River of Rocks

The white streak through the center of the valley below Hawk Mountain is the *River of Rocks*, boulder-sized leftovers from the glacier that pushed past this region 11,000 years ago. Visitors can hike a 4-mile circuit around the formation near the Blue Rocks Campground in Lenhartsville, circling down into the valley and back. Other hikers are just passing through: This is one of the most difficult stretches of the Appalachian Trail.

in the Appalachians, before cutting across Texas into Mexico, where they mass into millions. Hawk Mountain is one of the best places in the world for humans to catch the timeless spectacle. At this central Pennsylvania bird sanctuary, located off Route 61 near Pottsville, volunteers from all over the world annually track the flight paths of 16 species, from tiny kestrels to bald eagles, for the longest record of raptor population in the world.

Migration is hard work. Hawks, falcons, and eagles make it look easy, gliding at eye level past the sanctuary in numbers that can reach 1,000 per day in mid-autumn. It's easy to copy their laid-back style and sample their view by kicking back on a fall afternoon on the sunbaked boulders atop Blue Mountain. From the sanctuary's 1,300-foot summit, the views can extend some 70 miles. The Indian blanket of orange, yellow, and red foliage draping the ridge-and-valley landscape is *echt* ("pure") Pennsylvania.

Are you guaranteed to spot a golden or bald eagle? No. But here's a tip: Visit when the winds blow. "When there's a cold front over the Appalachians, we usually get northwest winds, and birds conserve energy by riding that deflected air current," says khaki-clad Jeremy Scheivert, a former education specialist at the visitor center (check hours online). Trails are open daily until dusk; book adult tickets ($10) online. From I-78, take exit 30 for Hamburg. Drive north on Route 61, then veer right to go north on Route 895. Turn right at Drehersville; call (610) 756-696 or visit hawkmountain.org.

If you prefer valley views to mountain views, the old *Wanamaker, Kempton & Southern Railroad* still operates steam engines near Hawk Mountain. The 6-mile ride boards just past the intersection of Routes 143 and 737 on 737, just north of Kempton, on Sun from May through Oct. Special evening excursions and other themed trips are also available. For a schedule call (610) 756-6469, or board kemptontrain.com.

Nine miles east of Hazleton, the *Eckley Miners' Village* gives you a chance to visit a spot that is part historic site and part living community. It is authentic, not because it has been re-created, but because it has never changed—the black silt heaps, open strip mines, and slag are ever present.

Eckley was a company town from its settlement in 1854 until 1971 and is now administered by the Pennsylvania Historical and Museum Commission. Its population of retired miners, widows, and children has dwindled to about 15. The village, covering 100 acres, is off Route 940. Follow the signs to the site, which is open Thurs through Sun 10 a.m. to 5 p.m. It is closed holidays except Memorial Day, Independence Day, and Labor Day. Admission is $8 per adult. For more information write to the village at 2 Eckley Main St., Weatherly 18255; call (570) 636-2070; or go to eckleyminersvillage.com.

Another coal locale is the **Pioneer Tunnel Coal Mine** in Ashland. The tunnel follows an anthracite vein that is nearly 200 feet thick in some places (huge by mining standards). You can take a half-hour tour ($10 per adult) in an open coal car pulled by a battery-powered mine motor. Another half-hour train tour ($7.50 per adult) goes around the outside of the mountain, not through tunnels. A steam locomotive, called a *lokie,* pulls the train past an open pit mine that was dug close to the surface with steam shovels and a "bootleg hole" where poachers dug out coal. To get to the Pioneer Mine, take Route 61 into Ashland, where it becomes Center Street. Turn left (south) on Twentieth Street and continue for 3 blocks. The mine is open for tours from Memorial Day to Labor Day, 10:30 a.m. to 6 p.m. daily. Call (570) 875-3850 or go to pioneer tunnel.com for hours in Apr, May, Sept, and Oct; closed the rest of the year.

Check out **Nesquahoning,** a mining town on Route 209, southeast of Hazleton. Nesquahoning is built on hills so steep that nothing seems level. Driving slowly, you can peek through a barbershop window to glimpse an elderly gentleman getting a haircut. In front of the homes, flowers spill from their beds over cement walls toward the sidewalk. In backyards women hang laundry to dry on clotheslines. Then you're through town, and signs usher you down the mountain into Jim Thorpe.

Little Switzerland

Until about 1950 **Mauch Chunk** was another Pennsylvania mining town whose economy fluctuated with the coal market, where miners lived in uncertainty and millionaires lived in mansions. Trying to survive, citizens of Mauch (rhymes with "hawk") Chunk and East Mauch Chunk donated a nickel a week to an economic development fund. In 1954 the towns merged and became **Jim Thorpe.** If you love small towns, you'll love Jim Thorpe.

Mauch Chunk's history is synonymous with coal mining and railway transport. Josiah White, a self-taught civil engineer and founder of the Lehigh Coal & Navigation Company, designed and invented a device to schlep his coal to his canal. He contrived the switchback railroad, which followed the Delaware

Canal to Philadelphia and the Morris Canal to New York City, and which jokers refer to as the first roller coaster. The 9-mile Gravity Road was completed in 1827; 10 wagons, each carrying one and a half tons of coal, traveled down Summit Hill powered entirely by gravity. Mules pulled the empty cars up the incline, then got a free ride down. After the demand for coal diminished, the train was used by tourists.

strange as it sounds

Of the 26 millionaires living in the United States before World War II, 13 had homes in Mauch Chunk.

Driving down the highway into the heart of Jim Thorpe, you quickly realize why locals call their home Little Switzerland. Park in a public lot (or at a meter, where a quarter still buys an hour) to explore the narrow, winding streets on foot. This area at the foot of the hills is Hazard Square. It quickly becomes obvious how it got its name. Drive and walk defensively.

On the square, in the *Jim Thorpe Railroad Station,* you can buy tickets for rides on diesel-powered locomotive trains through the mountains to Reading, round-trip, from Memorial Day through the weekend before Christmas.

The railway and an exhilarating bike trail both run alongside the Lehigh Gorge. Book ahead to bring your bike aboard. If you've neglected to pack your bike, rent one in town, and then ride the 25 miles one way from the Jim Thorpe station. At the terminus at White Haven, roll off the train and onto the trail to return at your own pace. These scheduled bike trains run seasonally one weekend a month; if your date is rained out, you can reschedule. For complete schedules and rates, contact the *Lehigh Gorge Scenic Railway* at lgsry.com or (610) 562-2102.

trivia

The town of Jim Thorpe has gone through several incarnations. At its founding it was known as Coalville. In 1815 it changed its name to Mauch Chunk, the local Native American term for Bear Mountain. Now it honors one of the United States' greatest athletes.

Drive up the hill on Route 209 to tour the *Asa Packer Mansion,* providing a dramatic contrast to the cabins of Eckley Miner's Village near Hazleton. Asa Packer worked his way from humble beginnings to become the founder and president of Lehigh Valley Railroad, founder of Lehigh University, and a philanthropist on a grand scale. In 1860 European craftsmen built the Victorian home, lavishly decorated and furnished in robber baron opulence. It stands today as it did when the Packers celebrated their 50th wedding anniversary, preserved rather than restored. Among the outstanding pieces is the

"Thanks, King"

Controversy in the Olympics didn't start with murder in Munich or bribery in Salt Lake City. In 1912 in Stockholm, Sweden, Jim Thorpe, a Native American from Oklahoma, won gold medals in the pentathlon and decathlon. King Gustav V, presenting the medals to the 24-year-old, said, "You, sir, are the greatest athlete in the world," to which Thorpe replied, "Thanks, King." When the International Olympic Committee (IOC) learned that Thorpe had earlier played semipro baseball, earning $2 a game, it demanded that he return his trophies, which he did. He later played baseball for the New York Giants, Cincinnati Reds, and Boston Braves and football for the New York Giants and other teams. After retiring from professional sports, Thorpe played bit parts in several Hollywood movies. When he died of cancer, penniless, in 1953, Oklahoma refused to build him a monument, so his widow started looking for a place where her hero husband could be buried with honor. She found Mauch Chunk and East Mauch Chunk, which voted to consolidate their communities as Jim Thorpe Borough. In 1982 the IOC reinstated Thorpe's amateur status and gave his family replicas of his gold medals. Thorpe's grave is on Route 903.

first-prize gas chandelier of the 1876 Centennial Exposition in Philadelphia, copied in the film *Gone With the Wind*. No wonder this place was named a National Historic Landmark. You'll find collections of carved walnut furniture, paintings, sculpture, crystal, and china. Brief tours are offered 11 a.m. to 4 p.m. Thurs through Sun. Admission is $6 for adults. Call (570) 325-3229 or visit asapackermansion.com for more details.

Asa gave his son, Harry, the brick-and-stone Second Empire–style mansion next door as a wedding gift. This house is lavish, too, with hand-decorated ceilings and Victorian antiques, including some pieces that belonged to the Packer dynasty. If the ***Harry Packer Mansion*** (Packer Hill) looks familiar, it's because the Gothic façade was the inspiration for Walt Disney World's Haunted Mansion.

The mansion now operates as a bed-and-breakfast inn, with 13 rooms. And if you like libations, you're in luck: every Fri and Sat evening from 4 p.m. to 9 p.m.,

trivia

In Mauch Chunk, now Jim Thorpe, miners in 1913 earned 23 cents an hour.

cocktails and fine wines are served to the public in the parlor or veranda. The mansion has mystery weekends and sometimes turns over the entire establishment to special celebrations, so be sure to call ahead. Write to 19 Packer Ave., Jim Thorpe 18229, visit murdermansion.com, or call (570) 325-8566.

One block south of Broadway, Race Street winds along the path once taken by a millrace and passes old buildings, more specialty shops, and the stretch of stone facades called Stone Row, built by none other than Asa Packer in 1848. Today longtime residents and shopkeepers live side by side with newly arrived artists and writers.

Don't miss **St. Mark's and St. John's Episcopal Church** at 21 Race St., considered one of the most notable late Gothic Revival churches in Pennsylvania. It was built in 1869 by Richard Upjohn, the architect who was responsible for the Third Trinity Church of New York City. St. Mark's is laid out in the form of a Latin cross, with an altar of white Italian marble, Minton tile floors, and two Tiffany windows. The reredo (which is the partition behind the altar), made of Caen stone, is a memorial to Asa Packer. Half-hour tours are available; check online for times and remember that the chapel may be closed for religious events. A $5 donation per adult is requested. The church is also the starting point for walking tours of downtown Jim Thorpe in warm weather. Call (570) 325-2241 or visit stmarkandjohn.org for more information.

While Jim Thorpe is a historian's heaven, it's also a sportsperson's paradise. The 100-mile-long Lehigh River, foaming with whitewater, runs right past it. Hiking and biking trails attract athletes from hundreds of miles away. Local outfitters Pocono Biking and Pocono Whitewater, on Hazard Square, offer all kinds of excursions and all the fun gear to enjoy yourself (poconobiking.com and poconowhitewater.com) For more information about the town, call the tourist center toll-free at (888) JIM-THORPE (546-8467), or visit jimthorpe.com.

Just outside of Jim Thorpe, overlooking Route 209 at the base of Mount Pisgah, is a memorial plaque on a large rock where the village of Northern Liberties used to be. In 1861 virtually all the village males between the ages of 16 and 26 volunteered to serve the Union in the Civil War; their wholesale death effectively destroyed the village by killing off its reproductive population. All that remains is the plaque memorializing the soldiers.

Bitter Memories: The Molly Maguires

In the late 1870s a group of men were hanged in the Mauch Chunk Jail (now the **Old Jail Museum** in Jim Thorpe) for murdering two mine bosses. The men were members of a group called the Molly Maguires, Irish immigrants who fled the famine and found a dismal existence in the mines of northeastern Pennsylvania. Poor pay and rotten working conditions led to a strike, which led to management's hiring a spy, which led to long-term controversy. Before the trial, which the coal companies financed, all newspaper reports called the men killers. See Sean Connery and Richard Harris in the movie *The Molly Maguires* and decide for yourself the guilt or innocence of the executed men.

Engineering, a Team Sport

Lehigh University, founded by (who else?) Asa Packer in 1865, prides itself on its excellent engineering department, so much so that its sports teams were nicknamed the Engineers. But in 1996, the school mascot became the Mountain Hawk. The school still uses the phrases "Brown and White" and "Engineers" about teams of the past but uses the winged nickname in the present. Lehigh has the longest-running rivalry in college football with **Lafayette College**, in nearby Easton; the teams have clashed annually for more than 140 years.

Consider **Country Junction** a transition from the sublime into the ridiculous. Yes, it's a hardware store. Yes, it sells chickens. Yes, it celebrates peach festivals with music and beer, and also rents dumpsters. Anyhow, it raises commerce to a fine art at 6565 Interchange Road (Route 209) in Lehighton, 4 miles west of I-476. Closed Sun. Call (610) 377-5050 or visit countryjunction.com.

Head down Route 209 to Route 33 for a visit to pre-anthracite Pennsylvania in two famous towns: Nazareth and Bethlehem. These namesakes of biblical cities are blessed with charm.

In **Nazareth** a folk landmark strikes a chord: **The Martin Guitar Company.** Beck, Sting, and Johnny Cash are among the many celebrity musicians who insist on this brand, made locally since 1839. (Elvis Presley loved Martins, too.) The pandemic closed the facilities to the public in 2021; check new tour times at the main factory campus, 510 Sycamore St., and the gift shop. Call (610) 759-2837 or visit martinguitar.com.

In **Bethlehem,** a thriving city of 72,000 that shares a metro area with Allentown, you'll find living history. Settled by Protestant Moravians on Christmas Eve, 1741, the city is still home to many members of that faith, which predated Anglicanism by a hundred years. Its elegant multipointed star, called Moravian, is today a symbol of the town.

Bethlehem is home to several colleges. On the south bank of the Lehigh River rises the almost-vertical hillside home of Lehigh University. Students and shoppers love Bethlehem's Main Street, a 19th-century gem with welcoming sidewalks, plenty of cafes, and Victorian storefronts. Its historic **Moravian Bookshop,** founded in 1745, claims to be the oldest bookstore in the world; it's also the student bookstore of nearby Moravian University. Over the years it has grown to encompass food items, a delicatessen, gifts (including Moravian stars of all sorts), and music. It's a friendly, very well-stocked place to browse. Open 7 days a week at 428 Main St. (610-866-5481) or shop online at moravianstar.com. A 21st-century addition to the town's cultural scene is **Steelstacks,** a

Peeps!

Peeps, the fluffy, nutrient-free marshmallow candy chicks that nest in Easter baskets all over the country, are produced by Just Born, a division of the Rodda Candy Company in Bethlehem. The company makes 1.5 million of the little guys each year. Emory University researchers subjected Peeps to a number of experiments several years back, testing their resilience in ovens, vacuum chambers, liquid nitrogen, and more. They proved virtually indestructible.

10-acre arts campus at the former site of the massive Bethlehem Steel works. In the past decade more than 1 million people have visited SteelStacks (steelstacks .org) to enjoy musical performances, films, community celebrations, and arena events including *Musikfest,* the largest free music festival in the nation.

In a huge 18th-century log home, the *Moravian Museum* (66 W. Church St.; 610-691-6055) offers 12 exhibit rooms. It's run by the Historic Bethlehem Partnership, which also operates five other period properties in town. In addition to workshops and the original living quarters of the first settlers, the sites include God's Acre, an egalitarian cemetery where Native Americans are interred alongside town leaders. Walking tours detail the industrious, God-fearing lives of those settlers, who were brutally attacked by local tribes in the 1750s. For details check historicbethlehem.org.

Shining just down the block, at 564 Main St., is the *Sun Inn,* which was the 18th century's place to see and be seen. It hosted Revolutionary War heroes in the 1770s; in 1792, 51 chiefs and warriors of the Six Nations Confederation, including Red Jacket, Corn Planter, and Osiquette, lodged at the inn on their way to Philadelphia to meet President Washington. The Inn is open for dinner Wed to Sat. To book go to suninnbethlehem.org.

How much is that doggie in the window? At *Pott's Doggie Shop* (known fondly as Pottsie's), 114 W. Fairview St. (610-865-6644), a great hot dog costs $2.35. Get all-American takeout here.

As you might guess, Christmas celebrations are a big draw in this town—with stars shining everywhere, Christmas markets, arts events, and performances by the city's famous Bach Choir. (Music's a constant, er, refrain here, with more than 1,000 performances a year.) Get the full lineup from the convention and visitor bureau at (800) 747-0561 or visit bethlehempa.org.

The Poconos

The *Pocono Mountains,* northern foothills of the Appalachian Range, are a year-round playground for the Boston-to-Washington megalopolis. The highest Pocono—the impressively named Mount Ararat, in Preston, Wayne County—towers 2,654 feet above sea level. Well, maybe it doesn't tower— some jokingly call the Poconos "the Pinocchios." Nevertheless, they're huge with East Coasters.

To see some of the more scenic and lesser-known parts of the Poconos, take Route 33 out of Nazareth and join Route 209 at Sciota. In its time Route 209 was a major highway, important enough for its construction to displace homes, cemeteries, and prize stands of sugar maples. This route has lost much tourist traffic to interstates; here and there you still see a failed group of tourist cabins predating today's motels or an abandoned gas station with weeds growing through the macadam. By today's standards 209 is narrow and slow due to the steep hills and curves, but the surface is in fairly good condition, trucks pull over to let traffic pass, and most of the countryside is lovely.

Continue north on Route 209, then turn right (south) on Old Route 115. Turn left on Lower Cherry Valley Road and follow the signs into the **Sorrenti Cherry Valley Vineyards,** a friendly little family winery. (From Route 33 take the Saylorsburg exit, then Old Route 115 south, and follow the signs.) For more information on visiting the Saylorsville vineyard, call (570) 992-2255 or visit cherryvalleyvineyards.com.

A quick jog back on Route 33 north takes you to Snydersville, which isn't much more than a gas station, a school bus stop, and antiques dealers in old homes. The names and proprietors may change, but this remains a good area for antiquing—the dealers are knowledgeable but not in the thick of the tourist traffic.

At Snydersville pick up Business Route 209 (paralleling the 4-lane Route 209) going south. Turn right on Hickory Valley Road and follow the signs to **Quiet Valley Living Historical Farm.** (If you start in Stroudsburg, take Business Route 209 north, turn left on Hickory Valley Road, and follow the signs.) Alice and Wendell Wicks, with their daughter and son-in-law, Sue and Gary Oiler, saw the possibilities for this centuries-old Pennsylvania German farm. The Wicks and the Oilers have invested work, time, and money in researching, repairing, and collecting furnishings and farm equipment. In 1963 they opened Quiet Valley as a living museum, showing how the original Pennsylvania Dutch settlers lived on this virtually self-sufficient homestead from about 1770 to 1913. The families restored the existing buildings to full function and reconstructed others that would have been there; for a while the Oilers lived in the top floor of the home. "We don't own it anymore," says Sue Oiler. "It's now a private, nonprofit organization. My home is in the middle of a nonprofit farm. In my head I know it's not really mine, but in my heart I care for it and love it as if it were." Check the calendar for farm tours and events: quietvalley.org.

Appellation Lehigh Valley

With a half-dozen vineyards sprouting between Jim Thorpe and Allentown, the area's *terroir*—the regional qualities imparted by soil and climate conditions—may one day be heralded for cabernets, chardonnays, and chambourcin, rather than coal. The vintners cooperate on special tastings and events year-round. Plan a day or weekend visiting the winemakers; go to lehighvalleywinetrail.com.

Trying to emulate the peaceful and mystical vibe of the Scottish isle of Iona, the pair of idealists who created this park named it for St. Columba (Colum Cille). The 6th-century founder of a monastic community, he protected the legacy of Celtic Christianity. The Pennsylvania park mimics its giant menhirs and stone circle and includes a meditation pond and an Infinity Gate. As Columcille's website (columcille.org) explains, it "suggests to all who enter that these are portals into a world of myth and mystery where the veil is thin between the worlds." All quarried locally, the stones are mind-bendingly old: 400 million years at their core.

Catch the ancient energy daily from dawn to dusk at *Columcille Megalith Park and Celtic Art Center.* It's located 3 miles from Quiet Valley Historical Farm. For more information call (610) 588-1174 or check columcille.org.

After the tour, consider picnicking in the grove. Quiet Valley is open mid-June to Labor Day, 10 a.m. to 5 p.m. Tues through Sat, and noon to 5 p.m. Sun. The last tour begins at 3 p.m. Cost is $10 per adult. For more information write to Quiet Valley Living Historical Farm, 347 Quiet Valley Rd., Stroudsburg 18360; visit quietvalley.org or call (570) 992-6161.

The Poconos offer options for every imaginable outdoor enthusiasm—as well as some unimaginable ones. For most of us, auto racing is a spectator sport, but the 2.5-mile racecourse **Pocono Raceway** is also home to the **Bertil Roos Racing School.** Go equipped with a driver's license, sneakers, gloves, and experience handling a standard shift. The raceway provides instruction, race cars, racetracks, colorful driving suits, and helmets. Your instructor will show you when to brake, when to accelerate, how to handle corners, and, pre-

Pennhenge

While "new megalith" may seem like an oxymoron, the ones erected in the late 1970s at *Columcille* (2155 Fox Gap Rd., Bangor) are worth a look.

sumably, how to pray for safety. Call Roos Mar through Oct at (800) 722-3669 or zoom to racenow.com. The office is on Route 115 in Blakeslee.

Consider popping into the **Pocono Cheesecake Factory** (Route 611, Swiftwater), where chefs prepare up to 100 cheesecakes daily. Watch through the giant window as almonds, raspberries, chocolate chips, and liqueurs blend into the dessert of your choice. As you choose between your wallet and your waistline, read the sign: "Life is uncertain. Eat dessert first." Open daily 11 a.m. to 7 p.m. Call (570) 839-6844 or visit poconocheesecake.com for menus and calorie counts.

Heading north on Route 611, turn east in Mount Pocono on Route 940, then north on Route 191. Eight miles up Route 191, in beautiful downtown LaAnna—wait, you missed downtown—you can visit **Holley Ross Pottery.** Daily from 9:30 a.m. to 5:30 p.m. (Sun from 1 to 5:30 p.m.), you can watch pottery being made and buy Fiestaware, gazing balls, and a variety of glass and ceramic items. The pottery showroom is closed mid-Dec through Apr, except by chance or appointment. Call (570) 676-3248 or go to holleyross .com for details.

Paintball is everywhere in the Poconos. If you like mayhem, paintball is for you. This competitive outdoor "sport" involves balls of water-soluble, biodegradable, nontoxic paint, which you shoot at your friends or enemies. (Yeah, it hurts for real when you get shot.) Ride a military troop transport to a mountaintop with a beautiful view—in order to inflict damage on your friends. Your $30-and-up all-day pass entitles you to 50 paintballs, all-you-can-use carbon dioxide as a propellant, and protective headgear and face mask. You can rent a camouflage suit, which might be a good idea since the games are called "attack and defend," "hostile takeover," and "total elimina-tion." Call ahead to reserve a field at **Skirmish USA** (1519 Route 903, Jim Thorpe; 800-754-7647; skirmish.com).

From Tanneries to Tannersville

Whether or not you stop in *Tannersville,* you'll certainly drive through it. While you're waiting for the traffic light to change, a bit of deep background: Early on, the Lenni-Lenape Indians lived in this valley in the foothills of the Poconos. In about 1750 John Larned bought the land and built a log tavern and two gristmills. Twenty-nine years later General Sullivan and his army, en route to the Wyoming Valley, spent the night in tents next to the tavern. In 1834 Jacob Singmaster built a large tannery, which became the village's main industry and inspired the change from Larneds to Tanners-ville. Fire destroyed several tanneries, but innumerable candle shops keep the heat on.

Bach to Bach

Founded in 1898, the all-volunteer Bach Choir of Bethlehem is the oldest Bach Choir in the country and gave the first American performances of Bach's Mass in B Minor and the Christmas Oratorio. It records and tours internationally, including appearances at BBC Proms.

For the back-to-nature gang—and even for people who prefer their nature on the National Geographic Channel—***Hickory Run State Park,*** especially the Boulder Field, is not to be believed and never to be forgotten. This area, now a National Natural Landmark (say that fast three times) has remained essentially unchanged for 20,000 years. Boulders up to 26 feet long cover an area 400 feet by 1,800 feet, and you're welcome to climb, scramble, or sit on them—if you can. Imagine a dish of 1-inch pebbles, and imagine an ant trying to navigate the terrain. The ground beneath the boulders is totally flat and free of vegetation. Staggering.

Of course, like any self-respecting state park, Hickory Run has trails, campgrounds, and picnic facilities. You may apply for hunting and fishing licenses and try your luck in the park's 15,500 acres. You can swim in summer and snowmobile, cross-country ski, and sled in winter. Hickory Run is immediately southeast of the intersection of I-476 and I-80, so it's hard to miss if you're in the area. Follow signs to 3613 State Route 534, White Haven 18661; call (570) 443-0400; or visit dcnr.state.pa.us/stateparks/findapark/hickoryrun/index.htm.

Delaware Water Gap

Here you are close to the ***Delaware Water Gap National Recreation Area,*** which runs along a 40-mile stretch of the Delaware River in New Jersey and Pennsylvania. Feeding the Gap are dozens of scenic waterfalls. The town of Delaware Water Gap marks the southernmost point of the 70,000-acre recreation area. ***Dingmans Falls Visitor Center*** (off Route 209 north of Johnny Bee Road), offers park information and a bookstore. Since hours vary seasonally, you might want to visit discoverpikepa.com.

Even in the 19th century this gap attracted the well-to-do for resort holidays away from the New York heat; Broadway's a 45-minute drive. Horse-drawn carriages and rafts transported early visitors until about 1856, when the Delaware and Cobb's Gap Railroad Company opened a track to Scranton. Native Americans called the area Pohoqauline, Pahaqalong, or Pahaqualia, all of which mean "river passing between two mountains." Its beauty lies partly in the contrasting colors of layers of quartzite, red sandstone, and dark shale that have been revealed as the river carved its path over geologic eons.

With light hiking, you can appreciate the Gap close up. Park in the Resort Point parking lot off Route 611, on the Pennsylvania side. Across the road stone steps take you to a trail paralleling a stream that goes up steeply for a short distance, then turns left onto a marked trail. The trail continues gently upward for about a mile; when you get to a waterfall, you can no longer hear the highway traffic. A little farther straight ahead, a large rock outcropping takes your breath away. It's picture-postcard pretty. In this area you can also drive into some well-marked overlooks from which you have a spectacular view without hiking. At one such place a souped-up red Chevrolet once roared in; a couple of teenagers slurping diet colas looked out, said, "There isn't anything here," and roared away. Pushing these types of people over the edge is against park regulations. For complete information on the Delaware Water Gap National Recreation Area, visit nps.gov/dewa or call (570) 426-2430.

The **Pocono Indian Museum** at 5425 Milford Road (Route 209) shows the history of the Delaware Indians in 6 rooms of collected artifacts. Some pottery is more than 1,000 years old, and weapons and tools have had only their handles reconstructed. The Delaware Indians wore simple deerskin garments, cut their hair short, and wore no feathers, except perhaps for ceremonies. Nor did they live in tepees. The museum and gift shop are usually open daily 10 a.m. to 6 p.m., but call first. Admission is $7 for adults. For more information visit poconoindianmuseumonline.com or call (570) 588-9338. Of course, you'll exit through the gift shop.

Bushkill Falls, called the Niagara of Pennsylvania, is easy to reach, 2 miles northwest of Route 209. Easy walking over rustic bridges and a nature trail of about 1.5 miles takes you through virgin forests and past a gorge with

Accessible Outdoors

All of the Commonwealth's state parks meet ADA standards, but Northeastern Pennsylvania, a crazy quilt of mountains and rivers, goes above and beyond, with wheelchair accessible scenic trails, fishing piers, sensory trails, and some audio descriptions. A quarter-mile handicapped access boardwalk trail brings you to the foot of Dingmans Falls (closed weekends), and the Pocono Environmental Education Center offers its Sensory Trail, a rope-lined 0.3-mile path open to all. Stretches of both the McDade Recreational Trail along the Delaware and the D&L Trail in Lehigh Gorge State Park accommodate wheelchair users. The Boulder Field at Hickory Run State Park is open to hikers—but a 5-mile one-way dirt road encircling the geologic formation allows another vantage point. For more ideas about easy access in the Poconos, visit poconomountains.com.

Eagle Etiquette

"The eagles are getting so friendly," marvels Maria Vernon at the Delaware Water Gap Visitor Center. While they don't actually wave, the birds have gradually become less afraid of humans. But please, don't scare them. To view the 200 or so bald eagles along the upper Delaware shoreline, the Eagle Institute recommends using the observation blinds at viewing areas to remain hidden from view. Avoid loud noises and use binoculars instead of moving close to the birds. And plan to do your bird-watching in midwinter—come spring, eagle parents don't want company while they're tending to their newborns (a sentiment most new mothers would share).

Maria recommends the Shohola Recreation Area, off Route 6, as a good viewing spot; Lackawaxen is good, too, she says. Basically, any spot with open, unfrozen water will afford an opportunity for viewing the raptors.

a view of 8 waterfalls, the largest of which is Bushkill, dropping 130 feet. Even with a cell phone, it's possible to take spectacular pictures. You may picnic, boat, and fish in the park. Some food is available. The park is open daily 9 a.m. to dusk Apr through Nov. Admission is $11 for adults. The park's operating calendar varies depending on the season, so call (570) 588-6682, or go to visitbushkillfalls.com.

At Dingmans Ferry, farther north on Route 209 but still in the Delaware Water Gap National Recreation Area, **Dingmans Falls,** the highest waterfall in Pennsylvania, pours down over 100 feet of rock with awesome power. On the same easy trail, in woods of hemlock and ferns, **Silver Thread Falls,** not quite as high but equally beautiful, is another stop worth a few photographs. In the park's nature center, you can study an audiovisual program, pick up a map, and talk to a naturalist about the falls and good trails—including easy ones—to walk.

From Dingmans Ferry it's only about 10 miles to Milford, a good place to spend the night. As a kid I remember discovering the **Hotel Fauchère.** My grandfather loved taking us to the place, and my brothers thrilled to the full-sized taxidermied bear guarding the men's room. I later found it has an interesting history, playing host to many New York celebrities in its heyday. One was D. W. Griffith, who filmed several early movies in the area. Now it's been transformed into a 4-star boutique hotel; the food is still magnifique (401 Broad St.; 570-409-1212; hotelfauchere.com).

Can you picture one of Dingmans Ferry's most famous natives, Chief Thundercloud? If you've got an old nickel, it's easy. He's thought to be the model for the iconic beaked profile on the obverse of the Indian-head coin (and for the last $5 gold piece minted in the United States). Though he was a Boy Scout in his youth, Thundercloud went on to quite a show-biz career, traveling with Buffalo Bill's Wild West show and P. T. Barnum. He also served as a model for sculptor Frederick Remington and artist John Singer. He's buried back in his hometown cemetery on Route 6/309 in Delaware Township.

The grandeur of **Grey Towers,** the Milford home of Gifford Pinchot, was the creation of 19th-century architect Richard Morris Hunt. Pinchot, a two-time governor of Pennsylvania, was a leading early conservationist and the first director of the US Forest Service. His wife Cornelia was a noted suffragette and gardener. While mansion tours are on hiatus, you're welcome to stroll the surrounding 100-plus acres at 122 Old Owego Turnpike; adult admission $8. Call (570) 296-9630 or visit greytowers.org.

In Milford stop at the **Upper Mill,** a 19th-century mill where water rushing over a 3-story-high waterwheel used to power a grindstone. The mill building, on the National Register of Historic Places, is open year-round. These days it produces more retail power, but that, fortunately, is thriving. The menu includes breakfast, lunch, dinner, and some scrumptious Asian specialties. From the cafe and bar, you can watch the waterwheel. The mill (570-296-5141; waterwheelcafe.com) is on Sawkill Creek at 150 Water St.

For a different kind of stay, go northwest from Milford on Route 6 to the **Settler's Inn,** a sophisticated 23-room country lodge furnished in Arts and Crafts style in Bingham Park. The menu features local produce and local trout, including the famous smoked-trout appetizer. The inn is within walking distance of local shops and near Lake Wallenpaupack, where you can go fishing and boating. For more information about Settler's Inn, at 4 Main Ave., Hawley 18428; call (570) 226-2993, or visit thesettlersinn.com.

trivia

Lake Wallenpaupack, an artificial lake north of Route 84, east of Route 191, covers old farmlands. Divers can still see stone walls, marking the perimeters of some farmers' pastures.

Upper Delaware Wilds

The Lackawaxen area remains unspoiled. Although the land along the Delaware River and the Lackawaxen River is privately owned, the stretch of the Delaware from Port Jervis to Hancock (both towns in New York) is protected under the Wild and Scenic Rivers Act. You'll find most of the historic and natural attractions along or near Route 590. The village of **Lackawaxen** (a native word for "swift waters") is named for the river that flows into the Delaware. If you're a fishing enthusiast, you'll like the Lackawaxen Fishing and Boat Access, operated by the Pennsylvania Fish and Boat Commission, which provides good fishing where the Delaware River runs deep and slow.

Across from the fishing access is the **Zane Grey Museum,** representing a classic American success story. Zane Grey was a handsome dentist. He attended the University of Pennsylvania, where he received his degree in 1896. "He played on the Penn varsity baseball team and was quite well known," says Dot Moon, former curator at the museum. "Baseball was very different than it is today. College baseball was a very big thing." After college Grey played baseball for the Orange Athletic Club in the Eastern League, which was considered a "gentlemen's league." Moon says that means they played for money but did not play on Sunday as "professional" baseball players did. In the off-season Grey practiced dentistry.

Grey's first article, a fishing story, was published in 1902. He gave up baseball after the 1902 season at the urging of his future wife, who encouraged him to devote himself to writing. In 1903 he wrote his first novel, *Betty Zane,* the story of his great-great-aunt who helped save Tennessee's Fort Henry during the Revolutionary War. He moved to Lackawaxen in 1905 to devote himself to writing and later said the Lackawaxen area was where he first experienced "really wild country." It's here that he wrote *Riders of the Purple Sage*, which created the swashbuckling Western genre in fiction and movies.

trivia

A popular horse race that was 5 miles long used to take place between Camptown and Wyalusing. The race is believed to have inspired Stephen Foster, who was visiting his brother in Towanda, to write "Camptown Races." Doo-dah.

After leaving Lackawaxen, Grey traveled extensively to exotic places, such as Tahiti and New Zealand, to research his books. They were so convincing that Hollywood took to them, and by 1918 he left for California to work with the people producing movies based on his books. His Lackawaxen home remains a museum containing mementos of his life. Grey and his wife are buried in the cemetery of St. Mark's Lutheran Church, built in 1848. The free museum is open in warm weather; for hours and details call the National Park Service at (570) 685-4871 or visit nps.gov/upde.

From the fishing access you can also see John Roebling's **Delaware Aqueduct,** the oldest suspension bridge in use today. Roebling (who designed the

Brooklyn Bridge but died before it was built) designed and built four aqueducts for the Delaware and Hudson (D&H) Canal; only this one remains. Completed in 1849, the aqueduct connected the canal between Lackawaxen, in Pennsylvania, and New York. The aqueduct fell into disrepair and was later restored by the National Park Service. Now it is sturdy enough to be used, a century and a half later, as an automobile thoroughfare. (Locals—and local signs—call it the **Roebling Bridge.**)

A nice place to stay is the **Roebling Inn** on the Delaware. It's on Scenic Drive off Route 590 in Lackawaxen. The white clapboard inn with green shutters and roof was built around 1870 and was used as an office for the D&H Canal company. The 6 guest rooms, decorated with country antiques, are modified for contemporary tastes with private baths, televisions, and queen-size beds; some rooms have fireplaces. From the inn you can walk to canoeing, golf, horseback riding, a bait shop, a lunch restaurant, a general store, white-water rafting, tennis, river swimming, and a couple of great places for dinner. For full details and reservations, write 155 Scenic Dr., Lackawaxen 18435; call (570) 685-7900; or visit roeblinginn.com.

You can find considerably more rustic accommodations at the **Sylvania Tree Farm** on the Delaware River in Mast Hope. It's a tree farm—a naturalist's paradise—where you can stay in a modern cottage or pitch your tent at a campsite. Mast Hope is one of those you-can't-get-there-from-here places. From Milford take Route 6 about 14 miles, go north on Route 434 for 3 miles, take Route 590 west to Lackawaxen, then turn right toward Mast Hope. The destination worth the trouble is 1,250 acres on the river with woods, fields, brooks, and seclusion. The privately-owned property is in the protected Upper Delaware Wild and Scenic River corridor, administered by the National Park Service. Watchful visitors sight bald eagles and blue herons in the valley and white-tailed deer, black bears, beavers, and foxes in the woods and fields. The fly-fishing crowd loves the farm's private stream. You can cross-country ski in winter, hike other times, and take canoe and rafting trips with nearby outfitters. In addition, the National Park Service gives tours of the river valley and several historic sites. Call (570) 685-7001. Find out more at sylvaniatreefarm.com.

trivia

Joseph Smith, founder of the Latter Day Saints movement, lived in Susquehanna County in 1830 while translating the Golden Plates for the *Book of Mormon.* See the historical marker at the site on Route 11 between Great Bend and Hallstead.

BEST ANNUAL EVENTS IN NORTHEASTERN PENNSYLVANIA

FEBRUARY

Kiwanis Winterfest
(272) 202-0123
sullivanpachamber.com
Mush! Each February the Kiwanis Winterfest celebrates all things frozen. The Presidents' Day Weekend event also includes an ice fishing derby, snowshoe races, and even a real sled dog race on the frozen lake at Camp Brulé, off Route 154 north of Forksville. Bundle up.

APRIL

Endless Mountains Maple Festival
Alparon Park, Troy
(570) 673-8871
maplefestivalpa.com
The last weekend in April, the Endless Mountains Maple Festival takes place in Alparon Park, Route 14, Troy. Of course it includes a pancake-eating contest. Adult admission is $4.

MAY

Bach Festival
Bethlehem
(610) 886-4382
bach.org

Music from the maestro: Each May for more than 100 years, Bethlehem's Bach Festival has showcased its glorious all-volunteer choir, which has even performed at the BBC Proms, the annual London music festival.

Farm Animal Frolic
Quiet Valley Living Historical Farm
(570) 992-6161
quietvalley.org
In May (usually the last 2 weekends) is the Farm Animal Frolic, a time for baby people to touch baby animals. No tours, just hens and chicks, sheep and lambs, pigs and piglets—you get the picture. Admission is charged (for humans).

JULY

Zane Grey Festival
Lackawaxen
(570) 685-4871
nps.gov/upde
A community tribute—more like a free town picnic—held on the museum's riverfront.

A Day Trip: Endless Mountains

Four adjoining counties—Bradford, Sullivan, Susquehanna, and Wyoming—form the **Endless Mountains Heritage Region.** More than 15,000 years ago, glaciers etched these stones, creating the North Branch of the Susquehanna River. Valleys that once held prehistoric agricultural settlements now hold modern farms—plus white clapboard churches, basket shops, and quaint bed-and-breakfasts.

Versailles, it turns out, is only a day trip from Scranton area. Early settlers thought the Susquehanna River vista looked like *la belle France*. So, in 1793,

AUGUST

Blueberry Festival
Montrose
(570) 278-1881
susqcolibrary.org
Try the annual Blueberry Festival the first week in August in Montrose. Alongside blueberry dishes from buckle pie to ice cream, the ladies of the Crazy County Quilters raffle off exquisite homemade designs to benefit the town library.

Riverfest
Towanda
(570) 265-2696
towandaborough.org
In late August Towanda concludes its weekend Riverfest with Fire Over the Susquehanna, a waterfront fireworks display. Infants can enter the Baby Crawl; adults can try the 5K Walk/Run.

Tomato Festival
Pittston
(570) 693-0704
pittstontomatofestival.com
Pittston holds a weekend Tomato Festival each August. The highlight: the in-the-streets, in-your-face tomato fights on Saturday. The $10 tickets include protective glasses. Splat!

SEPTEMBER

Milford Readers and Writers Festival
Milford
milfordreadersandwriters.com
A free weekend of events with noted authors in the historic county seat.

DECEMBER

Christkindlmarkt
Bethlehem
(610) 332-1300
christmascity.org
A European-style Christkindlmarkt with daily outdoor music, food, trees, crafts, and St. Nick marks the holiday season in downtown Bethlehem.

Peepsfest
Bethlehem
(610) 332-1300
steelstacks.org/festivals/peepsfest
The finale of the two-day celebration is the dropping of the 400-pound Peeps chick at midnight New Year's Eve.

those refugee royalists built an asylum for Marie Antoinette. Unfortunately, they waited in vain for the queen. Keep your head—and keep your eyes on the road—as you drive north on Route 6, above Wyalusing. The grounds are open May through Oct; hours vary. The $5 adult admission includes tours of the La Porte house, a later structure. Call (570) 265-3376 or get the full history from thefrenchazilum.com.

For more information on the area, stop at the **Endless Mountains Visitors Bureau,** 5405 Rte. 6 East, Tunkhannock 18657; (800) 769-8999 or (570) 836-5431. You can also visit endlessmountains.org.

Easton

My favorite Crayola color? Red violet. Nationally, folks vote for plain old true blue. Whatever your choice, take a tour of the **Crayola Factory,** which proves that crayon making hasn't changed much since it started here in 1885. The Crayola Factory is a happy place to visit, with craft stations, ball mazes, and clever depictions of the history of the company, now a subsidiary of Hallmark. The Crayola Store next door supplies a rainbow of chalk, glitter, clay, markers, and more. Both are at 30 Centre Sq. Book discounted day passes online for $22.99. For more information call (610) 515-8000 or (800) CRAYOLA or visit crayolaexperience.com.

The Crayola Factory shares Two Rivers Landing with the **National Canal Museum** (610-559-6613)—a natural for Pennsylvania, given the oceans of man-made waterways that crisscrossed the state in the 19th century. This is a well-designed little museum that illuminates the past with lots of hands-on displays, excellent short videos, and electronic timelines. Ten minutes out of town, at **Hugh Moore Park,** you can board the mule-drawn *Josiah White II* and float the 6 miles of the old Lehigh Canal that have been restored here. The *Josiah White II* sails June through Sept. One admission ticket ($12 for adults) admits you to the NCM and the barge rides. The park offers bike and watercraft rentals. Get details from the museum at canals.org.

trivia

A plaque on the riverbank in Easton claims it's the site of America's first Christmas tree.

Easton was a Native American settlement before it became one of Pennsylvania's first colonial towns. The Treaty of Easton, signed in 1758, promised local Iroquois, Lenape, and Shawnee tribes the right to their lands if they promised to become allies of the English rather than the French. The huge monument on the town square, however, commemorates the Civil War.

The route along the Delaware River between Easton and Philadelphia is a beauty. Take Route 32 South, particularly on a lovely summer afternoon, to return to the big city.

Places to Stay in Northeastern Pennsylvania

BETHLEHEM

Sayre Mansion
250 Wyandotte St.
(610) 882-2100
sayremansion.com
Mansion or carriage house accommodations on a downtown estate.

JIM THORPE

Hotel Switzerland
5 Hazard Sq.
(570) 325-4563
jimthorpedining.com
The town's oldest hotel, above the Molly Maguires Pub & Steakhouse.

Inn at Jim Thorpe
24 Broadway
(800) 329-2599
innjt.com
A collection of upscale rooms at three historic properties on Broadway.

SCRANTON

Radisson Lackawanna Station Hotel
700 Lackawanna Ave.
(570) 342-8300
radisson.com
Grand neoclassical dowager near the Steamtown National Historic Site.

STROUDSBURG

Penn Stroud Hotel
700 Main St.
(570) 421-2200
choicehotels.com
A member of Choice Hotels' Ascend Collection. Convenient to Camelback and Shawnee ski areas.

WILKES-BARRE

Woodlands Inn & Resort
1073 Rte. 315
(570) 824-9831
thewoodlandsresort.com
A full-service hotel with 2 restaurants, adjacent to Mohegan Sun Casino at Pocono Downs.

Places to Eat in Northeastern Pennsylvania

BETHLEHEM

Apollo Grill
85 W. Broad St.
(610) 865-9600
apollogrill.com
New American cuisine, serves lunch and dinner Tues through Sat.

EASTON

Pearly Baker's Ale House
11 Centre Sq.
(610) 253-9949
pearlybakers.net
A friendly pub in the heart of town.

JIM THORPE

Molly Maguires Pub & Steakhouse
Hotel Switzerland
5 Hazard Sq.
(570) 325-4563
jimthorpedining.com
Casual pub with a canopied deck.

MILFORD

Hotel Fauchère
401 Broad St.
(570) 409-1212
hotelfauchere.com
Elegant dining options in a hotel founded in 1852.

MOUNTAINHOME

Mountainhome Diner
Routes 191 and 390
(570) 595-2523
Comfort food destination near Buck Hill Falls. Closed Tues.

SCRANTON

Cooper's Seafood House & Ship's Pub
701 N. Washington Ave.
(570) 346-6883
coopers-seafood.com
Look for the striped lighthouse and pirate ship. Really.

SHAWNEE-ON-DELAWARE

Saen
Shawnee Square
(570) 476-4911
saenthai.com
Thai cuisine. Closed Mon.

SNYDERSVILLE

Snydersville Family Diner
6238 Business Route 209
(570) 992-4003
A sure-fire bet for breakfast, served all day.

TANNERSVILLE

Smuggler's Cove
2972 Rte. 611
(570) 629-2277
smugglerscove.net
Seafood and steaks for famished families, après-ski.

Selection of Pennsylvania's Covered Bridges

dairs Covered Bridge. Built 1864, rebuilt 1904. One of four covered bridges that
ban Sherman's Creek. Bridge is 150 feet long; Burr-truss construction. Route 274,
east of Andersonburg, west of Loysville; southwest Madison Township, Perry County.

Aline Covered Bridge. Built 1884, this bridge spans the North Branch of Mahantango
Creek. Span is 67 feet long; Burr-truss construction. Route 104, north of Meiserville,
Snyder County.

Bartram's Covered Bridge. Built 1860 by Ferdinand Wood. Span is 60 feet long, 18 feet
wide, 13 feet high; Burr-truss construction. The Bartram family was instrumental in having
bridge built. West of Newtown; Willistown and Newtown Townships, Bucks County.

Bells Mills Covered Bridge. Built 1950. Bridge is 104 feet long; Burr-truss
construction. Connects Sewickley and South Huntingdon Townships and connects
Route 136 to I-70. Last remaining covered bridge in Westmoreland County. Near
Wyano and Herminie.

Bistline Covered Bridge. Built 1884. One of four covered bridges across Sherman's
Creek. Also called Book's Covered Bridge. Span is 70 feet long; Burr-truss construction
with multiple king posts. Route 274, southwest of Blain, northeast of New Germantown;
Jackson Township, Perry County.

Blaney Mays Covered Bridge. Built 1882, this bridge spans Middle Wheeling Creek.
Queen-post-truss design, vertical plank siding, covered gable roof. Bridge is 31 feet
long, 12 feet wide. J. Blaney once owned land near here. Southeast of West Alexander
on Donegal Road, Claysville, Washington County.

Bogert Covered Bridge. Built 1841, it's the oldest bridge in the country. Span is 145
feet long across Little Lehigh River. Fish Hatchery Road, south of Allentown in Little
Lehigh Park, Lehigh County.

Bucher's Mill Covered Bridge. Built 1892. Also called Cocalico Bridge, it crosses
Cocalico Creek. Span is 64 feet long, 15 feet wide; Burr-truss construction. Cocalico
Road, off Route 272, south of Denver; East Cocalico Township, Lancaster County.

Cerl Wright Covered Bridge. Crosses north fork of Pigeon Creek. King-post-truss
system. Has outlived records of its builder and date of construction. Great view from
I-70. Sumney Road, northwest of Bentleyville overlooking eastbound I-70; Somerset
Township, Washington County.

Crawford Covered Bridge. Queen-post-truss construction. Bridge crosses Robinson
Fork of Wheeling Creek, 6 miles west of Finley, then 0.7 mile north of town on Route
3037, Washington County.

Ebenezer Covered Bridge. Spans south fork of Mingo Creek. Queen-truss
construction. Mingo Creek County Park, Kammerer, Washington County.

Jack's Mountain Covered Bridge. Built 1894. Crosses Tom's Creek. Bridge is 75 feet long, 14.5 feet wide; Burr-truss construction. State-owned; open to vehicles. Hamilton Township, southwest of Fairfield near Iron Springs, Adams County.

Jackson's Mill Bridge. Built 1875. Span is 95 feet long, 14.5 feet wide; Burr-truss support. Drivable. Township Route 412, 3.5 miles south of Breezewood, Fulton County.

Kidd's Mill Covered Bridge. Built 1868, restored 1990. Crosses the Shenango River. Span is 120 feet long; all-wooden-truss design patented by Robert Smith of Tippecanoe City, Ohio. Last historic covered bridge in Mercer County. Five miles south of Greenville on Route 18, then east.

Knapp's Covered Bridge. Burr-arch timber bridge constructed about 1860 over Brown's Creek. Span is 88 feet, 10 inches long. Said to be the highest covered bridge in Pennsylvania, at 36 feet above the stream bed. Burlington Township, Bradford County.

Kramer Bridge. C. W. Eves built the bridge in 1881 for $414.50. Named for Alexander Kramer, a local farmer, who also bid on its construction. Span is 50 feet long across Mud Run, a tributary of Green and Fishing Creeks, south of Rohrsburg on Rohrsburg Road, Columbia County.

McConnell's Mill Covered Bridge. Built 1874 over Slippery Rock Creek, just downstream from McConnell's Mill. Span is 96 feet long; built with Howe-truss support system. McConnell's Mill State Park, Slippery Rock Township, Lawrence County.

Sachs Covered Bridge. Built 1852 by David S. Stoner across Marsh Creek. Also called Sauck's Bridge. Red bridge is 100 feet long; lattice-truss design. Pedestrians only. Both Union and Confederate troops used the bridge in 1863. Waterworks Road between Cumberland and Freedom Townships; near Gettysburg, Adams County.

PENNSYLVANIA'S CAVES

Crystal Cave
963 Crystal Cave Rd.
Kutztown
(610) 683-6765
crystalcavepa.com

Laurel Caverns
200 Caverns Park Rd.
Farmington
(724) 438-3003 or (800) 515-4150
laurelcaverns.com

Indian Caverns
5347 Indian Trail
Spruce Creek
(814) 632-7578
indiancaverns.com

Lincoln Caverns
Route 22
Huntingdon
(814) 643-0268
lincolncaverns.com

Indian Echo Caverns
368 Middletown Rd.
Hummelstown
(717) 566-8131
indianechocaverns.com

Penn's Cave
222 Penn's Cave Rd.
Centre Hall
(814) 364-1664
pennscave.com

Thomas Mill Covered Bridge. This rural bridge in the midst of the state's biggest metropolis is 97 feet long and 14 feet wide. Access it by foot, bicycle, or horse along Forbidden Drive (so named because cars were always forbidden) between Valley Green Inn and Bells Mill Road, or from Germantown Avenue down Thomas Mill Road. Chestnut Hill section of Philadelphia.

TAKE A HIKE

Appalachian National Scenic Trail. Approach this 232-mile segment of the Appalachian Trail from Rouzerville, Franklin County. Its highest elevation is 2,000 feet. Along the beautiful route you'll find laurel and rhododendron blooming in late spring, historic sites, fall hawk migration, and fall foliage. For more information call (304) 535-6331 or visit appalachiantrail.org.

Black Forest Trail. Start in Haneyville and hike a 9.8-mile loop trail that gains 1,220 feet in elevation. Allow about 6 hours, and you will be rewarded with a section of the Black Forest Trail along Pine Creek Gorge. Pass a waterfall and the historic remains of the Black Forest Railroad, built to log much of this area. For more information call Tiadaghton State Forest, (570) 327-3450.

Eddy Lick Run. This trail is 7.3 miles long, and it takes more than 4 hours to hike. Starting at the trailhead at 2,292 feet, the loop gains another 950 feet in elevation. Walk past a logging railroad and traces of a splash dam, which permitted logging along streams that were too small to float logs, even in the spring flood. Most splash dams were made of logs and soil, so they were temporary, but this one was built largely of rock and is well preserved. For more information call Sproul State Forest, (570) 923-6011.

Maple Summit to Ohiopyle. To walk this trail, the southernmost section—and one of the most scenic bits—of the Laurel Highlands Trail, start in Confluence. The 11.3-mile-long trail requires several steep climbs—all worth the effort—for a total elevation gain of 1,700 feet. Allow at least 6 hours. The trail is contained within State Game Lands, No. 111. For more information call (724) 455-3744.

Table Rock. You can access this 4.2-mile easy trail near Dauphin and can cover it in a couple of hours. Allow time to take in the views from Table Rock. The wide swath cut for power lines allows for great vistas of the Susquehanna River.

For more trails—many more—visit trails.com. At last count it listed 265 Pennsylvania off-the-beaten hiking paths.

FINAL RESTING PLACES OF PROMINENT PEOPLE

Adams, Earl John "Sparky" (1894–1989). Slick infielder for Cubs, Pirates, Cardinals, and Reds. Starting third baseman for Cardinals' "Gas House Gang" of early 1930s. Tremont Reformed Cemetery; Tremont, Schuylkill County.

Ashburn, Richie (1927–1997). Baseball Hall of Famer who was twice National League batting champ with the Philadelphia Phillies. Also an original New York Met and a Phillies broadcaster for more than 30 years. Gladwyne Methodist Church Cemetery, southeast corner, directly behind the church; 316 Righter's Mill Rd., Gladwyne, Montgomery County.

Bailey, Pearl (1918–1988). African American vocalist and movie and stage actress. Began as dancer, won amateur contest in Philadelphia in 1933, sang with Big Bands. Starred in *Hello, Dolly!* Hosted a TV variety show. Autobiography: *The Raw Pearl*. Rolling Green Memorial Park; 1008 West Chester Pike, West Chester, Chester County.

Barry, Commodore John (1745–1803). Born in Ireland, Barry went to sea early and settled in Philadelphia by 1760. Commanded two ships. Became senior captain in US Navy. Called Father of the US Navy. Saint Mary's Catholic Church; 252 S. Fourth St., Philadelphia.

Barrymore, John (1882–1942). Stage and film actor, born in Philadelphia. Brother of Ethel and Lionel Barrymore, he debuted in 1903 and became a matinee idol. Triumphed as a stage Hamlet in 1922, then turned to films and radio. Married four times. Mount Vernon Cemetery; Ridge and Lehigh Avenues, Philadelphia.

Britt, Elton (1913–1972). "World's greatest yodeler" lies here—listen. Most famous song: "There's a Star-Spangled Banner Waving Somewhere." Independent Order of Odd Fellows Cemetery; Broadtop City, Huntingdon County.

Buchanan, President James (1791–1868). Fifteenth US president and the only one born in Pennsylvania. Woodward Hill Cemetery; Lancaster.

Calder, Alexander S. (1870–1945). Sculptor and painter, "Sandy" Calder was most famous for creating sculptures that move; artist Marcel Duchamp dubbed them "mobiles." Artist Jean Arp called Calder's stationary sculptures "stabiles." West Laurel Hill Cemetery, Pencoyd Section, Lot 200; 215 Belmont Ave., Bala Cynwyd, Montgomery County.

Croce, Jim (1943–1973). Top-10 folk-rock singer and instrumentalist. "'Cause every time I tried to tell you, the words just came out wrong, so I'll have to say I love you in a song." Haym Solomon Cemetery, Section B/B; Frazer, Chester County.

Day, William Howard (1825–1900). Prominent abolitionist, minister of A.M.E. Zion Church, orator, editor, and educator. Born in New York City; traveled in United States, Canada, and Britain on behalf of antislavery and free Black people. Lived after 1870 in Harrisburg, where he edited the newspaper *Our National Progress*. First African American elected to the Harrisburg School Board; later served as its president. Lincoln Cemetery; Lincoln and Carlisle Streets, Steelton, Dauphin County.

Dorsey, Jimmy (1904–1957). One of the musical Dorsey Brothers, he was a saxophonist, playing with his trombonist-brother Tommy (1905–1956). Together they were key figures of the Big Band era. Began their musical careers in Shenandoah, Pennsylvania, performing together until 1935. Later they led separate orchestras for 18 years before reuniting. Annunciation Cemetery; Schuylkill Avenue, Shenandoah Heights, Schuylkill County.

Drexel, Saint Katharine (1858–1955). Raised with status and wealth, she devoted herself to serving Native and African Americans and established many missions. She was beatified in 1988, canonized in 2000. 1663 Bristol Pike, Bensalem, Bucks County.

Ennis, Del (1925–1996). Slugging outfielder for the Phillies in 1950s, three-time All-Star, and member of 1950 "Whiz Kids." Hillside Cemetery, Lawnview Section, Lot 102; 2556 Susquehanna Rd., Roslyn, Montgomery County.

Pennsylvania Wineries

The website pennsylvaniawine.com offers a taste of wine-making activities throughout the state (though the most productive vineyards tend to be in the northwestern counties, near Lake Erie, and the southeastern part of the state). Winemakers say that the climate and soil hereabouts is similar to the Bordeaux and Burgundy regions of France; ergo, it augurs well for wine-making. Since wine is a subject with as many opinions as there are tasters, you'll just have to find out for yourself.

Here are a few of the wineries that have been consistent award winners in national and international tastings the past few years:

Blue Mountain Vineyards
7627 Grape Vine Dr.
New Tripoli
(610) 298-3068
bluemountainwine.com

Pinnacle Ridge Winery
407 Old Rte. 22
Kutztown
(610) 756-4481
pinridge.com

Chaddsford Winery
632 Baltimore Pike
Chadds Ford
(610) 388-6221
chaddsford.com

Presque Isle Wine Cellars
9440 W. Main Rd.
North East
(814) 725-1314
piwine.com

Nissley Vineyards and Winery Estate
140 Vintage Dr.
Bainbridge
(717) 426-3514
nissleywine.com

Winery at Wilcox
1867 Mefferts Run Rd.
Wilcox
(814) 929-5598
wineryatwilcox.net

Fine, Governor John S. (1893–1978). Governor of Pennsylvania from 1951 to 1955. Oak Lawn Cemetery; Wilkes-Barre, Luzerne County.

Forrest, Edwin (1806–1872). Actor born in Philadelphia; excelled in tragic roles. His rivalry with actor William Macready led to the 1849 Astor Place Riots in New York, where 30 people were killed during a fight. Episcopal Community Services; 225 S. Third St., Philadelphia.

Foster, Stephen C. (1826–1864). Popular 19th-century composer of folk songs and ballads. Penned "Oh! Susannah," "Camptown Races," and "Beautiful Dreamer." Lived in the Pittsburgh area most of his life. Allegheny Cemetery; 4734 Butler St., Pittsburgh.

Franklin, Benjamin (1706–1790). An American superstar, Franklin signed the Declaration of Independence; proved that lightning is an electrical phenomenon; wrote, printed, and published widely; and invented bifocals. Also known as a diplomat, philanthropist, statesman, and scientist. The 18th century's most illustrious Pennsylvanian built a house in Franklin Court starting in 1763 and lived there the last five years of his life. Christ Church Burial Ground; southeast corner of Fifth and Arch Streets, Philadelphia.

Frick, Henry (1849–1919). A Pittsburgh industrialist and philanthropist, Frick was instrumental in the organization of the coke and steel industries. His controversial management style while chairman of Carnegie Steel led to the bloody Homestead Strike in 1892. Homewood Cemetery; 1599 S. Dallas Ave., Pittsburgh.

Furness, Frank (1839–1912). Influential Philadelphia architect. Designed Victorian buildings between 1870 and 1900. Laurel Hill Cemetery, Lot 94, Section S; 3822 Ridge Ave., Philadelphia.

Garroway, David (Dave) (1913–1982). Television host. Originally a disc jockey on Chicago radio, he appeared on NBC-TV. First host of *Today* show (1952–1961); hosted *Wide, Wide World* (1955–1958). West Laurel Hill Cemetery, Washington Section, Lot 49; 215 Belmont Ave., Bala Cynwyd, Montgomery County.

Gathers, Hank (1967–1990). Hank "The Bankman" Gathers was the last college basketball player to lead the NCAA in both scoring and rebounding. Mount Lawn Cemetery; Eighty-fourth Street and Hook Road, Sharon Hill, Delaware County.

Gridley, Captain Charles Vernon (1844–1898). Commander of Dewey's flagship USS *Olympia* in the Battle of Manila Bay, 1898. Dewey's order, "You may fire when you are ready, Gridley," opened the battle in the Spanish-American War. Lakeside Cemetery; East Lake Road, Erie.

Hopper, Hedda (1890–1966). Gossip columnist, born Elda Furry in Hollidaysburg, Pennsylvania, one of nine children. Worked in theater, became a fashion commentator on a Hollywood radio station. Eventually her column appeared in 85 metropolitan papers, 3,000 small-town dailies, and 2,000 weeklies. Rose Hill Cemetery; Altoona, Blair County.

Jarvis, Anna (1864–1948). Her mother had hoped "sometime, somewhere, someone will found a Mother's Day." When her mother died, Jarvis, living in Philadelphia, did it. The first Mother's Day was May 12, 1907. President Woodrow Wilson made it official in every state, and the day is celebrated now in more than 40 countries. West Laurel Hill Cemetery, River Section, Lot 499; 215 Belmont Ave., Bala Cynwyd, Montgomery County.

Kahn, Louis I. (1901–1974). This 20th-century architect designed the Salk Institute for Biological Studies in La Jolla, California, and the Yale Center for British Art and Studies in New Haven, Connecticut. He taught at Yale and Penn. Montefiore Cemetery; 600 Church Rd., Jenkintown, Montgomery County.

Mansfield, Jayne (1933–1967). Actress born Vera Jayne Palmer in Bryn Mawr, Pennsylvania. Known for sultry movie and stage roles, including *Too Hot to Handle* and *Will Success Spoil Rock Hunter?* Fairview Cemetery; Plainfield near Pen Argyl, York County.

McKean, Thomas (1734–1817). Signed the Declaration of Independence. Laurel Hill Cemetery, Section G, Lot 210; 3822 Ridge Ave., Philadelphia.

Mead, Margaret (1901–1978). Anthropologist who redefined and expanded the field of anthropology, the science of human culture. Born in Philadelphia, she was ambitious and always controversial. Did field work in Polynesia, Melanesia, and Nebraska, among other sites. President Jimmy Carter awarded her the Presidential Medal of Freedom. Buckingham Friends Cemetery; Lahaska, Bucks County.

Moore, Marianne (1887–1972). Modernist poet. Studied at Bryn Mawr College and Carlisle Commercial College; worked at US Indian School. Known for her eccentricity, devotion to baseball, and keenly intelligent poetry. Evergreen Cemetery, Lot 91, Area G, Grave 5; 799 Baltimore St., Gettysburg, Adams County.

Peale, Charles Willson (1741–1827). Portrait painter who was a Democratic member of the Pennsylvania Assembly. He established the Portrait Gallery of the Heroes of the Revolution (1782) and founded the Peale Museum of natural history and technology (1786). His most famous painting is *The Staircase Group* (1795), portraying his sons, Raphaelle and Titian. Married three times, he had 17 children, many of whom were artists. St. Peter's Churchyard; occupies a city block bounded by Third, Pine, Fourth, and Lombard Streets, Philadelphia.

Pitcher, Molly (1754–1832). Mary Ludwig Hays McCauley was dubbed Molly Pitcher while carrying pitchers of water to her husband and other thirsty soldiers during battle; heroine at Battle of Monmouth. Old Graveyard; South Hanover Street between Walnut and South Streets, Carlisle, Cumberland County.

Rizzo, Frank (1920–1991). Commissioner of police department of Philadelphia, where he lived all his life. Called himself "toughest cop in America." Twice elected mayor of Philadelphia (1972 and 1975). Holy Sepulchre Cemetery, Section S, Range 1, Lot 136; Cheltenham Avenue and Easton Road, Cheltenham Township, Montgomery County.

Rush, Benjamin (1742–1813). Signed the Declaration of Independence. Christ Church Burial Ground; Fifth and Arch Streets, Philadelphia. Other signers buried at Christ Church Burial Ground include Jacob Broom (1752–1810), Pierce Butler (1744–1822), Joseph Hewes (1730–1779), Francis Hopkinson (1737–1791), Robert Morris (1734–1806), and George Ross (1730–1779).

Russell, Lillian (1861–1922). Actress and singer born in Clinton, Iowa. This popular, flamboyant blonde beauty was known for her unreliability. Starred in 24 musicals between 1881 and 1899. Allegheny Cemetery; 4734 Butler St., Pittsburgh.

Sully, Thomas (1783–1872). Learned art from relatives, began painting portraits in 1801. Studied with Gilbert Stuart and Benjamin West. Returned to Philadelphia; painted technically polished and elegant portraits. Laurel Hill Cemetery, Section A, Lot 41; 3822 Ridge Ave., Philadelphia.

PENNSYLVANIA WEB ADDRESSES

golfinpa.com
link to the links

groundhog.org
eternal replays of February 2

paroute6.com
virtual drive across the northern tier

pennsylvaniawine.com
wineries

visitpa.com
tourism in Pennsylvania (official state site)

visitphilly.com
tourism in Philadelphia

visitpittsburgh.com
tourism in Pittsburgh

Index